The Way of Belle Coeur

A Woman's Vade Mecum

Sibyl Vana Reynolds

Copyright 2015 © Sibyl Dana Reynolds
All rights reserved, including the right to store, reproduce or transmit
this book or portions thereof in any form whatsoever without prior
written permission of the author.

Illustrations by Judy Alkema

ISBN: 1490404961
ISBN 13: 9781490404967
Library of Congress Control Number: 2013911066
CreateSpace Independent Publishing Platform
North Charleston, South Carolina

*For my mother,
Barbara Lee Carduff,
with love and gratitude*

Contents

Introduction xi
    Community, Companions, and Sisters xiii
    The Practice of Lectio Divina xvi

**Before You Begin Necessary Tools for
the Journey** xxvi

    Getting Started: Your Journal and Codex . . . xxviii
    Archaeology of the Soul xxxvii
    A Prayer of Embarkation xliv

**Book I: The Way of Belle Cœur:
A Spiritual Template** 1

    The Four Pathways 6
    The Path of Spirit 8
    The Path of Sacrament 14

Community and Personal Sacraments 15
The Path of Sisterhood 33
Spiritual and Creative Intentions 37
The Contemporary Sisterhood of
Belle Cœur 42
The Beguines' Legacy:
Our Ancestral Heritage 53
The Path of Service 65

Book II: The Four Chambers
The Alchemy of Sacred Practice 76

Six Applications for Exploration. 79
The Chamber of Devotion. 81
The Myriad Forms of Devotion 81
The Chamber of Craft 87
The Sacred Life-Artisan and Her Senses... 96
The Chamber of Story 105
The Portundae 109
The Chamber of Study. 115
Six Responsive Practices for Enrichment 117

Book III: The Compass 122

The Center: Jesus the Christ, the Beloved 123
True North 123
The Season's of Life's Journey
with the Beloved. 126
The Circle: Wisdom Sophia. 131

Book IV: The Wisdom Keepers of
Belle Cœur 138

A Meditation. 141
The Belle Cœur Iconotypal Portraits 147

Contents

Beatrice, the cook and soothie 147
Cibylle, the waif 153
Comtesse, the needle worker 159
Gertrude, the carpenter 165
Goscelin, the scribe 172
Grace, the child 179
Helvide, the herbalist 184
Henriette, the doll 190
Imene, the midwife 196
Mabille, the chanteuse 201
Marie, the helpmate 205
Myrtle, the crone 207
Petronilla, the prophetess 215
Ravenissa, healer for God's creatures 221
Sabine, the counselor 226
Mary and Martha 232
Your Iconotypal Self Portrait 243

**Book V: The Labyrinth and
Chartres Cathedral** 249

The Chartres Cathedral Labyrinth 251
The Sacred Made Visible 257
Visual Prayer Tags 258

Book VI: Seasonal Inspiration 260

The Belle Cœur Perpetual Calendar 261
The Qualities of Time 291
The Moon and Her Cycles 296
Monthly Reflections 301

Book VII: Foundational Fundamentals 352

The Twelve Holy Mysteries 354

The Twelve Elements of Wonder 363

**Book VIII: Illumination, Co-creation, and
the Sacred Imagination** 372

    The Sacred Life-Arts: Seven
    Facets of Illumination 372
    The Intuition and the Sacred Imagination . . . 400
    Six Steps to Fulfillment 404

Book IX: The Oratory 410

    The Daily Hours. 412
    Marking Time. 418
    Prayers for Particular Needs 422
    Sacred Rituals. 426
    The Feast of Life. 432
    The Fast 442

Book X: The Belle Cœur Lexicon 448

    Belle Cœur symbols 449
    Belle Cœur Vocabulary 454

Bibliography. 461
Acknowledgements 465
Belle Cœur Resources 469

*"You must find the cathedral, the sanctuary,
and the oratory hidden within you.
We will meet you there, in spirit. We implore you to
gather a circle of kin for shared study of this sacred
manuscript. Read between the lines, and meditate
upon the symbols offered here. Look for the allegories
to reveal the hidden knowledge within these pages.
Use what you discover as you would a map to
help you find the way to your destination.
You will learn through our stories how our sisterhood
chose to live in beauty, with holy passion for God, how we
transfigured our world in the time of the sword. The lessons
for the art and craft of sacred living are offered here."*

Petronilla,
Ink and Honey

Introduction

*...an eager anticipation for my
future kept me alert
to the sights and sounds
that surrounded me at
the beginning of
my great adventure.
(I&H: 21)*

The Way of Belle Cœur is ancient and new. It is a spiritual pattern to quicken, inspire, and nurture a woman's passion and longing for...

- ❖ *Spirit*, through her ever-deepening relationship with the Divine Presence, the Sacred Feminine, and Jesus the Christ, the Beloved.
- ❖ *Sacrament*, expressed symbolically through ritual and celebratory blessing.
- ❖ *Sisterhood*, among kindred spirits as a contemplative and spiritually creative community.
- ❖ *Service*, through the meaningful sharing of her gifts and talents to benefit the Greater Good.
- ❖ *Devotion*, as the full embodiment of her sacred connection through prayer and spiritual practices.
- ❖ *Craft*, as her manifestation of beauty and personal creative forms of sacred expression.
- ❖ *Study*, through the ongoing exploration of sacred wisdom and mystical teachings.
- ❖ *Story*, as her fully lived, recorded, and enduring legacy for future generations.

The Vade Mecum

The Way of Belle Cœur is a Christ-centered contemplative, co-creative, spiritual cosmology rooted in sacred iconotypal wisdom and expressed through spiritually grounded, creative practices. Belle Cœur spirituality is inspired by the medieval story of the sisters of Belle Cœur as depicted in my novel, *Ink and Honey*. It is recommended that you become familiar with *Ink and Honey* to fully experience the creative inspiration and spiritual practices offered within this *Woman's Vade*

Introduction

Mecum. The two books when studied together create a complete body of work through the combined experience of story and sacred practices.

Derived from the Latin, *vade mecum* means *go with me.* During the Middle Ages, a *Vade Mecum* served as a spiritual handbook for pilgrims while they journeyed. Illuminated parchment pages were wrapped in hide and hung from the belt or carried in a knapsack during pilgrimage to various holy sites across Europe. The *Vade Mecum* was a hand-scribed compendium of prayers, maps, and spiritual inspiration. The sacred practices, prayers, and iconotypal wisdom within the pages of this book are intended to serve as a contemporary *Woman's Vade Mecum* to inspire *you*, a wise woman and spiritual pilgrim of the third millennium.

Belle Cœur community, companions, and sisters

It's important to note that *The Way of Belle Cœur* may be experienced as an independent spiritual study or shared as a group process. Belle Cœur spirituality can be celebrated in a variety of ways according to your particular acclimation and needs. Refer to the Belle Cœur Resources section at the completion of this book to learn how to access additional online information regarding the following forms of experience.

   I. **Community study**
       An existing women's community (a prayer group, spiritual book club, etc.) may choose to

study and incorporate the Belle Cœur prayers and practices for the group's spiritual and creative enrichment.

II. **Companion of Belle Coeur**
A Companion of Belle Cœur desires a solo (cloistered) journey as a private, personal, creative, and spiritual experience. The Belle Cœur companion weaves the practices and prayers of the Way of Belle Cœur into her life as led by the Spirit.

III. **Sister of Belle Cœur**
The process to become a Belle Cœur Sister includes a period of discernment, and participation at a Belle Cœur spirituality retreat, and online study and interaction. Sisterhood circles form through active participation and connection with a committed, intentional community.

Your personal spiritual journey is a lifelong, inner, and outer pilgrimage. Sharing the journey with sisters on the path adds another level of experience and deepening with kindred spirits.

The concept of *sisterhood* has remained a constant theme within women's lives for centuries. An intentional and co-creative community circle provides a sacred container for women to gather, share, and curate our stories. Together, we support one another as we develop our crafts and spirituality. In this way, we create our personal and collective legacies for future generations.

While many women are called to seek the company of kindred spirits, others feel led to a contemplative and solitary form of spirituality. Within the Way of

Introduction

Belle Cœur, as mentioned above, there is a continuum of inclusivity for diverse forms of spiritual and creative expression. Whether actively involved as a sister or reflectively connected as a companion, we experience unity through shared Belle Cœur devotional practices and daily prayers.

Shifting paradigms and inclusivity

While writing *Ink and Honey*, I imagined the possibility for the creation of a contemporary, contemplative community to share Belle Cœur spirituality. The eventual result was the founding of the Sisterhood of Belle Cœur. You will become acquainted with many of the sisters of our community through their shared wisdom and stories within these pages.

It's important to mention as we begin, there are also male readers who feel spiritually and creatively stirred by the story of *Ink and Honey*. The hunger for community and a return to particular forms of creative and spiritual expression are not limited to the feminine gender. To the male readers of this book… thank you for your interest.

The tenets of compassion, love, and generosity combined with an appreciation for beauty, order, and simplicity are values shared by women and men that seek to know God and serve humankind. While *The Way of Belle Cœur* is written from a feminine perspective it's important to stress that today's global and cultural needs call for both genders to come together to bring about the balance of masculine and feminine attributes. Over two thousand years of patriarchal abuse have been detrimental to both sexes. Collectively, we must heal the wounds of sexism and find a way forward as we ride out the current global, spiritual, and cultural tsunami of shifting paradigms.

Throughout this book, you will find enclosed parentheses with corresponding page numbers for pertinent and referential text for *Ink and Honey*. Example: (*I&H:* 36-38). You're invited to cross-pollinate your reading experience as you refer to the noted pages of *Ink and Honey* in accompaniment to this text. The practice of lectio divina, outlined below, is encouraged wherever you see Scripture or (*I&H*) refererences.

The practice of lectio divina

Lectio divina (sacred reading) is an ancient three-part spiritual practice. Scripture, literature, poetry, sacred texts, and other forms of the written word may be used as the focus for the practice of lectio divina.

I. *Lectio*
Read aloud, slowly the chosen passage of the particular work to savor each word. Read the entire passage a second time. The second reading may be done in silence. During the

second reading notice a word or phrase that feels illuminated with meaning and/or resonance for you.
II. *Meditatio*
Meditate upon the illuminated portion of the reading.
III. *Contemplatio*
Contemplate the illumination with regard to the encapsulated personal relevance and inspiration.
IV. *Oratio*
Finally, offer your response to God as prayer silently or aloud.
V. An optional fifth step of lectio divina is to journal your reflections and revelations.

Women's wisdom and anamnesis

Women have always discovered innovative ways to embody sacred feminine wisdom. Ancient knowledge has been passed through a collective and personal ancestry within the stories, music, poetry, prayers, and crafts of those who came before you. You carry the colorful and diverse elements of women's wisdom within your bones. Your sacred understanding and knowledge are a work in progress, gathered throughout your lifetime. Sources for your particular feminine wisdom include: your familial stories, education, religious and spiritual experiences, and the ever-changing cultural messages and mores.

Your wisdom comes alive within you through your intuitive understanding and your dreams, visions, and mystical experiences. It is this latter form of "knowing" that holds particular emphasis for the Way of Belle Cœur.

The concept of anamnesis (intentional recollection) is helpful to "grow the wisdom" (*I&H:* pp. 46, 47, 63, 66, 134) and to curate, archive, and pass along our individual and shared spiritual and creative legacies. The conscious examination of women's *her*story, the patterns of how our ancestors lived, created, worshipped, and experienced community, inspires and informs our contemporary lives.

Circles and sharing

During the past thirty years I've had the privilege to facilitate numerous women's spiritual/creative retreats and workshops. On many occasions I have witnessed a phenomenon that occurs when women gather in community to share their stories. Within the circle, a safe and nurturing space for group process, women experience a deep connection with one another.

From an intentional place of heart-centered sharing the participants explore, express, and imagine what it means to be spiritually attentive and creatively inspired women. They listen to one another with compassionate interest. The circle is an ancient form that offers a container where personal and collective transformation is possible.

Introduction

While sharing, studying, and crafting together, women often remember and begin to reconstruct the lost and forgotten facets of their spiritual wisdom and creative gifts. Within the inner space of a circle of kindred spirits it's possible to collectively reclaim previously hidden, sacred, and feminine wisdom. Within a prayerful and intentional circle, the participants' questions, stories, and shared wisdom are held with sacred awareness and the work of the soul becomes a central focus.

Reflect

- ❖ How do we personally and collectively appreciate our connections with our feminine ancestor's ways of living, being, creating, and experiencing the holy?
- ❖ How do we retrieve and repurpose ancient sacred wisdom to inform our spiritual understanding and creative lives today?
- ❖ How do we claim and express the emerging legacy of *hope and wisdom* we feel called to live and share with the women of the future? (*I&H:* 252, 254, 272, 432, 475, 480)

Iconotypes, reflections, and seasonal inspiration

I believe that through the mystery and power of women's shared stories, the iconotypal feminine spirits of long ago sisterhoods mysteriously transcend space

The Way of Belle Cœur

and time to impart their lost and forgotten wisdom. Within the numinousity of sacred space the palpable spiritual inspiration from our ancestors infuses the present day with ancient reckoning and guidance. In Book IV: The Wisdom Keepers of Belle Cœur you will explore the iconotypal portraiture of the sisters of Belle Cœur from the story of *Ink and Honey* and discern your personal iconotype.

The iconotypes reveal how sacred feminine wisdom recorded within our bones is also alive through our connections with the elements of air, fire, earth, water and spirit, through the natural world, and all of Creation. In the story of *Ink and Honey* Goscelin, the scribe studied the properties of nature while she copied the sacred volumes of *Dominions and Graces*. You will find references to *Dominions and Graces* and a perpetual Belle Cœur calendar in Book VI: Seasonal Inspiration.

Each section of this *Vade Mecum* offers the opportunity to "Reflect" with a series of discernment questions and journal prompts to inspire your creative heart and spirit. As we prepare to begin the journey to discover the Way of Belle Cœur, I invite you to contemplate the following questions:

- ❖ Can you imagine the possibility that in a far away place, hidden from view, there is long forgotten, sacred, and ancestral feminine wisdom, awaiting discovery to inform our lives today?
- ❖ How might the reclamation and renewal of a precious cache of shrouded, ancient, sisterly,

Introduction

spiritual, and creative knowledge change your life and also benefit our world?
- Is it possible that Wisdom Sophia (the Sacred Feminine) is returning through the spiritual/creative awakening of women today within their prayers, rituals, and expressions of the sacred life-arts?
- Are we experiencing inspiration, individually and collectively, on a cellular level to prophetically embrace our spiritual and creative gifts as our heritage and legacy for the future?
- Do you resonate with the call to make an inner pilgrimage? Are you called to serve as a spiritual midwife for the birth of a spiritual and creative renaissance to foster beauty, hope, renewed wisdom, and healing for yourself and our world?

Commitment

As you prepare to set out on your inner pilgrimage to explore your spirit and express your creative heart it's beneficial to know that unexpected emotions may arise while you work with the material. The cultivation of personal truth and wisdom stirs the soul. Thoughts and feelings can intensify during the process as new concepts emerge to challenge the familiar.

Though the journey is ultimately transformative and inspirational, it should be acknowledged that traversing the landscape of the heart and soul might periodically be arduous and challenging. It takes courage to make a pilgrimage whether inwardly or outwardly. The call to make a spiritual quest deserves prayerful discernment and preparation.

Once the inner pilgrimage begins conscious and fierce commitment, focus, intention, spiritual practice, and prayer are required. Periods of silence, reflection, contemplation, study, and sacred creation are the luminous tools for the journey. It's helpful to have a field guide to provide support along the way.

The Way of Belle Cœur offers a map for the woman who feels called to explore and longs to experience the four pathways: *Spirit, Sacrament, Sisterhood, and Service* and the four alchemical chambers: *Devotion, Craft, Study, and Story.*

The cartography

Within the pages of *Ink and Honey,* readers are introduced to the daily life of the sisters of Belle Cœur through their prayers, rituals, and connections with the natural world, as well as, through their sacred crafts and artmaking. Goscelin recorded the day-to-day routine at Belle Cœur within the pages of her illuminated manuscript, the sisterhood's journal and legacy. The depiction of the scribe's spiritual wisdom is for the reader's interpretation.

The ancient tenets and tempo of daily life portrayed in the story of *Ink and Honey* reveal a template that consists of four wisdom paths and four alchemical chambers to enrich and inspire your creative heart and spirit. The cartography of *The Way of Belle Cœur*

Introduction

found here in the first three chapters (Books I-III) provides spiritual and creative enrichment for existing women's communities and offers sustenance for the woman called to study independently.

In Book III you will explore the meaning of the template's circle (the all encompassing container) representative of Wisdom Sophia in her many forms. The circle surrounds the pathways and chambers of Belle Cœur. You will also learn about the center, the beautiful heart, of the circle, Belle Cœur.

Within the center of the equidistant cross is the sacred compass that reveals True North as Jesus, the Cosmic Christ. The Cosmic Christ…refers to the anointed one who fulfills the universe in all its parts (Ephesians 1:23).

Jesus, God, Yaweh, the Divine Presence, the One, the Creator, the Holy Spirit, is referred to throughout this book as the *Beloved,* in the spirit of Christ's enduring presence as our Beloved life's companion. He is our spiritual brother, teacher and mentor, confidante and friend.

An invitation

Throughout this *Vade Mecum* you will find the invitation to "Create." Prayers, sacred practices, journal prompts; spiritual and creative exercises, and additional forms of guidance are offered as sweet honey from the hive of inspiration for your spirit.

Be sure to read *Before You Begin: Tools for the Journey* immediately following this introduction, where you'll

The Way of Belle Cœur

be guided to prepare your Belle Cœur Journal and Sacred Wisdom Codex. Your journal and codex will become your steadfast companions as you write, create, and craft a personal legacy of wisdom.

Going forward

We currently inhabit a season of human evolution that reveals an invisible and strangely palpable opening in time and space. Could it be that we are being invited to move through myriad shifting paradigms ever deeper into the Mystery of God's infinite Love?

We are navigators of countless changes that our rapidly growing and ever-changing technological world places before us. Often it can feel as though we are finding our way through a carnival house of distorted mirrors and crooked rooms.

This time in history and *her*story requires innovation, curiosity, stamina, and perseverance to discover new ways of living and being, sharing and serving. There are unlimited possibilities when we examine our personal journeys and study the legacy of ancient, feminine, sacred wisdom as the taproot of our understanding.

The spirits of *Ink and Honey's* sisters of Belle Cœur return within these pages to offer their postscripts, iconotypal guidance, and inspiration. Their stories blend with those of today's Belle Cœur sisters as a living legacy of sacred knowledge and feminine understanding.

Introduction

May *your* story continue the tradition to "grow the wisdom" for future generations while blessings flow to you and through you...as you journey the Way of Belle Cœur.

Sibyl Dana Reynolds
Sister of Belle Cœur
Winter 2015

Before You Begin
Necessary Tools for the Journey

Your Journal and Belle Cœur Sacred Wisdom Codex

Before you begin your journey to navigate the pathways, chambers, and iconotypes of Belle Cœur, it's important to gather a few essential provisions. Please carefully read the preparatory guidance offered here to ensure your full experience of the various creative and spiritual practices.

To receive full benefit from the material offered within this *Vade Mecum* it is recommended you designate a journal for your responses to the reflection prompts and creative exercises. Your journal is an essential tool for your inner journey. Imagine it as

Before You Begin Necessary Tools for the Journey

your alchemical workbook and sacred container where you will record your questions, revelations, and inner discoveries.

In addition to your journal, your *Belle Cœur Sacred Wisdom Codex* (a blank book you will embellish and make your own) will become your personal wisdom text. Imagine this very special book as a work in progress and compendium for all that inspires you. The codex differs from your journal in the following way.

The journal is where you process and work through your questions. It's your personal workbook, a place to brainstorm, reflect, and fully examine your questions, reflections, ideas, etc.

The codex is your wisdom text. Imagine it as your contemporary version of an *illuminated manuscript.* The codex is where you will record the insights, self-knowledge, and revelations you glean through your reflections, creative experiences, and spiritual exploration. The codex ultimately becomes the polished distillation of what is discovered within your journal process. No previous art experience is required to craft your codex. The codex can also be imagined as a scrapbook for your soul.

Your codex is where you will record the extracted essence of your particular and unique wisdom that rises like cream from your explorations in your journal. Your creativity has free reign as you write, paint, draw, and collage your stories, wisdom, alchemical understanding, and spiritual revelations within the pages of your codex. Again, no previous artmaking experience is required.

Note: *It's helpful to think of your codex as an ongoing work in progress. Inspiration for your codex will develop over time as you work with the material in this book. When to begin to create your codex is a matter of personal preference. The process of gathering materials for your Codex will help you to get underway.*

You are infinitely creative. It's important to emphasize that while guidelines are offered here, <u>you cannot make an "artistic" nor intellectual mistake with regard to how you choose to use your journal or craft your codex.</u> Total freedom of self-expression is essential and encouraged. Follow your intuition to reconnect with your sense of childlike wonder and fearlessness. Give yourself total creative permission!

Getting Started
Your Journal and Codex

- ❖ Designate a journal of your choosing (your current journal or one you choose especially for this purpose) as an accompaniment to this book. Your journal will become your personal version of your Belle Cœur Workbook.
- ❖ Your journal is the place to thoroughly explore your questions to "grow your wisdom."
- ❖ Use the journal as a place to scribe your responses to the reflection prompts you'll find throughout this *Vade Mecum*. Become like Goscelin when her teacher, Brother Paul,

Before You Begin Necessary Tools for the Journey

invited her to make notes in the margins as she copied sacred texts (*I&H*: 64-65). You're invited to make notes in the margins of not only your journal, but this book as well.
- ❖ Choose a journal that suits you. Go to your local art supply or stationary store and explore all the varied styles of journals: small, large, spiral bound, hardcover, softcover, lined, unlined. Select the one that feels right for your way of self-expression.
- ❖ After you've chosen your journal select a second blank book to serve as your Belle Cœur Sacred Wisdom Codex. It's recommended that you choose a hardcover sketchbook that is at least 11 inches by 14 inches in size. Your codex will become your contemporary illuminated manuscript. It will hold *your* inspired prayers, prophecies, revelations, sacred wisdom, drawings, illuminations, and creative expressions in creative ways.

A reverent and sacred process

- ❖ The codex is the place to record your most important distillations from your work within your journal and inspiration gathered from other sources. The codex will become your "sacred wisdom text." The creation of your codex, if you choose, can evolve as a lifelong spiritual and creative practice. Imagine a shelf filled with volumes of codices full with written and visual expressions of your wisdom.

- ❖ When you take time to journal and/or craft your codex, do so with reverence and ritual. Light a candle, offer your prayer of intention, and pause to center your heart and spirit. You may want to anoint the covers of your journal and codex with sacred oil as a blessing for the work you are about to begin. You're invited to write a dedication on the first page and date each entry for future reference. The important thing is to make your journal and codex your own.
- ❖ Begin your journal with your written intention for your inner pilgrimage.
- ❖ Envision your Belle Cœur wisdom books as sacred vessels where you are free to fully express your truths and to respond and reflect in whatever way you choose. It is advisable to write a disclaimer somewhere within the first pages of your journal as protection for your most intimate and private thoughts. In your own words, feel free to express the following: *To anyone who may find this book. PLEASE READ NO FURTHER. This journal (or codex) is a sacred container for my personal, innermost, thoughts and feelings. Your respect for my privacy is appreciated. Thank you. If found please return to: (Add your name, address, or whatever information you desire).*
- ❖ **It's important to reiterate: <u>There is no way you can express yourself incorrectly. You cannot make a mistake.</u>** Guidelines are offered to help you get

Before You Begin Necessary Tools for the Journey

started, but it's important that you give yourself permission for full creative freedom to explore the material and record your discoveries in whatever way suits you best.
- ❖ Keep your journal and codex in a secure place so you will feel free to express yourself fully.
- ❖ Keep your Bible nearby as reference for the Scripture notations and for the practice of lectio divina. Please note in this book that inclusive language sources have been used where full Scripture passages appear. Women often feel overlooked and disregarded due to the weight and prevalence of masculine oriented rhetoric within the context of everyday cultural messages. The shift to the use of inclusive language is an ongoing educational and intellectual process.
- ❖ Mark your calendar to create time for your personal study of *The Way of Belle Cœur*.
- ❖ It is helpful when beginning a new study to offer a prayer of commitment to the work as your spiritual practice. You'll find an example for this type of prayer following this introduction. Be creative and create your own prayer if you wish, or initiate a personal ritual to sacralize your time for journaling and study.
- ❖ Allow spaciousness for contemplation and reflection in the midst of your reading experience. Take time to b r e a t h e, contemplate, savor, and reflect as you explore the content.
- ❖ Gather an assortment of writing tools: colored pens, markers, and colored pencils into a box or basket to keep near your journal and codex.

The Way of Belle Cœur

Be creatively fearless. Feel free to add color to illuminate your notations. You may also want to paste inspirational images cut from magazines or copies of personal photographs to the pages.
- ❖ You may wish to dedicate your journaling to a particular prayer need: a prayer for healing for a friend or beloved, the needs of the homeless, world peace, the protection of earth's children, the renewal of the planet, etc. Listen for the Beloved's guidance to inspire your creative heart.
- ❖ Carry this *Vade Mecum* and your journal with you. Imagine yourself as a pilgrim while you traverse the daily landscape of your life's journey. You may want to create or designate a tote bag for your journal and *Vade Mecum*. You might also craft a bookmark or add colorful ribbons to mark the pages.
- ❖ Enter your exploration of this book through your sacred imagination to deepen your experience. Explore the story of *Ink and Honey* and place yourself in the spiritual presence of each of the characters, as though you are in the presence of a dear friend. Allow *The Way of Belle Cœur* to lead you along the four wisdom paths and through the four alchemical chambers to new vistas of spiritual and creative understanding.
- ❖ You're encouraged to read passages aloud, particularly those that hold a charge of resonance for you. In ancient times verses, prayers, and stories were read repeatedly on street corners, in churches, and shared between

pilgrims while they journeyed. Passages were memorized to share with others because many people were illiterate and the few existing books of that time were scribed by hand. Perhaps you will be inspired to commit to memory one of the archetypal wisdom offerings as a remembrance of one of the sisters of Belle Cœur and her influence for your journey.

❖ You may wish to call together a circle of friends to study and experience *The Way of Belle Cœur*. Community study opens new pathways for exploration and enrichment.

Symbols, words, and imagery

Words and language are of course, our most common and natural form of communication. However, as you begin to explore Belle Cœur spirituality it's important to acknowledge the value of the translation of words to become symbols and images. Symbols and imagery become iconographic when we meditate upon the deeper meaning. While writing this book I have contemplated various words and topics, ancient and new, to inspire your spirit and sacred imagination and found them to be symbolic.

Meditate upon the words that appear here. Notice what feelings arise with your associations and be aware of any symbols or images that emerge. Make sketches or find images in magazines to represent the words symbolically and add them to your journal or codex. As you explore

The Way of Belle Cœur

the Belle Cœur template it's important to be open to receive symbols and images to express the concepts you'll encounter. Dream imagery informs life's experience and understanding. Pay attention to your dreams.

Create a personal lexicon of symbols and images, a visual language as you journey the Way of Belle Cœur. Additional symbolic inspiration will be explored later in Book X.

sisterhood pilgrimage amulet

alchemy tree of life sacrament

prayer prophecy ministry

labyrinth cathedral sanctuary

manuscript ritual illuminations

Keep your journal nearby while you continue reading. Record the various questions and revelations that arise. Contemplate additional words that hold radiant meaning for you. Make your symbolic, alchemical, and iconographic connections and add them to your journal. Later, distill your wisdom from your journal (workbook) and scribe it within the pages of your codex then add your illuminations as creative and colorful touches.

Before You Begin Necessary Tools for the Journey

Lineage and inspiration

Our journals are often well-worn, coffee and tear stained, dog-eared and smudged. A woman's journal is a cherished possession and a sacred vessel that contains the stories of her day-to-day circumstances. Within the secret pages of our journals we record our ideas and dreams and explore the questions and concerns that shape our lives. We rant. We rave…and we pray. All of these outpourings and more deem the journal, "A Workbook for Everyday Life."

Belle Cœur spirituality invites a creative and sacred way to document, curate, and archive your stories and wisdom, inspired by the ancient craft of the illuminated manuscript. This doesn't mean you need to become a calligrapher or graphic designer to craft your Belle Cœur Sacred Wisdom Codex. Rather, the codex is a very personal creation uniquely brought to life through your imagination and creative spirit.

Goscelin, the scribe of Belle Cœur in the story of *Ink and Honey,* was the creator of the Belle Cœur manuscript (codex). The community's stories, herbal and midwifery wisdom, as well as, their prayers and prophecies were recorded on the parchment pages. Envision yourself as the scribe and illuminator (enlightener) of your sacred wisdom codex while you express and record your deepest truths, visions, wisdom, and images.

Illuminations

First, a bit of background regarding the creation of illuminated manuscripts and the codex may be of interest. The word, codex or codices (plural) signifies an ancient manuscript in book form. The word, codex, is derived from the word, *caudex*, the Latin word for tree bark. The codex began to replace the parchment scroll as the form for delivering illustrations and text in Western Europe between the first and third centuries.

There were many advantages to placing parchment sheets between boards rather than rolling them. A flat parchment allowed the use of thicker pigments and illustration became important as another way of telling a story or sharing information. With the arrival of the seventh century, monasteries were predominantly responsible for the production of books in the form of illuminated manuscripts. (*I&H:* 36, 42, 46, 59, 64, 207)

The illuminations (hand painted and colorful illustrations, borders, and flourishes) of the manuscripts were a sacred art form that required great practice and skill. The word illumination means, "to enlighten." The luminous colors used to embellish a manuscript's text often included silver and gold. The craftsperson creating the illuminations was called the *illuminator* and could also be the *scribe*. At the beginning of the Middle Ages, illuminators and scribes most often worked in a scriptorium at a monastery. By the end of the medieval period many illuminators were lay people. When printing presses began the mass production of books, the art of illumination became

Before You Begin Necessary Tools for the Journey

rare though some printed books were embellished with handcrafted illuminations.

In contemporary times the invention of e-books with their slick surfaces and lighted displays portends a very different form for sharing information, story, poetry or prayer. The invitation within the concept for a Belle Cœur Sacred Wisdom Codex is to enter the realm of the sacred imagination to connect with your creative spirit. When the codex is opened to a blank page a vast landscape awaiting creative discovery is revealed. There is spaciousness for the manifestation of beauty as a framework to accompany your written story and/or wisdom. You become the creator of your illuminated world within the pages of your codex.

The Way of Belle Cœur invites each sister to be the curator and archivist of her life's journey. You are encouraged to craft your *Belle Cœur Sacred Codex of Feminine Wisdom,* while you work through the processes in this *Vade Mecum.*

Like each of the sisters of Belle Cœur in the story of *Ink and Honey,* you carry and express particular feminine wisdom that is unique and iconotypal to you. Over time you will discover your individual methods for gathering and crafting your codex.

Archaeology of the soul

The thoughtful process of excavation of self-knowledge, for our purposes, is referred to as the *archaeology of the soul.* The intention to bring forth the highest meaning within an experience, whether

The Way of Belle Cœur

the experience is uplifting or challenging, is spiritual work.

Consider the archaeologist who digs for clues to explore the true nature of an ancient culture. The dig reveals relics and objects from the past. These are cleaned, examined, studied, and carefully sorted, labeled, and cared for. Later the findings are curated and displayed. Ultimately, new wisdom is extracted from the previously lost and buried antiquities to eventually be shared with others.

The excavation of lessons and meaning from your personal experiences is a similar soulful undertaking. Become the archaeologist of your inner world and your soul will reveal previously hidden beauty and wisdom for your life.

Preparation for gathering

An archaeologist would not begin her work without the proper equipment to contain whatever treasures she might discover. You, too, will need to create a special container for the gatherings that you will eventually place upon the pages of your codex. A basket, a shoebox, or other suitable vessel will work nicely.

Alternatively or additionally you may also choose to use an assortment of categorically assigned envelopes or folders. These may be embellished, if desired, and made beautiful. The bits and pieces you collect into your containers, envelopes, or folders will eventually find their way, in one form or another, to the pages of your codex.

Before You Begin Necessary Tools for the Journey

Suggestions are provided here for how to begin to collect the fragments of clues that will lead to the discovery of *your* sacred wisdom. Some of the recommendations are in the form of a question to be used as a reflection prompt and stepping stone for your discernment process. Other suggestions are invitations for specific collection activities. Choose the topics that hold personal resonance and explore them.

The list that follows offers recommendations for where to dig, and also indicates the various kinds of things to gather, archive, and curate as you begin your inner and outer excavation for your sacred wisdom. Incorporate prayer, intention, and reverence as part of the gathering practice. In this way, gathering becomes a creative sacrament.

Gather

Spend time to explore the following options to help you discover the ephemera (all things made of paper) and other elements to include within the pages of your codex. The gathering process is an ongoing practice. Initially, however, gathering is essential to set the stage for compilation and ultimately the creation of your codex.

It's important to reiterate that you <u>cannot make a mistake</u> with regard to the curation and creation of your sacred codex. This will be your unique creation according to <u>your</u> wisdom and creative desires for expression. Take these guidelines and make them your own.

The Way of Belle Cœur

Your creativity and sacred imagination are encouraged to create additional collection categories that will be uniquely meaningful for you. Imagine additional possibilities in addition to the suggestions in the list below.

Categories may include but are not limited to the following:

- ❖ Gather samplings of colors and textures that inspire you. These may be magazine images, fabric swatches, paint chips, things found in nature, etc. This is a valuable way to incorporate swatches of fabric you've held dear for years and years. You can also scan objects and things from the natural world on your printer or at a local copy store and print copies of your finds.
- ❖ Contemplate your favorite songs and music that evoke an emotional response. What instrument(s) interest you? If you play an instrument look for an image to represent your musical passion.
- ❖ Who are the famous and not so famous figures and people of "*her*story" and history that inspire you? Find images of at least three persons (living or deceased) that you would like to imagine as *spirit-mentors*. Gather photos to represent these persons either literally or symbolically. Often libraries will sell out of date magazines for a nominal charge or give them away. The bargain table at your local bookstore is also a good source for a variety of inexpensive image filled books to inspire your process.

Before You Begin Necessary Tools for the Journey

- Who are the ancestors and friends in your life that have been your most beloved teachers and mentors? Look for images to represent these important people.
- Gather photos, letters, and personal cherished relics belonging to your beloveds (your grandmother's earrings, your mother's gloves, etc.). Scan these objects on the computer and print them.
- Sort through your favorite recipes and copy particular favorites. Peruse magazines and gather images of foods you consider nourishing for your comfort, healing, or for renewed energy.
- Browse online for images pertaining to mythology, works of art, or other creative pathways that interest you. Local art/craft galleries are also good places for exploring the imagery to represent your personal aesthetic.
- Gather all sorts of imagery that inspires your spirit and creative heart.

Collect the following:

- Favorite poems that inspire you.
- A list of films you would enjoy watching time and again.
- Quotations that speak to your heart and spirit.
- Imagery of any kind that elicits an emotional response.
- Copies of cherished photographs from your life's journey.

- Imagery of animals, plants, landscapes, weather, etc. that interest you.

Gather spiritual sustenance

You have begun your collection of inspiration for your codex to reflect your creative heart and spirit. Next, you're invited to move to an interior experience to contemplate your personal longings, spiritual discoveries, and questions. This phase of gathering for your *Sacred Wisdom Codex* will focus on your soulful wisdom.

The following prompts are for your reflection as you begin:

- From what source(s) do you draw strength when life is challenging?
- What activities, practices, or experiences restore you when you've been living through a desert or spiritually arid time?
- What forms of prayer do you turn to time and again?
- How do you nurture your creative heart and spirit?

Contemplate the following questions and suggestions as you gather the words, images, prayers, and inspiration that spiritually sustain you. Add these to your assigned folders, envelopes, or containers. Allow the Spirit to lead your process.

Before You Begin Necessary Tools for the Journey

- ❖ What specific Scriptural or sacred text passages hold special meaning for you?
- ❖ Do you have favorite images of Christ, the saints, spiritual teachers, mystics, or other persons as representations of your spiritual anchors? Copy these images and add them to your codex.
- ❖ Look for images, or make copies of photos to portray the meaning and presence of sacred space for you.
- ❖ Copy refrains and passages from sacred writings, hymns, music, and personally valuable teachings that have inspired your journey.
- ❖ Copy prayers, litanies, worship services, and other perhaps more unconventional writings that celebrate the Divine Presence.
- ❖ Take a photo of a collection of your most treasured sacred objects.
- ❖ Most of all, allow the Spirit to reveal to you the deepest truths of your heart and soul and imagine these in a personal and creative way.

The creation of your codex is an iconographic process. By virtue of your prayer and intention the process of crafting your codex will create a sacramental portal to self-understanding as you honor your life's journey. Your *Belle Cœur Sacred Wisdom Codex* will become your personal reliquary to contain your inspiration, spiritual sustenance and enduring legacy.

A Prayer of Embarkation

Beloved, receive my prayer…

I am eager to explore, express, and imagine new possibilities to quicken my spiritual understanding and enliven my creative heart.

I call upon the spirits of my ancestors to awaken the sleeping knowledge within my bones. I ask for the spirit(s) of…(add the names of your ancestors) to accompany me as I make my inner pilgrimage of remembrance.

I call upon Wisdom Sophia to ignite the fires of creative passion beneath my breast, and to burn away my fears.

I pray for Creation to reveal her secrets in ways that will both inspire and inform my heart and mind.

I call upon my Highest Self to unveil my genuine gifts and sacred truths.

Oh, Beloved, enkindle my curiosity to illuminate the Way of Belle Cœur, as I grow my wisdom to enrich my life through personal acts of service for the greater good.

I long to serve as a spiritual midwife in this time of shifting paradigms. May I become a purveyor of beauty, a conduit of hope, and an illuminator of the pathway to peace.

In the name of the One who calls me to begin this sacred work, I pray.

Amen

Book I
The Way of Belle Cœur
A Spiritual Template

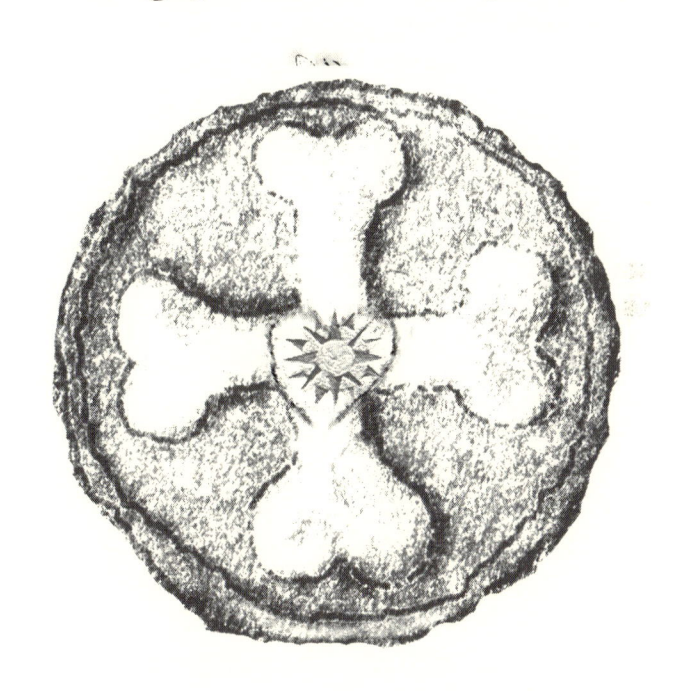

The Way of Belle Cœur

Overview

The Way of Belle Cœur is a map, a meditative pattern, a sacred template and cosmological imprint. Belle Cœur cartography reveals a visionary landscape where you're invited to explore four sacred pathways and four alchemical chambers. As you become familiar with the symbolic form of the equidistant cross within the circle, you'll discover an illuminated map leading you to spiritual and creative fulfillment.

The Belle Cœur symbol and template is created from two ancient forms, the *equidistant cross*, enclosed within a *circle*. The equidistant cross represents the principles of inclusivity, equality, and balance. The circle symbolizes eternity, the entirety of Creation, and the wholeness of body, mind, and spirit.

The four arms of the cross correlate to four wisdom paths representing *Spirit, Sacrament, Sisterhood* and *Service*. Each path also shares a relationship with a particular season of the year.

The quadrant spaces within the circle form four alchemical chambers. Each chamber houses a particular theme illustrative of creative and spiritual practices. The themes include: *Devotion, Craft, Story* and *Study*.

The center of the cross represents the indwelling Beautiful Heart (*Belle Cœur*) of Jesus, the Cosmic Christ, our *compass*. He is our eternal True North and our refuge, guardian, and guide for life's journey. Jesus Christ is referred to here as the *Beloved*.

The four wisdom paths (the passageways), the four alchemical chambers (the practices), and the heart of Belle Cœur (the compass) are held within the container

Book I The Way of Belle Cœur A Spiritual Template

of the sacred circle representing *Wisdom Sophia* (the Spirit of Creation and Sacred Feminine).

The entire symbolic template of the Way of Belle Cœur is paradoxically ancient and new, mystical and practical, virtual and real. The image of the equidistant cross, held within Wisdom Sophia's circle of Creation, is a metaphysical imprint and map. The Way of Belle Cœur is an invitation to live a spiritually aware, sacred, generative, and creative life. The practices, sacraments, and wisdom you'll discover here invite dedication to service for the Greater Good through prayer, the creation of beauty, and the peaceful presence of indwelling hope.

The sacred Belle Cœur template expresses a renewed feminine cosmology to enrich daily life experience. The call radiating from the center of the cross encourages the cultivation and practice of sacred awareness, creative imagining, and compassionate service. Belle Cœur spirituality is rooted in the acknowledgement of the individual's spiritual and creative gifts (charism).

Additionally, the spirituality of Belle Cœur is also a study for established women's communities experiencing a desire to commit to spiritual sisterhood. Through the practices and prayers of Belle Cœur spirituality, a community creates the opportunity to discover the group's collective creative and spiritual charism.

The sign of Belle Cœur

In the story of *Ink and Honey* we learn that a worn wooden sign hangs near the door of the sisters' home at Belle Cœur. In the center of the sign is a rusted cross within a blue painted circle. (*I&H:* 12, 84)

The sign of Belle Cœur is the medieval equivalent of a logo or icon in today's world. In the story it is depicted as the symbol the sisters use for blessing one another and others that arrive at their door in search of healing and prayer.

In today's world, sisters and companions of Belle Cœur, share the same sacred and symbolic gesture. Blessing is offered with the touch of index and middle fingers to the lips. Next, fingers gently touch the heart-space or on the forehead of the one receiving the blessing, while they form a cross.

- ❖ We make the cross by first, drawing our fingers downward and saying, "In the name of God, our Creator…"
- ❖ We draw the crossbar of the cross with our fingers while saying, "Jesus, our Beloved…"
- ❖ Lastly, we enclose the cross with a circle traced by our fingers while saying, "…and Wisdom Sophia, our Mother."

The blessing concludes as the fingers draw a circle to enclose the cross. This final gesture completes the sign/blessing of Belle Cœur. (*I&H:* 85)

Inspiration for the contemporary and contemplative spirituality of Belle Cœur was drawn from the *Ink and Honey* story. Additional enrichment came from Goscelin's copies of Dominions and Graces, the sisterhood's shared rituals, Myrtle the crone's teachings, and other key practices, rituals, and prayers. (*I&H:* 50-61, 274-276, 142, 240).

Book I The Way of Belle Cœur A Spiritual Template

A Sister of Belle Cœur shares her wisdom

"*The Belle Cœur symbol marks a path and a place where the fire of the sacred imagination encompasses the heart of feminine creativity. A true joining. From this hearth within, my life becomes my devotion. The sisterhood of spirituality of Belle Cœur is my monastery, a true and inspiring gift.*"

Trish Morris
Sister of Belle Cœur and Life Artisan

Une petite leçon de français

As we prepare to begin to explore Belle Cœur spirituality it's important to share the literal meaning of *Belle Cœur* (*Beautiful Heart*), as portrayed in the context of the story of *Ink and Honey*, and the material within this book. When I began writing *Ink and Honey*, I felt called to give a feminine emphasis to French grammar in order to convey the essence of the English term, *beautiful heart*. Here's a little French lesson to explain….

In French the heart is *le cœur*. Cœur, according to French grammar is a masculine word. Technically, the correct masculine form of the French adjective for the word, beautiful, when used in conjunction with the word *cœur*, should be *beau* (masculine), rather the feminine adjective, *belle*.

However, as the author of a story centered on the *beautiful* heart in relationship to feminine understanding I took poetic license. I chose to break the rules and use the feminine adjective rather than

The Way of Belle Cœur

the grammatically correct, masculine adjective. Hence, the concept of *Belle Cœur* was born.

I share this information for clarity's sake for all readers, particularly French-speaking or those well versed in French. Rest assured, this is not the first time in my life I have chosen to break the rules, nor undoubtedly, will it be the last.

The Four Pathways
Spirit, Sacrament, Sisterhood and Service

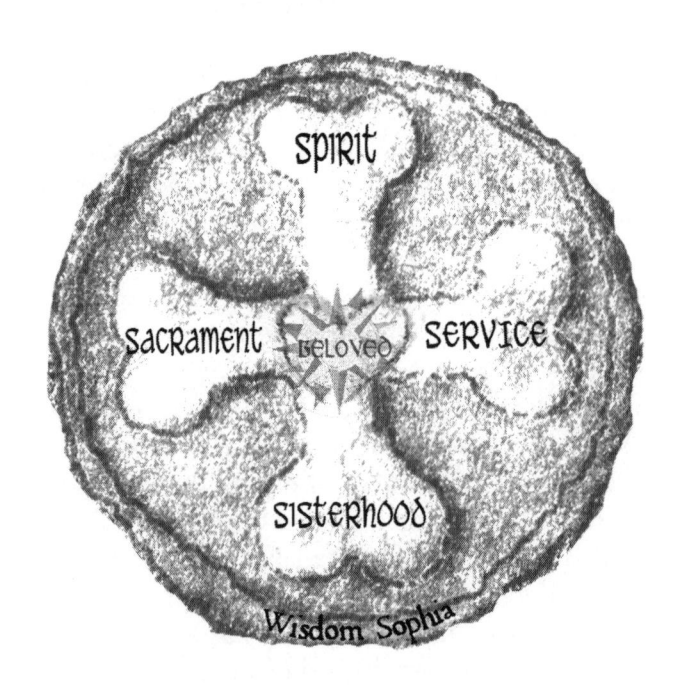

Spirit

Sacrament — *Beloved* — *Service*

Sisterhood

Wisdom Sophia

We begin our journey with the exploration of the four paths Belle Cœur spirituality. The four branches of the equidistant cross within the circle represent four interrelated spiritual paths. Each path (branch) also corresponds to one of the four seasons.

The seasons are important in relationship to the Way of Belle Cœur. Every year we circumnavigate the seasons. Each season affects, body, mind, and spirit in profound and subtle ways. The quality of light, the weather, the temperature, and also the various cultural and familial traditions that vary throughout the year… all of these seasonal aspects affect our senses and our sensibilities.

Certain segments of life's journey are cyclical and patterned. We experience the seasons as markers of time. The seasons remind us of the processes of birth, life, death and resurrection. The seasons' metaphoric correlation with the four pathways adds another level to each path's meaning. We'll explore the seasons in greater detail in Book VI.

The Four Pathways and corresponding seasons

- *Spirit relates to spring*: a season of new beginnings, birth and resurrection, and greening.
- *Sacrament connects with summer*: a time of flourishing gardens, flowing streams, and vibrant color.
- *Sisterhood is associated with autumn*: a period for reflection, hearth keeping, and gathering in.
- *Service pertains to winter*: a season for sharing, contemplation, and completion.

The Way of Belle Cœur

Each path represents a foundational aspect for Belle Cœur spirituality. It's important to note that the paths may be explored as an individual study for personal awareness or as a group process with your community.

The Path of Spirit

*Longing filled my spirit
to know God more deeply
and to serve Jesus
and His mother...
(I&H: 7)*

The path of spirit is the first path. It marks the seeker's point of embarkation to explore the Way of Belle Cœur. Spirit corresponds with spring and leads to opportunities for renewal, transformation, and spiritual maturation.

There is a spark of Divine creative fire within each soul. The Creator that set the universe in motion and created all living things also "...knit you together in your mother's womb." (Psalm 139:13)

Imagine that within your spirit you carry not only the sacred imprint of your place of origin (the heart of God), but also the marking of your soul's purpose. These blessed gifts given to you by the Beloved as you were "knit" together, are held within the sacred flame that burns eternally within your spirit. This branded eternal flame of illumination, unique to you, will continue to burn brightly after your bones have become dust. The flame can never be extinguished, though at times it may grow dim when life's distractions and challenges pull the spirit off course.

When you sense an unnameable longing within your spirit, it may be the signal that your sacred flame is in need of kindling. A sense of yearning can also be a signal that it's time to enter a season of learning to grow your wisdom through study, a pilgrimage, or other spiritual and/or creative exploration. Longing and yearning invite you to stoke your spirit and creative fire through imaginative new experiences or sacred practices.

The wisdom path of Spirit reflects the Divine Presence within you and the relationship of your heart and spirit with the Beloved. This path is relevant to the totality of your journey with God in all aspects of your life. The wisdom path of spirit is the path leading to love, forgiveness, justice and compassion…for yourself, your beloveds, your community, and *all* of creation.

The spiritual desire to become part of a sacred community is often realized as a root cause of feminine spiritual longing. It's important to realize, however, that the desire for kindred sisters is both outer and inner. As your spirit searches outwardly for your kindred sisters and community there must also be, in tandem, the exploration of your deepest resources and wisdom within *your Self.*

Your particular creative orientation and personal relationship with God, the Holy Spirit, Wisdom Sophia, and the Christ within, set the foundation where you will build your interior reliquary to hold your sacred wisdom. Your unique spiritual journey will reveal inspiration, guidance, and synchronicity like stones, one by one, to create your path. A path leading you deeper and deeper into the landscape of your spirit and your distinctive and unique relationship with the Beloved.

A Sister of Belle Cœur shares her wisdom

"As a child I knew there was a voice other than my own informing my days. Like a friend without a face it warned me of dangers and directed my understanding. That voice still guides me today. Spirit is its name. This Sacred Feminine voice, as I understand it, speaks truth and places upon my path those meant to accompany me on this journey. I am never sure whether I am to be the teacher or student. More often than not, Spirit proves I am meant to be both. Constantly, I feel this manifests as a blessed assurance."

Katherine Hempel
Sister of Belle Cœur

Spirit and community

With regard to community, the circle (a *sisterhood*) of women is a collective response to the women (*the sisters*) who feel called to share their stories, co-create, and grow together spiritually. Each woman comes to sisterhood carrying her life's joys and challenges, creative and spiritual gifts (charism), her shadow, passions, secrets, and sacred wisdom. These personal facets of her inner iconotypal self-portrait are influenced and colored by her beliefs, cultural and familial background, faith journey, unique visions, and her hopes, and dreams.

For the spirit of a woman to grow and flourish, she must be honored for her particular wisdom and spiritual/creative gifts. She may also desire the compassionate witnessing of her story as she seeks to re-member her true nature, the full radiant realization of her Self.

The path of Spirit is unique for each woman. It's the initiate's pathway where she learns to give her Self the permission to explore her spirituality and relationship with the Beloved in ways that are right for her. It's the essential path that must be traveled as a place of engagement with the essential needs of her creative heart and spirit. Walking the path of Spirit leads a woman to enter a season of intimacy with her Self and the Beloved.

The path of Spirit is also a developmental path for a sisterhood or committed intentional community. Just as there is a sacred flame burning within the spirit of each woman, a flame also burns within the collective spirit of a sisterhood and/or a circle community. The wisdom path of Spirit is the primary and foundational path leading to the Way of Belle Cœur.

It's important to reiterate that not every woman is called to become part of a community (sisterhood). Belle Cœur spirituality is spacious and respects the individual. Along the continuum from companion to sister, there's also the possibility for a woman to feel called to seek solitude, either periodically or permanently, not unlike an anchorite or hermit in the monastic tradition. This state of desired solitude may apply to Belle Cœur sisters, as well as, companions.

In monastic communities it's not uncommon for a monk or nun to request time away from the community. Often, when this happens he/she will retreat to a hermitage to experience time alone with God. Acknowledging one's rhythm, regarding the need for interaction with others and those moments when silence and solitude are called for, is important for spiritual growth and wellbeing.

The Way of Belle Cœur is inclusive and offers a wide breadth of possibility for the introvert and the extrovert. There is freedom for myriad forms of spiritual and creative expression, as well as, the acceptance of solo and/or community involvement.

A Sister of Belle Cœur shares her wisdom

"The path of spirit I have been following this year has opened up new and exciting possibilities for me. I have closed doors to many areas of my life that I thought I needed to close, only to realize I am blessed and enriched through Jesus Christ and no matter what I do, as long as my gaze is upon him, I am accepted and loved. One area I closed was my belief that I must do the right thing for God. It opened new meaning for me to realize my life has always been acceptable to God and that what I enjoy within my heart and soul is what I am to do in my every day life. I live in the moment, allowing the Spirit to reside in me, and I in Spirit."

Carolyn Hewitt
Sister of Belle Cœur

Book I The Way of Belle Cœur A Spiritual Template

Reflect

With regard to personal insight, you're invited to contemplate and respond to the following questions with your first responses. Resist the urge to edit.

- One simple step I can make towards the path of spirit is…
- My deepest longings at this moment in time are…
- When I imagine the flame within my spirit I see…
- When I consider beginning an in depth exploration of my spirit, I…
- When I envision making my spiritual journey a solo experience, rather than in community I feel…
- The concept of sisterhood is/is not important for me because…
- If I became part of an intentional spiritual community (sisterhood), I feel that I have the following spiritual, leadership, and creative gifts to offer…

For existing spiritual communities or Belle Cœur circles, the following reflection questions are intended for your group process and discussion:

- How is God informing the life of our community in the here and now?
- Do we need to revisit our intention and vision for our community?

The Way of Belle Cœur

- How do we define the health of the spirit of our community?
- What invitation is the Beloved offering our community at this time, with regard to our collective spiritual growth for the betterment of the whole?
- How is the Spirit calling us to nourish the soul of our sisterhood/community?
- What are some creative ways to add kindling to our collective soulful fire?

The Path of Sacrament

When accompanied by prayer,
a floor swept clean,
a tidied cupboard,
or a sprig of rosemary
thoughtfully placed on a pillow
are sacramental gestures of faith.
(I&H: 349-350)

The experience of sacramental observance is ancient. Throughout the ages there has been a belief that spiritual meaning could be transferred to objects or events, to transform the ordinary into the extraordinary. Primitive cultures believed they could influence the weather through their various sacramental rituals. Many religions today embrace a variety of sacraments including: marriage, communion, baptism, ordination, and penance, among others.

Belle Cœur Sacraments

For those following the Way of Belle Cœur the path of sacrament is two-fold. Sacramental expression includes personal, intentional practices of devotion and prayerful worship, and also community spiritual practices including diverse forms of celebration and ritual. The path of sacrament resonates with the season of summer.

The celebration of sacrament frequently incorporates elements from nature including: earth (flowers), air (incense), fire (candles), and water (water and oil for blessing/anointing). Sacramental expression is colorful and symbolic. It stems from the primal nature of human experience and therefore has a taproot within the fecundity of Creation.

The path of sacrament is the path of sacred awareness, creative intention, and prayerful presence. This path leads to blessings and enrichment for your spiritual wellbeing. Belle Cœur spirituality encourages sisters and their communities to create sacramental celebrations, as they feel guided by the prophetic inspiration of the Spirit.

The Way of Belle Cœur

Personal Sacrament

The key tenets for the creation of personal sacraments are *sacred awareness, creative intention,* and *prayerful presence.* In this way, your morning walk becomes sacramental as you pray for others, while you breathe in the peace of God's presence within the sunlight and shadows on the path before you. When you dress for the day, as you offer the Morning Prayer of Belle Cœur (Book IX), the simple act of putting on your clothes becomes a sacramental experience. The preparation of a meal becomes sacrament as you chop vegetables and stir your prayers and love into the soup you'll serve your family at suppertime. Your evening bath is a sacrament as the water cleanses away the stress and anxiety of the day and you prayerfully shed your cares in preparation for rest, renewal, and dreams.

The path of sacrament pertains to specific daily and celebratory rituals, and the sacramental observance of life's transitions and rites of passage.

A sacrament by definition in relationship to the Way of Belle Cœur may be expressed as an outward demonstration of prayerful and heart-centered recognition of the Divine Presence within the present moment.

Sacraments are celebrated to reflect a sister's inner awareness of the Beloved's presence, benevolence, and grace. Sacraments may also be co-created within the sister's community, to acknowledge collective mindfulness of the spiritual practices, occasions, and celebrations that hold meaning for the whole. A sacrament may evolve and change form in accordance with the ebb and flow of a sister's personal spiritual development, or the ongoing particular needs of a community as it emerges into the fullness of its charism.

Sacramental rituals to honor and celebrate daily experiences

Imagine your creation of sacraments through the incorporation of intention, prayer, and beauty to bless and honor the following ordinary moments, life transitions, and occasions:

- ❖ The simple act of the preparation of your first cup of morning tea or coffee. Breathing in and breathing out, you take a sip and offer a prayer for someone in need.
- ❖ As you prayerfully prepare a meal, contemplate mealtime as a sacrament of shared communion with those around your table. Break bread together as a prayerful acknowledgement of the Beloved's presence within each person.
- ❖ As the day begins you consciously and prayerfully select your clothing and adornment. Consider the sacramental potential within the act of dressing (vesting) for the day or for a special occasion.
- ❖ While you prayerfully (sacramentally) clean and bring order to the various rooms within your home, make your bed, fold laundry, and/or arrange your workspace. Consciously and

reverently create sacred space for yourself and those who will cross your threshold.
- ❖ When you or your beloveds prepare to leave your house. You may wish to offer a prayer for protection and sacramental blessing for yourself or beloveds as you (they) journey. Additionally, offer a prayer for your home's safekeeping while you're away. When you return, remove your shoes as you cross the threshold with a prayer of gratitude for a safe arrival.
- ❖ When visiting a friend who is ill, or an elder celebrating a milestone birthday, offer the sacrament of anointing and/or a blessing.

Sacraments for transitions, celebrations, and life's passages

Imagine creating a sacrament to honor moments of transition and celebration. When you're creating and celebrating a sacrament be mindful to incorporate a variety of elements to activate the senses such as: incense, candles, water, color, music, and things from nature.

The creation of sacramental observations to mark life's passages, both festive and somber, may be celebrated but not limited to the experiences listed below. Contemplate how you would prayerfully sacralize these moments and occasions, and be sure to add additional opportunities for sacramental observance that come to mind.

Book I The Way of Belle Cœur A Spiritual Template

How would you create a sacrament to honor the following experiences and occasions?

- The commencement of a new job
- A change of residence
- A pregnancy
- A birth
- For the healing of a woman/family following a miscarriage
- At the onset of illness
- A vigil for the dying
- For the blessing a new relationship
- An engagement
- A marriage or acknowledgement of a partnership (Book IX)
- For peace and closure when a relationship ends
- A birthday
- Forgiveness and/or reconciliation
- An anniversary of a marriage, partnership, union or special event
- At a time of healing or transformation (Book IX)
- To honor the blessing of good news
- When planting flowers or gardening
- The blessing of a new animal companion
- The commencement of a new journal
- The first day of a creative project or course of study (Book IX)
- The day of a young girl's menstrual onset, or the announcement of a pregnancy
- A celebration to honor the remembrance of the life of a beloved on the anniversary of his/her death

- ❖ A celebration to acknowledge the change of seasons
- ❖ Sacred observations during the liturgical year: Advent, Christmas, Lent, Easter, Pentecost, Ordinary Time
- ❖ The celebration of breaking bread together… a sacrament to be shared with your community or shared with family as inspired by the movement of the Spirit

Community sacraments

In the context of community, sacrament takes form through a shared need and desire for sacred celebration, the honoring of a transition, or other particular desire for ritualized prayerful acknowledgment.

Contemplate the following examples of sacraments to be used within a community experience when…

- ❖ your community reunites for your annual retreat.
- ❖ a sister experiences a celebratory life event: a new career path, the birth of a child or grandchild, the completion of a major project or the fruition of a vision or dream, or a birthday marking the beginning of her wisdom years.
- ❖ a sister moves through a major life transition such as: marriage, divorce, the death of a

partner, spouse, or beloved, or the experiences the onset or recovery from illness.
- ❖ a sister dies.
- ❖ the community commences a project, service, or ministry.
- ❖ there has been a challenge or shadow experience within the community and healing is called for.
- ❖ when a sister is called to leave the community or called to enter into a time of solitude.

The sacrament of anointing and blessing

"Pray my sisters, before you touch the sick; ask for your hands to become instruments of healing; open yourselves to become Christ's love and mercy."
(*I&H:* 157)

Those who follow the Way of Belle Cœur are compassionate carriers of hope and healing. The sacrament of anointing is an ancient practice to offer Christ's peace with a blessing. Anointing has been used for centuries for a variety of somber circumstances including illness (for healing) and when death is imminent (final blessing). Anointing is also a celebratory sacrament for various rites of passage such as: birthdays, anniversaries, a time of departure for a journey, or the commencement of new work, and so on. A recipe for anointing oil and blessing prayers are provided in Book IX.

A Sister of Belle Cœur shares her wisdom

"Before I start my workday as a hospice chaplain I pray the Scripture, 'I go to prepare a place for you, that where I am, you may also be.' This reminds me that Jesus is present in the patient's room, even before I arrive, preparing a place for my arrival.

Being present to the dying becomes sacramental as I gently place my hand on the person's forehead or heart to offer prayer and blessing. Death sometimes occurs in that very moment.

I have been a channel for the Beloved as an outward and visible sign to the tender transition of the 'also life' of that person. The awe of this sacramental presence is palpable, gentle and serene and in that moment we are simultaneously held inside God's grace."

Chaplain Sheryll Shepard
Sister of Belle Cœur

The Sacrament of Table Community

Belle Cœur spirituality celebrates the Sacrament of the Feast of Life where <u>*all are welcome*</u> to the table to prayerfully join in the breaking and sharing of "bread for the journey" and to drink from "the cup of compassion." (*I&H*: 473-474)

The Feast of Life is a celebration of the Beloved's teachings and promise of new life in the Spirit. Communities may decide to celebrate the Feast of Life every time they gather, or seasonally, or whenever they need the nourishment of an Agape (spiritually loving) celebration. This sacrament is also meaningful when it is shared personally with family or friends. (Book IX)

The Sacrament of Naming a Charism

Belle Cœur spirituality recognizes the multitude of spiritual and creative gifts belonging to others. Individual charisms are acknowledged within a Belle Cœur sisterhood circle (or Belle Cœur spiritual community) and the Sacrament of Naming is offered according to a sister's charism and calling.

For example, a sister may have the necessary creative skills and feel inspired to record the legacy of her sisterhood. She shares her calling with her sisters. With the community's blessing and agreement the sister then receives the Sacrament of naming as *Keeper of the Stories* or *Guardian of the Sisterhood's Sacred Codex*, or another title appropriate for the recognized calling.

Sisters that feel called to enter into solitude may also choose to be named by the community as, *Anchorite* or *Cloistered Sister*. There are many ways to serve as a sister beyond the boundaries of community activities. Sometimes this means a sister steps into a solitary role. Her gift of spiritual presence endures when her physical presence is no longer active.

There is an endless list for possible namings, including the *Keeper of Prayers, Baker of the Bread, the Keeper of the Portundae, the Keeper of the Hearth,* and so on. Additional sacramental namings may be called for according to the needs of a particular community and the respective charisms and callings of the various sisters. A community ritual for the Sacrament of Naming is outlined in Book IX.

A Sister of Belle Cœur shares her wisdom

"I am the "Keeper of Prayers" for our sisterhood and a Shalom-making Artisan. I have always been a woman of prayer, and I have always turned to quilting, knitting, and weaving in times of both joy and sorrow. For many years, I designed and made quilts, some to celebrate births and others that came through my fingers as I dealt with fears and uncertainties. Several years ago, I attended a prayer shawl retreat. I learned to pray for the ones who would receive my shawls as I knitted. I also began weaving dolls that expressed the joy of women's wisdom. Working with my hands became my way of praying.

Through the Way of Belle Cœur my praying and crafting literally become one. When my sisters named me to be the Keeper of our prayers, I knew we needed something that could embody our prayers, especially since our sisterhood is spread all over the country. I was inspired to make a prayer quilt. Our quilt of blue, gold, and honeybees expresses our identity as sisters of Belle Cœur. Our names and who we are in our sisterhood are written around the edge, and our prayers are written on the meandering labyrinth of the quilt's pattern. One of my sisters described my craft as alchemy. I take the sorrows of our prayers and change them into a quilt that wraps us in Shalom—wholeness of body, mind, and soul."

Book I The Way of Belle Cœur A Spiritual Template

Deborah Hansen
Spiritual Director and Sister of Belle Cœur

The Sacrament of Creative Expression

Inspiration is a miraculous phenomenon. This morning before I began writing I was looking through my photos, the way one sorts through twigs and branches in search of useful kindling to build a fire. I was seeking fuel to stoke my creativity. In my search I came upon many images pertaining to artmaking, writing, and an array of pictures reflecting the creative process.

The thought was sparked as I added my photographic kindling to my creative fire, that the generative and life giving acts of artmaking, writing, and other forms of expression are sacramental by nature. Fundamental to any form of creativity is the engagement with the sacred imagination. The sacred imagination is the mystical place within you where the Spirit's inspiration merges with your particular gifts and talents as co-creative energy.

With the arts in mind, it's important to acknowledge the Sacrament of Creative Harvest. The exploration of various forms of artmaking, writing, and all manner of creative processes when passed through the lens of sacred awareness become sacramental.

Three years ago when I began to write this book, I carefully harvested my journals in search of morsels of inspiration to fuel my writing. I came to realize that the art and the reflective practice of reviewing and culling

The Way of Belle Cœur

the journal is a sacred undertaking. I was inspired when I began to revisit the first journal of my harvest to light a candle and offer a prayer for guidance for what would be most essential and helpful for my writing.

In this way, harvesting my journals became sacramental. With the turn of each page I felt myself slowing down. I began to receive blessings of discovery through a found word or a forgotten idea scribbled in the margin.

Inspiration lived in the pages of my past journals. Not because I was so wise and prophetic to have provided it. Rather, because through God's grace and the sacrament of sacred awareness and harvesting, I was guided to unearth and reclaim nuggets of treasure. Those fragments and shards of cultivated and archived journal entries are woven within these pages.

The sacrament of harvesting journals is a way to become the curator and archivist of your life's journey. I invite you to contemplate receiving the Sacrament of Creative Harvest that awaits you within the pages of your past journals. Sacred wisdom, creative inspiration, and guidance for your life waits within the pages of the old, dusty notebooks stacked on a shelf or buried in boxes in the attic.

Gather your journals. Light a candle, sit quietly in prayer with a chosen volume in your lap then lay your hands upon it and bless it for the stories it so faithfully received. Open it with reverence, while you savor and commune with what awaits you, as you look to the past to inform your present. When you encounter anything that holds the potential of reliving old wounds or regrets, acknowledge the feeling with prayer for it to be released. Take a deep breath and return to the present moment where all is well. Receive the gift and sacrament of a well-harvested journal as nourishment for your creative spirit.

The Sacrament of Dreaming

The sacred practice of the recollection and recording of your dreams and the creation of art, writing, music, etc. inspired by your dreams is potentially informative and life giving. Your dream life provides clay gathered during your nocturnal wanderings to be sculpted as guidance to inform the day. The cultivation and honoring of dreams is a sacrament. If you consciously record your dreams and dream images, it's quite possible that your waking life will reveal new depths of inspiration and sacred awareness.

In many cultures dreams are honored as wisdom stories, as visitations by spirit teachers, and there are special shamans within tribal and primitive cultures to help the dreamer interpret her dreams. In our culture dreams rarely receive a similar level of sacramental attention and recognition. Paying homage to dreams through recall, exploration, and expression enriches the dream-life and brings revelations and new potential for soulful living to your waking-life.

Here are a few ways to bring your dreams into two and three-dimensional form to anchor them within waking reality for a closer look. Think of your dreams as visitors you would like to become better acquainted with. In the way you would cultivate a friendship with new acquaintances you can entertain your dreams, invite them to stay, and pay close attention to their stories. In this way, dreams become sacramental offerings from your unconscious and beyond.

Invite the dream

The first step is to create an environment to welcome your dreams. It's important to take a look around your bed before you put your head on the pillow. Do clutter and the shards of the day surround you? Your bedroom should be a place of tranquility and sanctuary. When you cross the threshold into your *dream chamber* you should experience a sense of relaxation. Sacralize the space you sleep in with beauty, intention, and attention.

Before sleep it's important to sweep away the accumulated dust of the day from your inner world. Just as you outwardly remove your make-up or clothes as you prepare to go to bed, you must also make a shift inwardly. When you set your alarm for morning, try tuning the radio to a classical music station and set the volume at the lowest level possible, to allow you to gently awaken.

Enjoy a warm bath imbued with lavender oil, play soft music, slip into fresh linens, and release your concerns upon the pages of your journal before you close your eyes. This ritual of preparation becomes a Dream Sacrament that will help to clear the path for nocturnal visitations to the dream world. Prepare your space and your body and spirit to receive your dream visitor.

Record your dream

Have a blank book and a pen handy to record your dream, or dream images, and fragments as soon as you awaken. Think of your dream journal as a sacramental vessel, a blessed container to hold the stories of your dreams.

If a dream should cause you to awaken during the night, scribe it in your journal. As the light of day or the alarm returns you to consciousness, lie still for a time and be aware of any images, thoughts, or feelings that surface for your awareness. Next, notice your body. Are you curled in a fetal position or stretched out like a cat basking in the afternoon sun? What can your body tell you about your dream?

Slowly reach for your dream journal. Record the date and time and write anything you can recall about your dreams. Write your dream or dream fragment in the present tense as though you are reliving the dream. You are inviting your dream visitor to stay to become better acquainted.

Engage the interpreter

Dreams speak in the language of symbols. Decode your dreams to discover a way to translate the symbolic imagery into a tangible and recognizable form. List the various symbols and write all the meanings you attach alongside. Circle the one or two meanings that feel resonant with the story of your dream or hold potency for your present day life.

Engage your creative sacred imagination as an interpreter to assist the process. Have a few simple art supplies handy as the first step towards dialoguing with your dreams.

In a basket near your dream journal keep some colored pens or pencils. Make a quick sketch of prominent dream symbols. This is a good starting point for creative exploration of your dreams.

Honor your dream

Take time to get to know a dream as a way to honor your symbolic life. Make a visual prayer card to represent your dream's story. This is a powerful creative process that will yield an additional layer of understanding through a two-dimensional symbolic representation.

Create
The Sacrament of Visual Prayer Card Reflection

A visual prayer card is a small, collaged representation of a particular prayer intention or a symbolic interpretation of a dream. Visual prayer cards are created with a specific intention, through a spontaneous and intuitive process.

Book I The Way of Belle Cœur A Spiritual Template

Materials

An assortment of collage materials such as: magazines, castaway photos, and bargain art books
A glue stick
A stack of 4" x 6" unlined index cards

The Process

Gather several magazines or collage materials of your choice. Notice images that draw you in. Clip or tear out the images that hold the most resonance for you.

A good source for meaningful images is old photos, the castaways that didn't make it into albums or scrapbooks. You might also check the bargain table at the local bookstore where you can find wonderful and very inexpensive illustrated books with imagery that's perfect for your visual prayers.

When perusing your photo collection, select the images that catch your eye. Look for a portion of the photo that holds your attention and cut it into a square or rectangular shape to become a miniature photo. Make copies with your printer of favorite photos then trim the copies.

Keep a basket of supplies near your workspace including: an envelope filled of assorted clipped images, a glue stick, scissors, and 4" x 6" unlined index cards (these work nicely as a background). Have everything within reach for those moments when you need to pause for inspiration. When you notice you're feeling

The Way of Belle Cœur

overwhelmed by your list of "shoulds" stop *doing* and make a conscious shift to a sacramental state of *being*.

Light a candle, make a cup of tea, and listen to quiet music or rest in silence. Next, spend a few moments consciously breathing in and breathing out. Offer a prayer and with soft focus (as though entering a waking dream) look through your collection of images. The intention is to find a few pictures that hold inspiration and guidance for the present moment or images to reflect a recent dream.

Cut and arrange your selection of images on the blank card and glue the pieces of your visual prayer collage into place. Words and phrases torn or cut from magazines might also be added, though it's often beneficial to step away from the world of words to simply rely upon imagery to create the visual prayer. There's really no way to make a mistake with this process. Allow your creative heart to guide you.

Rather than over thinking the placement of images in a perfectionistic way, craft your visual prayer intuitively…as a dreamlike encounter. When a visual prayer is created with reverence and prayerful intention for the experience becomes sacramental.

After the visual prayer is complete, title and date the back of the card for future reference. Then reflect upon the sacrament (the blessing and grace) within your visual prayer collage. On the reverse side of the card, jot your immediate thoughts and feelings, or scribe a poem, haiku, or prayer in response to the story within the imagery.

Completed cards can be stored in a photo album, basket, or index file. Often, the simple act of randomly drawing a previously made visual prayer card can become a sacramental moment of blessing when time is scarce to create a new one.

The creation of visual prayer cards for a friend or beloved in need of spiritual upliftment, healing, and/or comfort is also a contemplative and valuable form of prayer. Three or four visual prayer cards tied with a ribbon are a wonderful offering of blessing.

The entire process to create a visual prayer collage takes fifteen to thirty minutes or less. Time and time again when I've created a visual prayer card I've felt an internal shift from frustration and overwhelm to inspired calm. Crossing the bridge from doing to being through the creation of visual prayer cards is a centering and sacramental creative practice

The Path of Sisterhood

*As their community grew,
each woman's gifts bloomed
into loving action,
an offering to God
and the sisterhood.*
(*I&H:* 107)

Communities of women, like branches on the Tree of Life, stem from an ancient taproot. Perhaps women's circles have endured throughout time because they are connected to an ineffable and invisible lineage of feminine, sacred wisdom winding throughout history and *her* story.

Overview

The Path of Sisterhood can be related to the season of autumn. In the fall we experience time for reflection, hearth keeping, and gathering for the harvest. Within the heart of the sisterhood, we share the bounty of our spiritual and creative gifts with one another as we contemplate our ministries and service for the greater good.

Through my experiences and interactions as a spiritual director and retreat facilitator for the feminine spiritual/creative process, I have witnessed remarkable and numinous connections among women when they gather together as spiritual sisters. Within the circle of an intentional community, women have the opportunity to share, co-create, dream, study, serve, and vision in the Way of Belle Cœur.

The sacred container of sisterhood holds a community in an atmosphere of safety where sisters feel confident to share their stories, embrace silence, pray, create, celebrate beauty, and break bread. It could be said that there is sacrament within the spirit of sisterhood. Through the profound connection of Christ's presence within each woman the value of her wisdom and Spirit-filled contribution to the whole is acknowledged and appreciated.

Book I The Way of Belle Cœur A Spiritual Template

The path of sisterhood leads to an intentional, collectively wise, spiritually centered and service oriented community. The circle is our form as the representation of wholeness, fulfillment, and the unending continuation of the ancient lineage of sisters.

When a woman has traveled the wisdom paths of Spirit and Sacrament, she may feel called to journey the path of sisterhood. Her search for a sacred community of kindred spirits (her spiritual sisters) is sacramental by virtue of her personal intention to grow her wisdom in community.

The path of sisterhood enriches and fortifies the spiritual growth of each sister. Through the sisterhood's support, acknowledgement, and respect for each sister's spiritual and creative gifts (her charism), every sister takes her place on the rim of the community's circle as an equal. Those who follow the Way of Belle Cœur and call forth a sisterhood circle are ecumenical and inclusive. They welcome diversity, and honor and respect each woman's particular charism.

Individuality and varied forms of self-expression are essential for the health of the sisterhood. Inclusivity with regard to cultural and religious/spiritual experience, sexual orientation, and political views is also essential. The unifying and fortifying underpinnings throughout Belle Cœur spirituality manifest through our shared forms of devotion and prayer.

We listen to one another with compassion. To the best of our abilities we practice non-judgment. When difficulty arises we acknowledge the challenge before us with prayer, reflection, and open discussion. We offer whatever issue arises to God and prayerfully engage the wisdom of every sister to assist a resolution.

Belle Cœur sisterhood circles are intentional communities. The basic intention for each circle is to honor one another. Each sisterhood circle also has an expression of charism that is particular and unique to the community. There is creative freedom for a circle to celebrate and serve in myriad ways. Belle Cœur sisterhood is a contemporary, contemplative, spiritual, and creative community.

We continually rely on Christ as our model of love, compassion, forgiveness, non-judgment, and service for the greater good. Jesus, our Teacher, is at the center of all we are and all we do. We cannot lose our way with the Beloved as our compass and True North.

Who we are

We are 21st century women: single, married, widowed, divorced, and partnered. We are diverse in sexual orientation, shape, size, and hair color. We are mothers, maidens, crones, artisans, writers, beekeepers, retired and active clergy, and spiritual directors. Women who choose to follow the Way of Belle Cœur are grandmothers, aunts, doctors, godmothers, chaplains, hearth tenders, poets, and professionals. Religious backgrounds among the sisters are also diverse. We are a blend of introverts and extroverts. An important commonality is that we have all been seeking and journeying most of our lives to know ourselves, to grow closer to God.

Our diversity reflects how each sister is called to participate. Diverse forms of response and involvement with regard to active Belle Cœur participation run the gamut along a continuum. Some women feel called to leadership. They organize, orchestrate, and plan structure for Belle Cœur retreats, gatherings, online interaction, and they facilitate Belle Cœur Sacred Life-Arts workshops. There are also sisters that choose to be less participatory with regard to community activities. Solo practitioners (companions) of the Way of Belle Cœur are also prayerful, contemplative, and reflective.

There is room for all manner of participation, non-participation, experience, and personal acclimation. Each woman is respected and honored for her unique and personal call. Again, our commonality rests within the center, within the heart of Jesus.

Spiritual and creative intentions

To follow the inner call to the Way of Belle Cœur is to follow one's heart towards a direct experience and relationship with the Divine Presence within and without. This is soul-work that requires a ready openness to the Mystery and fearless creative expression.

For those who are discerning the call to sisterhood or those who are called to a solo companion journey, the following suggested guidelines of spiritual and creative intention are offered for your inspiration. The appropriate associated aspect of Belle Cœur spirituality for each guideline is in parentheses. Please

The Way of Belle Cœur

reflect upon these intentions as the Spirit reveals how you might embody and make them your own.

As a sister/companion of Belle Cœur, I intend…

- ❖ to express my life to the best of my ability through co-creation with God, moment by moment. To live within a river of ever-flowing prayer while I listen with the ears of my heart for the Beloved's guidance, and draw from the well of my feminine wisdom. (Spirit/Devotion)
- ❖ to reconnect with the spirits of my ancestors, feminine *her*story, and the Divine Feminine to learn from the legacy of the ancients to inform my present life. (Wisdom Sophia)
- ❖ to contemplate the meaning of my soul's contract while I step confidently into my creative and spiritual gifts. (Iconotypal Study)
- ❖ to thoughtfully, prayerfully, and appropriately respond to the needs of others. To practice self-care so I may remain healthy, centered, and whole as I continue my life's journey. (Service)
- ❖ to commit to working towards an organic and evolutionary daily sacred practice in alignment with my personal spiritual understanding. (Devotion)
- ❖ to humbly express my creative and spiritual gifts, given to me by God. To cultivate beauty, order, and simplicity within my environment and in the world. (Craft/Service)
- ❖ to keep a personal journal as a workbook for my life's journey, in order to distill and grow my wisdom, to be recorded in my Sacred Codex as

my enduring legacy of feminine knowledge and experience. (Story/Craft)
- to use my inner eyes to recognize the symbolic, energetic, and metaphoric meaning of places, objects, dreams, and life's synchronicities. To offer blessing and anointing for healing and celebration. (Sacrament/Spirit)
- to pray for and support my sisters, companions, and beloveds. (Devotion/Service)
- to practice the tasks of daily life: creating, cooking, bathing, laundry, etc., as sacred life-arts. To engage my sacred imagination to seek a creative solution when I am challenged by a problem or conflict. (Craft/Spirit)
- to continue to study and learn from the Holy Scriptures, the teachings of the ancient mystics and contemporary spiritual teachers, and through life's everyday moments and relationships. (Study)
- to speak my truth clearly and authentically with passion and compassion. (Spirit)
- to balance my inner Mary with my inner Martha through my needs for contemplation, reflection, and solitude combined with sacred action, activism, and community life. (Sisterhood)
- to serve as Christ's hands, heart, ears, and eyes in the world. (Service/Spirit)
- to regard nature as the Living God made visible and to honor all of creation in her myriad forms. (Wisdom Sophia)
- to foster radical beauty, peace, hope, and wisdom as a living conduit for God's mercy and grace. (Service/Craft)

Those who follow the Way of Belle Cœur share...

- ❖ devotion to personal daily spiritual practice and prayer.
- ❖ passion for creativity and sacred artmaking as forms of spiritual expression.
- ❖ mindful, compassionate service and/or ministry to foster healing and hope for our world.
- ❖ respect for each woman's unique call with regard to her participation within the sisterhood.
- ❖ recognition for the evolutionary movement of personal response to the sisterhood in accordance with prophetic guidance through Spirit.

Onward we go

We carry the sisterhood tradition forward, inspired by the medieval monastics and the Beguines in ways that are acclimated for our lives today. We will explore the Beguine movement later in this section.

There is beauty and sacredness woven into the rituals, prayers, and spiritual experience of all the religions of the world. Shared prayers, sacraments, and spiritual/creative practices are drawn from many inspirational sources and religious traditions while the heart of the Way of Belle Cœur remains Christ-centered.

Book I The Way of Belle Cœur A Spiritual Template

A Sister of Belle Cœur shares her wisdom

"I never had a sister, so the Belle Cœur sisterhood serves as a family of sisters for me. I am amazed at how close I feel to a group of women that I was only in physical presence with for five days. Our communications since our time together has been ongoing and very dear to me. I feel that I could call on any one of these women for support, for encouragement, for virtually anything I needed and they would be there for me – like a sister. Even though we are far apart, we continue to grow and learn together and support each other in trials and in successes."

Millie Park Mellgren,
Sister of Belle Cœur

It is often a vital human need to feel part of a community. Women throughout time have gathered in circles and perhaps the yearning for the *circular* experience of community is a cellular memory encoded in our DNA.

The Way of Belle Cœur invites the *re*-membering of the beauty, truth, and purpose of life's journey for each of us. We personally incorporate sacred practices into the everyday, and bring ritual, prayer, and contemplative ways of being to our women's circles.

Here is how Goscelin, in the story of *Ink and Honey*, describes the importance and value of simple ritual for her community, the sisterhood of Belle Cœur.

*"The rituals of daily life sustain us.
Prayer is added to all we do to feed our spirits.*

The Way of Belle Cœur

We taste it in Beatrice's bread. It grows in Helvide's planting of the herbs and is heard with every strum of Mabille's playing on her lyre."
Later she goes on to say....
"The beauty is in the blending of how each demonstrates her vision of the sacred." (*I&H:* 349)

The Contemporary Sisterhood of Belle Cœur

Soon after *Ink and Honey* was released I began receiving e-mails and calls from readers. They wrote to share how the story of the sisterhood of Belle Cœur rang a bell of resonance and longing within their hearts. With the arrival of each message I felt God calling me to enter a time of prayer and discernment. I prayed to know how to respond to the readers' longing for community and sisterhood.

My personal desire to be a sister, to be part of a women's spiritual community was seeded within me sixty plus years ago, when I attended my first day of parochial kindergarten. My family was Episcopalian. We lived next door to a Catholic church and for convenience's sake I was enrolled there at Holy Angels School.

Sister Maria Giovanna, my teacher, and her community of teaching sisters inspired my child's heart with a profound spirituality that continues to inform my life. From the very first day when I attended Mass with my schoolmates, I wanted to become a nun, a sister. I wanted to be just like Sister Maria Giovanna, prayerfully present to God with sisters, in community.

Soon after my introduction to Catholicism and sisterhood my family moved to another town. My longing for a monastic life never left me, rather it continued to grow stronger throughout the years. In my early teens I begged my mother and father to allow me to enter the local convent. My parents were not in favor of this idea.

My girlhood spirit had become mysteriously intertwined and devoted to the ritual, prayers, and spirituality of Catholicism. My calling to conversion to Catholicism and to enter the convent to become a nun continued until I was sixteen.

Choices

In my junior year of high school I met the boy who would one day become my husband. We went away to college and were married soon after. Three years later I gave birth to our daughter and next our son arrived to complete our family. Motherhood was a blessed and cherished season of my life.

When I fell in love with my husband I was called to follow a path that was very different from cloistered religious life. In later years I became a grandmother and another sacred chapter of life's journey began.

Throughout the years my inner desire to traverse the path of sisterhood awaited exploration. The first step on the sisterhood path commenced for me when my children were grown and on their own.

I was inspired to call a women's circle of like-minded kindred spirits. We met quarterly at my home to celebrate the changing seasons, to pray together, to break bread and share our personal stories. Several committed souls from our community formed a smaller circle and we gathered regularly to meditate, pray, and express our spiritual questions. It was during this time that I received the inspiration commencing my twenty-two year writing journey of *Ink and Honey*. (*I&H*: 483-487)

My teachers prepare the way

I felt that the story that would eventually become *Ink and Honey* would portray the sisterhood of Belle Cœur as a community that was independent from the Church. I was clear that my characters were a private and rather radical order of sisters for their time. They were Christ-centered, devoted to Jesus' mother, Mary, and also to Mary Magdalene. Their covenant ensured they could choose to leave their community at any time and they were free to marry if they desired. Their sisterhood's service was expressed through their devotion to continual prayer and caring for the sick and dying, as well as, feeding and tending the poor. (*I&H*: 86-87)

My characters began to reveal their sacred life-arts to me. I learned their ways of gardening, cooking, candle making, tending the hearth, creating sanctuary, bread baking, and so on. It was revealed to me, through the writing, how sacred everyday tasks when imbued with prayer and intention become a sacrament. Every action by the sisters in my story, whether great or small, was illuminated with prayer or ritual, contemplation or sacred expression. While I wrote, Goscelin, Beatrice, Petronilla and the others spilled forth their sacred mysteries, one by one.

October 2003 was my initiation to consciously recognize my deep and fervent inner call to create a sisterhood. The following is an excerpt from my journal during that time.

My recent dreams have been filled with sacred imagery… a folded black and cream-colored nun's habit, a scapular with the monogram, MM (Mary Magdalene?) is presented to me by St. Michael. Christ speaks to the ears of my heart, "Work from the center… out." Finally, I am handed the folded nun's habit and told, "Start a new order."

My call and longing for sisterhood took root. Meanwhile I worked to complete the manuscript that would eventually become *Ink and Honey*. At the time the working title for the novel was XII (Twelve). I continued to express my thoughts in my journal.

I am beginning to realize that the characters of XII are teachers with instructions for how to create the new order, the Sisterhood of Belle Cœur. The Blessed Mother, Christ, and Mary Magdalene are the matrix (template). I am praying for guidance for how to begin.

The Way of Belle Cœur

It would take ten more years of journaling, contemplation, prayer and the completion and deliverance of *Ink and Honey* for the Spirit's fertile gift of inspiration to gestate to fruition. At a personal level, what I learned during those ten years was instrumental for my understanding of how to call forth, create, and nurture the birth of Belle Cœur spirituality.

At long last in 1999, while the process of writing *Ink and Honey* continued, I converted to Catholicism. Four years later I discovered an international movement, Roman Catholic Women Priests, had begun a formation program for Roman Catholic women called to ordained ministry. I learned that their women bishops were ordaining women in Europe, Canada, and the U.S.

I was accepted into the ordination preparation program and two years later I was ordained as deacon and a year after celebrated priestly ordination. Eventually, I was called by our region's community and elected as the first Roman Catholic woman bishop of North America. I served as bishop for the Western Region of the organization until a sudden illness required me to retire.

During my yearlong healing process and recuperation I came to realize that God was calling me to serve in another way. I discerned after months of prayer, journaling, and long conversations with my spiritual director that God's call is organic and evolutionary.

My desire to follow prophetic obedience required my ordained life to take a turn. I became clear I was to follow the path of the writer. When I recovered from illness I picked up the thread of the story of *Ink and*

Book I The Way of Belle Cœur A Spiritual Template

Honey and continued to write. Four years later it came to fruition.

Several years later, after the release of *Ink and Honey*, I began to contemplate the meaning and heart of Belle Cœur spirituality. The journey continues...

I have shared this piece of my personal story because you may be experiencing a time in your life when you are feeling called to step away from the familiar to begin something new. It takes courage to change the course of one's life. I have come to understand through the many unexpected challenges and detours of my life's journey that God's call for the soul is *not* static. An initial and particular calling may evolve with the passage of time and organically lead to another path. However, even though circumstances may require a change of course to begin again, the original call will always remain a foundational steppingstone on the path for wherever God leads you.

❦

When *Ink and Honey* was at last in print and I reread it. It was then that the story clearly revealed to me how the Belle Cœur sisters shared four distinct pathways of development: *Spirit, Sacrament, Sisterhood* and *Service.* It also became clear they expressed their spirituality, their prayers, and their faith through four forms of spiritual practice: *Devotion, Craft, Study, and Story.*

The Sacred Feminine, experienced throughout Creation as the plants, animals, stars, and changing seasons, were revealed to be essentially informative

The Way of Belle Cœur

for the Belle Cœur sisters' way of life. Core to their lives was an abiding faith and profound relationship with the Beloved.

The emergence of Belle Cœur spirituality began to take shape. The four pathways, four practices, the reliance on Jesus at the center, and the circular, encompassing nurturance of Wisdom Sophia, represented the holistic patterns for life's spiritual/creative journey. All of the elements fit within the sign of Belle Cœur that is the sacred symbol of the equidistant cross, encompassed by the circle. The symbol became the template for the Way of Belle Cœur.

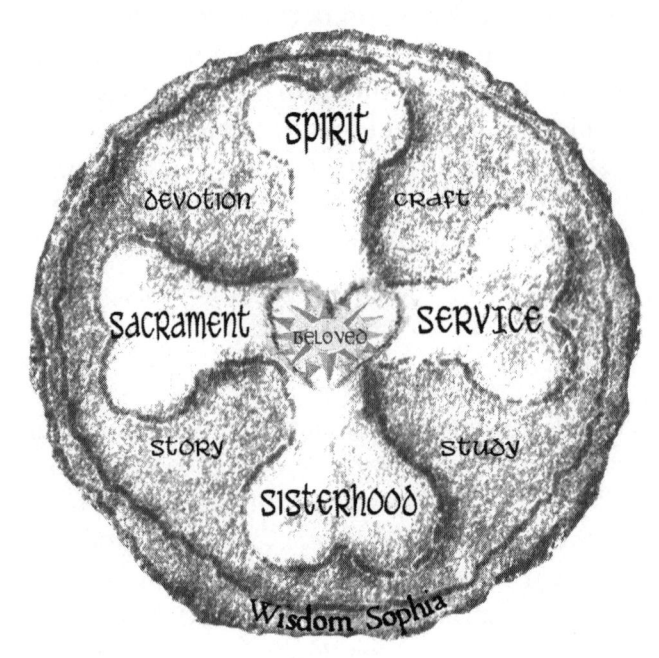

Book I The Way of Belle Cœur A Spiritual Template

The intention

At long last in 2013, the way of Belle Cœur spiritual and creative program was prepared and the invitation was shared for a five-day autumn retreat. I celebrated when all was finally ready for those who would respond to the call to Belle Cœur.

I turned to a fresh journal page...

My intention for the first Way of Belle Cœur Retreat is to call a circle of Christ-centered, open-minded, and openhearted women to gather together to pray, study, create sacred art, and share their wisdom in community. I intend to offer a spiritual and creative template, the Way of Belle Cœur, inspired by the depiction of the sisters of Belle Cœur in the story, Ink and Honey. *Our new community will rely upon God's guidance with respect for one another's wisdom, as we individually and collectively explore Belle Cœur spirituality.*

A Belle Cœur Sister shares her wisdom

"As we sat together in circle, shared laughter and tears; as we listened deeply to one another's stories, celebrated ritual, meditated, prayed and created art together, I knew I had found what I'd been seeking for so long—my spiritual home, my sisterhood, my center."

Mary Montayne,
Sister of Belle Cœur

The circle: the relational form for Belle Cœur

Central to Belle Cœur community participation is the form for our group process, the circle. We have learned that the circle surrounding the equidistant cross of the Belle Cœur template represents: wholeness, inclusivity, equality and the spiritual aspects of Wisdom Sophia and Creation. The circle is also the form we embrace when a Belle Cœur community meets for a retreat or other activity.

We arrange our chairs in a circle: place a candle upon a small table at the center as our altar. The candle flame represents the Light and Love within the presence of the Beloved.

To fully understand the circle as a sacred container where guidance, dialogue, problem-solving, and shared story may be held and processed in a sacred manner, read *The Circle Way: A Leader in Every Chair* by Christina Baldwin and Ann Linnea. The PeerSpirit model of circle, taught by Christina and Ann, is foundational to Belle Cœur spirituality. The same model may be incorporated for existing women's groups, community circles, and for business settings.

The basic three principles for the circle where all are respected as leaders include:

I. Leadership rotates among <u>all</u> circle members.
II. Responsibility is <u>shared</u> for the quality of experience.
III. Reliance is on <u>wholeness</u>, rather than on any personal agenda.

Book I The Way of Belle Cœur A Spiritual Template

During a Belle Cœur retreat or whenever Belle Cœur sisters gather, we sit in sacred circle together at the beginning and ending of the day. In silence, we prayerfully light the candle in the center as we begin our circle time. This is our tangible reminder for all, that whatever is shared among us is blessed by the Beloved's presence. It represents our compass and the flame marks True North.

Our seated bodies form the rim of the circle representing the Sacred Feminine as Wisdom Sophia and the Spirit of Creation. Christ is at the center. The container for our stories is strong and alive with the Divine Presence.

An assigned "guardian" of the circle keeps track of time to allow an equal measure for everyone. She is also responsible for monitoring the circle energetics. The guardian may choose to ring a bell to call for a period of silence to honor what has been shared or to signal a need for a break, etc.

Each woman takes her turn "checking-in." She holds a sacred object as a "talking-piece" and without interruption she shares her story, weaving it thread by precious thread as part of the community's tapestry of wisdom. Those on the rim of the circle listen compassionately, without judgment or comment. It is a rare thing to be truly listened to, to have our stories witnessed without the listeners trying to fix or judge us.

This model of circle establishes guidelines to ensure that a measured depth of respect, and reverence is present for each woman and her story.

During our circle time we experience, "...*the blending of how each demonstrates her vision of the sacred.*" (*I&H*: 349-350)

The longevity and healthy development of a spiritual circle is dependent upon rotating leadership. A circle should function autonomously according to the particular ebb and flow of the needs of circle members.

Within a community circle, there is co-creation, collaboration, and commitment. When participation and responsibilities are shared all come away feeling replenished, renewed, included, and inspired.

A Sister of Belle Cœur shares her wisdom

"My Belle Cœur Sisters are my kindred soul tribe. Finding these diverse and spirit guided women meant discovering long-lost beloved family with whom I share interests and connections: a love of the Divine, a commitment to craft and service, a call to create authentic relationships, an open heart filled with love and respect for all creatures, and a deep desire to walk softly with divine intention and leave the world a better place in as many ways possible."

Pamela Sampel, OblSB
Sister of Belle Cœur

Book I The Way of Belle Cœur A Spiritual Template

Community, communication, and connection

Perhaps you're currently a member of a women's spiritual circle or community. If so, you may feel called to share this book with your members to blend the Belle Cœur spirituality within your current circle's practices.

In our technological world, those who follow the Way of Belle Cœur stay in touch through e-mail, social media, and online connections. In this way we become the continuation, a golden thread in the tapestry of an ancient feminine tradition. We remember we are connected with the great ancestral lineage of women's stories and wisdom.

The Beguines' Legacy

Our Ancestral Heritage

*It was their desire as the sisterhood
grew in numbers to remain free,
independent of the Church's rule,
neither taking vows nor donning
the veil of the nuns,
free of vows of obedience
to the bishop.* (*I&H:* 106)

It's important for those called to the Way of Belle Cœur to understand the taproot connection we share with our medieval European sisters, the Beguines. The courage and spirituality of the Beguines inspired my depiction of the Belle Cœur sisterhood in the story of *Ink and Honey* and informs the foundation of the Way of Belle Cœur.

In recent years there have been several excellent books pertaining to the history and *her*story of the Beguine movement. In this section, you will receive an abbreviated introduction to familiarize you with the importance of the Beguines in regard to the call for women's communities today. Please visit the Belle Cœur Resources information section of this book to learn how to access additional sources pertaining to the Beguines.

Who were the Beguines?

In the mid-twelfth and thirteenth centuries in Belgium, France, Germany, and the Netherlands women shared a similar longing. Rather than accept one of the two choices available for most women of their time, either become married or enter a convent and take the vows of the Church, the Beguines responded with the creation and establishment of a third way. They began to create Christ-centered and independent women's communities of varying sizes and configurations.

The Beguines pursued personal spiritual growth and development while they remained free from the traditional and more restricted ways of the religious sisters. They didn't follow an established rule of any kind, by choice, each beguine community co-created a particular covenant or rule of life that was then scribed and/or memorized. Amendments were made according to the community's changing needs. This document outlined the spiritual and also practical aspects for the particular sisterhood.

Beguine communities were independently formed. Typically six or more women would gather together and eventually establish residence in one of the women's homes. There were also solo Beguines who lived on their own, demonstrating that Beguine life was unique for each individual and each community. They mirrored the Scriptural archetypes of Martha and Mary. They were very active and service oriented, as well as, deeply prayerful and contemplative.

Women were invited to live within a particular Beguine community for a year as a trial period. At the end of the scripted time if the community and the woman were comfortable together, there was a ceremony of welcoming. Following this experience she stayed with the community for another year or so. When the initial two years were complete, and the woman's desire to become part of the community was expressed and approved by the members, she received the traditional clothing of the Beguine. Their garments were simple in design, made from wool, gray or beige, with a hooded cape.

Rather than take the veil and vows as nuns of the Church, the Beguines often combined their resources to purchase homes (beguinages) where they could live and work with faithful like-minded kindred spirits. They lived simply in apostolic poverty. They supported their communities as tapestry and lace makers and

The Way of Belle Cœur

through other forms of creative expression. They practiced chastity, yet, were free to marry if so inspired. They encouraged the spiritual lives of others through their use of metaphors and images. The Beguines experienced a perpetual longing to go ever deeper into the heart of Christ.

The Beguine way of life provides guidance for today's woman who yearns to know the Divine Presence more dearly. The spirits of the Beguines encourage her to trust her mysterious and numinous intuitions and to revisit ancient feminine wisdom, sacred texts, Scripture, and the teachings of the Beguines. The Beguine legacy invites the rediscovery of creative forms and spiritual language to communicate the transcendent feminine experience.

There was diversity in the ways the Beguine communities functioned, while a devout love of Christ and simplicity and order were central and universal to Beguine spirituality. They were charitable and hardworking as they fed the poor and cared for the sick.

Beguines were radical revolutionaries for their day. They were tolerated and also tormented by Church authorities. The Beguine way of life provided an alternative to vowed monasticism or life as a "layperson." However, over time their *middle-way* was suspect to many and often seen as heretical.

The Beguine movement thrived for several decades but by the end of the thirteenth century it fell under suspicion for some of their teachings that inferred the possibility and importance of direct guidance from the Holy Spirit rather than through Scriptural study.

Over time many beguines were branded as heretics and died at the stake. However, they left us a legacy of sacred wisdom recorded within their ecstatic poetry and writings. Examples of their profound spirituality, spousal love for Christ, and fervent imaginative fire of the soul can be experienced in the works of Marguerite Porete, Mechtild of Magdeburg, and Hadewijch of Antwerp, to name a few.

The taproot of the Beguine tradition lives on

Contemporary life calls women to community in new and creative ways. While most organized religions move through a period of transition, women *and* men are seeking alternative forms of worship and pathways to spiritual nurturance, fulfillment, and service to others.

With regard to women's communities, we have medieval inspiration and wisdom left to us by the Beguines to draw upon. Many women today (individually and collectively) are seeking spiritual growth and sacramental celebration. They gather together in living rooms, the workplace, coffee shops, and community centers. They share the stories of their journeys, break bread, study Scripture and explore spiritual thought while they honor one another's gifts and life's passages. Online women's communities are also forming. The weaving of global circles of women provides new opportunities for collaboration, study, prayer, and service across the planet.

The Beguines were creative and courageous, innovative and imaginative. Perhaps their spirits are calling to us now through our dreams and sacred imaginations. The Way of Belle Cœur clears forgotten pathways leading to a deeper relationship with the Beloved, as it revisits and reclaims the ancestral legacy and teachings of the Beguines.

Reflect

- ❖ How will we, as contemporary, creative, and spiritual women respond more fully to the invitation and call to community?
- ❖ How might we reimagine the traditions and wisdom of our medieval sisters to bring it alive again for our time?
- ❖ What new forms of worship sacrament, and celebration await us if we dare to revisit the past to inform the present?

Weaving past, present, and future

"There is a Sisterhood among women, that transcends time and space." (I&H: 483)

Synchronicity is a mysterious phenomenon. In the spring of 2015, The Reverend Mary Anne Dorner, a retired Episcopal priest and Belle Cœur sister, traveled with her husband to Europe. Before leaving for her journey she began to read extensively about the Beguines and she was inspired to contact the Benedictine sisters at Begijnhof de Wijngaard (the medieval Beguinage of the Vineyard) in Bruges, Belgium. Sister Mary Anne's request for an interview was approved and an appointed day and time were scheduled for her visit.

A few weeks before her pilgrimage to the beguinage Sister Mary Anne dreamed she delivered a copy of *Ink and Honey* to the nuns that now live there. She shared her dream with me and I provided her with a copy of the book and a personal note to deliver to the sisters. The following is Sister Mary Anne's reflection of her introduction to the beguinage and interaction with the sisters.

A Sister of Belle Cœur shares her story

A Sacred Reflection on My Visit to Brugge
June 12, 2015
"I carried the book, Ink and Honey, *across the ocean, from the New World back to the Old. It came to rest on an ancient wooden table in the guest room of the medieval Beguinage of the Vineyard in Bruges. The Benedictine Sisters received their gift and touched the author's name.*

'Sibyl. Do you know Sibyl?'

I told them, 'Yes, she is the founder of our emerging Sisterhood of Belle Cœur which was inspired by this book.'

Then we were invited deep into the cloister, into the biblioteca, where an ancient, leather bound manuscript was opened to us. I looked inside and saw black diamonds and squares, some with tails and apostrophes. My heart quickened as I realized that I was looking at a masterfully inked medieval hymnal of Gregorian chant. Underneath the notes were streams of Latin words from the Psalms. When I reached my hand out to touch this sacred hymnal, I felt a mysterious and mystical connection to the Beguines, the Benedictines, and the Sisters of Belle Cœur. I felt our Beloved drawing us all together into one sisterhood...across time and space."

The Reverend Mary Anne Dorner
Sister of Belle Cœur

Carrying the sisterhood forward

Sister Mary Anne and many other women who have discovered the Beguines feel a resonance with their spirituality and way of life. They also resonate with the Beguines love for Christ, and their abilities of creative sacred awareness. It's remarkable to learn that Beguine communities continued for centuries, though their numbers diminished with time.

Marcella Pattyn, the last Beguine, died in Belgium at age 92, on April 14, 2013. With Marcella's passing an eight hundred year old spiritual tradition also breathed its last breath...or did it? Again, synchronicity seems to have come into play.

The invitation for the first Way of Belle Cœur retreat went out in the spring of 2013. The gathering took place in October of that same year, six months after the passing of the last Beguine. Perhaps it is a blessed synchronicity that Belle Cœur spirituality, inspired by the Beguines, picked up the torch from Sister Marcella's spirit to continue the tradition of an independently formed, creative, Christ-centered, spiritual sisterhood.

Book I The Way of Belle Cœur A Spiritual Template

⌒▩⌒

Those who practice Belle Cœur spirituality follow in the footsteps of dedicated, hard-working, spiritual women. They are not unlike the Beguines, Benedictines, and the countless fervent and faithful believers who journeyed the Holy Road, solo and in community.

Our commonality with our ancestral sisters rests within our inclusive, creative, compassionate, and Christ-centered spirituality. The connection to the taproot of ancestral spiritual sisterhood stems from our shared faith and love for the Beloved, our fierce prayers, and our sacred life arts as expressions of passionate beauty from our creative hearts.

As Goscelin, the scribe of Belle Cœur describes...

> *Each of us does her best to bring her prayers,*
> *wisdom, and sacred life art to each day...*
> *The beauty is in the blending of how each*
> *demonstrates her vision of the sacred.*
> *As sisters of Belle Cœur, we believe God*
> *speaks to each of us in a unique way.*
> *Our rituals and prayers unify us and hold*
> *us in a common shared center.*
> *We are united through our practices*
> *that reflect our love for God,*
> *while the outward expressions of our*
> *spirits are often very different.*
> (*I&H*: 349-350)

The Way of Belle Cœur

The feminine desire for community

As we learned from the Beguines, circles of women have gathered throughout the ages. A sacred and intentional circle is both a container and vehicle where women can collaborate and co-create with prayerful and intentional presence.

In primitive times, women sat in circle, around the fire, to paint their prayers and stories on cave walls. When Jesus was on earth and even today, women have gathered to sing praises to God in tents beneath the desert moon.

The Middle Ages called women to monastic enclosure, a cloistered life behind stonewalls and iron gates where they studied and prayed...in circle. The Beguines, of that time, chose to gather in community in houses throughout the Netherlands, France, Belgium, and Germany to care for the sick and the poor. Eventually, in the early 20th Century, Susan B. Anthony and a small circle of women met in her dusty attic to birth a movement that would eventually ensure the vote for women living in the United States. Increasingly, as we have observed, there are *virtual* circles of women who create blogs, online study and discussion forums, and social media pages as new forms of community.

Questions for contemplation

In the introduction of this book we explored how women today are longing to experience spiritual and creative community to discover sacred practices to enrich and merge their spiritual lives with everyday moments. This particular yearning raises the following questions for women of the third millennium living within a fragmented, technological, fast-paced culture.

- ❖ Inspired by our ancestral sisters, the Beguines, and Belle Cœur spirituality, how do you imagine a covenanted, intentional, spiritual and creative women's community might benefit your life and today's global needs?
- ❖ How do you nurture your creative heart and spirit to bring your best self to your personal life and your community?
- ❖ What are the sacred practices and creative exercises you currently embrace to help you to grow the wisdom of your soul?

Nothing can replace the energetic exchange that occurs within a circle of women that gather to share a common intention and focus. Circles of women praying together, creating, collaborating, and sharing stories and wisdom…this is a very fundamental and necessary form for the facilitation of the global and personal change we long for.

I have witnessed a feminine collective need to *gather* in the midst of the chaotic and transformative time we're living in. Questions arise as I contemplate the incredible abundance of women's wisdom that flows through chat rooms, on social media pages, and discussion forums.

- ❖ What is the Spirit inspiring and inviting women to bring forth as we share our stories and wisdom with one another at this moment of technological and global connection?
- ❖ Is there something we're missing with regard to the spiritual and creative potential of online community sharing?
- ❖ How can those of us who are longing for the sacred in everyday life and those yearning to grow spiritually best serve and be served through an online community experience?

Finding our way

We are women finding our way together as we make a pilgrimage of remembrance through our virtual and real time communities. The intention to is to birth a spiritual and creative renaissance to encourage new forms of spirituality informed by our devotion, story, study, and craft to foster extreme beauty for the increasingly dark times we currently experience.

"There is a sisterhood among women that transcends time and space..." and women are being called to the doorway of *her*storical legacy to reclaim and to share the stories and wisdom of women to foster hope in the world. We are called to gather on the rim...

Book I The Way of Belle Cœur A Spiritual Template

Reflect

- ❖ When I contemplate the word "sisterhood" I feel…
- ❖ When I imagine myself contributing, co-creating, and interacting with others I envision…
- ❖ My global vision of contemporary sisterhood can be described as…
- ❖ When I reflect on my connection to the ancient, ancestral and future sisterhood circles/communities, what arises for me (visually, sensually, emotionally and spiritually) is best expressed in this way…

The Path of Service

Pray we continue to grow
in service to God, our Creator,
to Jesus, our Beloved,
and to you, Mother,
guardian of Creation.
(*I&H*: 184)

The path of service is foundational for a Belle Cœur sister's personal ministry and the shared collective ministry within her community. Service as a form of *ministry* begins as a calling within the heart of a woman and within the heart of a community. The path of service is related to the season of winter and the elements of fire, heart, night, gestation, spider, hawthorne, transformation, ashes, burning logs, smoke and gold.

Ministry and service take root from the desire and longing to support, bear witness, and offer assistance in alignment with human physical, spiritual, emotional needs, social justice issues, and ecological crises.

Service becomes tangible through the intentional sharing of a sister or community's creative and spiritual gifts as resources to provide support for transformation and healing for the Greater Good. There are endless ways to be of service both individually and through intentional and prayerful co-creation with others to provide outreach. The path of service leads to making a difference in the world in both subtle and profound ways.

A woman's service becomes ministry through her prayerful intention and response to the experience of feeling called to serve in a specific way. The same is true with regard to a collective service or ministry born from a particular charism and calling associated within a community as a whole.

The many forms of service

It is important to mention that service may be *actively responsive* to a designated need such as: preparing food for the homeless, visiting the sick and homebound, orchestrating fund-raising events for charities, etc. Service may also be *actively passive*; through the practices of personal or intercessory global prayer, prayer shawl knitting, letter writing to shut-ins, and additional *contemplative* forms of service.

There are myriad ways for a woman and her community to minister. Prayerful intentional service becomes ministry. The call to service and ministry is also an invitation to respond creatively.

In service for the Beloved

Service as ministry is directly related to the center of the Belle Cœur template. Serving the greater good in the name of the Beloved is a calling, as sixteenth century nun and saint, Saint Teresa of Avila, instructs through her prayer:

> *"Christ has no body now but yours.*
> *No hands, no feet on earth but yours.*
> *Yours are the eyes through which,*
> *He looks compassionately on this world.*
> *Yours are the feet with which He walks to do good.*
> *Yours are the hands with which He blesses all the world.*
> *Yours are the hands,*
> *Yours are the feet,*
> *Yours are the eyes,*
> *You are his body,*
> *Christ has no body now on earth but yours."*

To imagine our selves as Christ's earthly body adds a full measure of responsibility to life's journey. This understanding is a call to open our hands and hearts to share our gifts and talents, and to keep our eyes and

The Way of Belle Cœur

ears alert to recognize and acknowledge injustice and suffering. Through service as ministry we offer and share Jesus' love with the people of God. Discernment and prayer are required as each woman contemplates how the Holy One is calling her or her community to serve.

We live in a time of shifting paradigms. For many we find ourselves living through a season of disorientation, displacement, and discouragement. Nature and all of Creation are in dire straits. Our Divine Mother, Wisdom Sophia, needs our assistance. We are called to shine a light on the global, environmental, and interpersonal challenges we face and to offer our hands and hearts in service for the healing of our planet, her people, the animals, and all of Creation.

༺༻

In the story of *Ink and Honey*, the sisters of Belle Cœur fed the poor and cared for the sick and dying. They shared their hope and wisdom whenever possible, and prayed continually for the needs of others as they tended the earth and her creatures. Ravenissa spoke the languages of deer, mouse, and crow as she healed the animals. Helvide shared her wisdom through her knowledge of the healing properties of herbs, minerals, and plant life. (*I&H*: 3, 95, 109, 146)

Service and ministry are directly related to the concept of *tending*. When something or someone is tended it is cared for, nurtured, looked after, and prayed for. When we choose to tend another through the ministry of compassionate service, we are often graced to *cherish* the one we are tending. *Tending* and *cherishing* are twin attributes for those called to service and ministry.

Reflect

I invite you to contemplate how you serve the Greater Good, individually and collectively. The topic of service must be a primary topic for discernment in our communities, as well as, a subject for personal contemplation. Thoughtful, dedicated, sacred, and intentional *action* is called for. Let us serve as spiritual midwives to assist the birth of hope, charity, and compassion in our world through our works of loving service and our genuine words of encouragement.

Seek ways to fearlessly express God's Love.

Share love. Celebrate love.
Serve love as a Sacrament.
Express love. Inspire love.
Reveal love. Seek love.
Embrace love. Nurture love.
Live in love. Die in love.
Embody love...eternally.

In this time of increasing polarization in our world it is easy, and in some cases habitual, to quickly judge how someone is different or "other." Whether it's a difference of religion, cultural beliefs, race, sexual orientation, generation, socio-economic background, or political viewpoint.

However, the spiritual invitation when we meet someone in the context of our day-to-day relationships is to seek to discover the place of common ground. The Beloved's invitation is to always seek the place where there is a shared desire, longing, and/or vulnerability. From the threshold of shared and universal human need, the possibility to open the door to the pathway of acceptance and love is revealed. Belle Cœur spirituality offers love as the antidote for fear.

Holy outrage…a catalyst for service and ministry

It has been said that the emotion of anger takes hold when something or someone that a person cherishes or values is threatened. Outrage occurs when injustice, abuse, neglect, violence, betrayal, and suffering are witnessed or experienced.

When a person is consumed with rage that is never processed, darkness takes up residence within the heart and spirit. Unacknowledged rage has the potential, over time, to grow like a cancer and become something very unholy and dangerous.

If the feelings of rage can be recognized, acknowledged, and transformed to become passion for finding solutions and transformative methods to resolve the instigating issue, then the outrage becomes Holy through grace and awareness. In other words, the outrage becomes a catalyst for blessing and change for the greater good through conscious, active service and prayerful, intentional ministry.

Book I The Way of Belle Cœur A Spiritual Template

The following meditative schemata is offered for your reflection...

Holy outrage yields passion.
Passion begets service and ministry.
Service and ministry inspire solutions
to support healing, and resolve conflict.
Solutions, healing, and resolved conflict foster peace.
Peace gives rise to hope.
Hope encourages renewal.
Renewal aids the healing of broken hearts.
Healed hearts beget Love.

God needs lovers. Choose to love and offer hope without an agenda for a desired outcome. There is no greater service than when the only desired outcome is to share love and foster hope within another.

Forgiveness and compassion are love's helpmates. Generosity is love's child.

Spill love into everyone and everything you do. Be in gratitude and amazement as you empty your pitcher of love while it mystically refills to overflowing. This is the nature of love.

A question arises to be used as my daily guidepost. It is a question that opens a space to be filled with healing, inspiration, and creativity. It is a question that leads to the pathway of indwelling peace and the Source of unending love.

The Way of Belle Cœur

How will I choose to express love through my next action, word, response, or creation?

Beauty is the by-product of love. Be love and beauty will follow. Light gravitates and radiates from love. Be love and ignite the light and the love within others.

The divine spark, the love and light of the Beloved and Sophia Wisdom, are every human's birthright. God's love endures and we are made, body and bone, hearts and spirits from that same love to become ad*ministers* of love, to serve love, to live immersed within love.

Five daily questions for a minister of love

- ❖ How will I share the blessing of being alive with someone today?
- ❖ Where in my life do I recognize the presence of fear, greed, mistrust, and judgment and offer the antidote of love?
- ❖ How am I called to minister to my spirit with love?
- ❖ Who in my life today needs to know that he/she is loved? How will I respond?
- ❖ What form of beauty will I create to freely share today in the name of love?

Book I The Way of Belle Cœur A Spiritual Template

A Belle Cœur Sister shares her wisdom

Path of Service

In the beginning were the stone circles
on Mother Earth – silent yet speaking
for all humanity – man and woman.

My voice, baptized by the Sacred Spirit
and freed in the heart of the labyrinth
began its Journey of Faith.

The Path led me to the wounded and forsaken,
to the sick and grieving, and to wisdom's blessings,
the teachers and healers.

I listened and submitted to the Call
of prayerful hope, joyful music,
promised healing and the Presence of Infinite Love.

In Circles of Grace, I share worship, compose and say prayers,
make Eucharist visitations in response,
to the outrageous legacy
of the Gospel of Jesus Christ.

Carol Luster
  Sister of Belle Cœur

Reflect

- When I imagine myself as Christ's body on earth I feel...
- Where do I share the service/ministry of tending?
- Who and what (in my personal life and globally) do I truly cherish?
- I experience "holy outrage" when I witness or think about...
- How do I feel called to service/ministry in response to my feelings of holy outrage?
- How do I currently offer service for the greater good?
- When I think of the various ways of *being in service*, I imagine...
- My definitions for service and ministry are...
- When I imagine myself "in ministry" I see myself...
- When I contemplate co-creating ministry/service with others I envision...

Create

- Without editing, create a list of all the forms of service you can imagine where your creative and spiritual gifts would be beneficial. Spend time in prayer and discernment with each act of service on your list. Choose two opportunities for serving that hold the most potential for

Book I The Way of Belle Cœur A Spiritual Template

your actualization. Research and explore your two choices to discern your primary choice.
- ❖ In community, invite each sister to share her primary choice. Notice the common themes among the all of the various choices. In prayer and discernment begin to draw forth how and where the Spirit is calling your community to serve.
- ❖ Be creative as you and your community: explore, share, imagine and actualize the call to serve God's people, Creation, and the myriad needs of our world.

Book II
The Four Chambers
The Alchemy of Sacred Practice

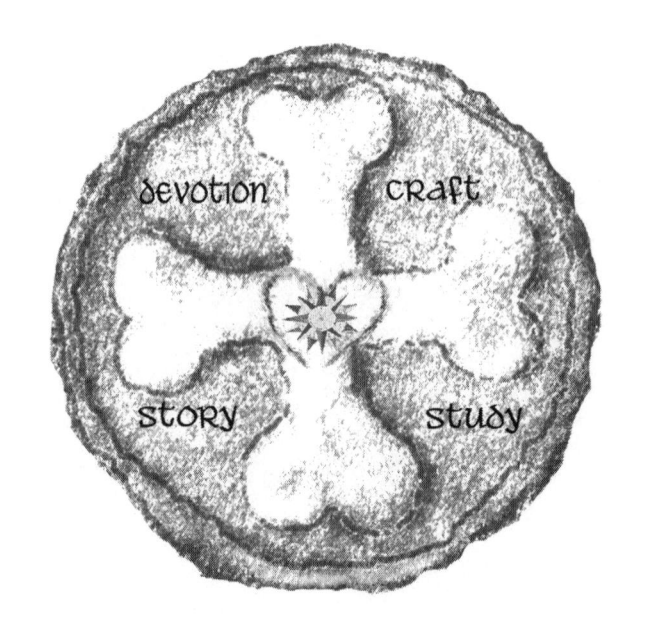

Book II The Four Chambers The Alchemy of Sacred Practice

Overview

Embedded within the Belle Cœur template there are four spaces where the pathways of the cross intersect. Each space represents a particular sacred alchemical chamber containing spiritual and creative sacred practices. The four chambers are: *Devotion, Craft, Story,* and *Study.*

Each category of practice serves as a vessel of possibility that holds myriad creative and spiritual opportunities for your exploration. The chambers may also be imagined as cells within a honeycomb. Each cell (chamber) contains practices, like nourishing honey, offered for your spirit.

Circumnavigate the chambers to discern which form of practice may be applicable for your particular needs and present circumstances. Taste the practices, as you would taste a variety of honeys, to determine the experience that will nourish your spiritual/creative appetite.

The chambers (forms of practice) are organic and evolutionary in nature. Each chamber may grow, change, and develop in accordance with your needs or the desires of a particular community. Engage your sacred imagination to prayerfully engage with the various practices suggested throughout this section. Make them your own.

Alchemy and Belle Cœur spirituality

The original pages
(of the sacred mystery texts)
were encoded with emblems

The Way of Belle Cœur

*and alchemical formulas,
illuminations of exotic birds,
kings and queens, the sun and the moon,
eagles and salamanders.*
(*I&H:* 41)

The pursuit for spiritual, intellectual, emotional, and physical transformation is alchemical. Alchemy is an ancient art that incorporates fundamental laboratory processes to purify metals. In medieval times it was said that the alchemist's work was to turn base metal into gold. The metaphor that is encapsulated within this concept is more philosophical than scientific. Alchemy can be seen as a process of transformation for the spirit through self-knowledge.

The alchemical process invites consideration, contemplation, and also responsive action. Alchemy is a trial and error process. The alchemist gains knowledge through success and failure, alike. The alchemist's tools include a vocabulary of symbols, sacred wisdom codices, and a variety of implements.

The alchemical journey to self-knowledge is labyrinthian. There is a process of the repetitive retracing of steps, spiraling in and out, again and again. However, with each spiral turn towards the previous challenge new knowledge is gained through intellectual and spiritual revelations within the layered experience. Eventually the repetition of gleaning wisdom and releasing old patterns proceeds to open a portal to a numinous level of understanding.

In the alchemist's laboratory the medium in the retort (a glass vessel) undergoes a process of continual change. Sometimes the ingredients appear to boil and bubble. There may be variations in color and temperature, and often the contents become still as though nothing is happening. All the while, the substance is being purified and transformed. This is the alchemical procedure, not unlike the human process of spiritual transformation.

Alchemy is also connected with the totality of the Universe. The astrological properties of the stars and planets (*shinorage* (*I&H:* 165), with the Sun and the Moon representing the masculine and feminine are central to the alchemist. Additionally the seasons are believed to alchemically carry wisdom and messages. It's important for the alchemist to note how the cadence of her life mirrors the rhythm of the natural world.

The Way of Belle Cœur's alchemical chambers: Devotion, Craft, Story and Study are your laboratories of discovery. Become the alchemist as you seek to grow your wisdom and spiritual understanding through a variety of spiritual practices. Discover your sacred tools and your symbolic vocabulary. Observe your relationship to the changing seasons and record your findings in your journal and codex.

Six Applications for Exploration

It is helpful to note there are six fundamental applications (not unlike alchemical processes) that may be engaged as you explore the various chambers. These applications will provide a way for you to adjust your level of deepening for a specific practice. Explore each alchemical application and refer to them often. Discern which of the following applications works best for you with regard to your current spiritual/creative practice.

I. ***Observe***: Pay close attention to what you see, feel, hear, and experience during a specific sacred practice. Record your sensory observations in your journal and scribe your gleaned wisdom in your sacred codex.
II. ***Arrange***: Collect, sort, arrange, bundle, and repurpose elements (sacred objects, things from nature, vessels, ephemera, etc.) that are part of your sacred practice. Make the creation of beauty a formational tenet of each practice you explore.
III. ***Tend***: Study the hours, days, months, seasons, cycles of your life with sacred awareness as you incorporate practices, one by one. Cultivate a gardener's heart as you nurture and tend your sacred experiences.
IV. ***Pray***: Express your prayers, personal creed, rituals, and sacraments as creative outpourings of your love for the Beloved. Prayer is the ever present, continual, conduit of grace that runs throughout all of the pathways and chambers of Belle Cœur.
V. ***Imagine***: Co-create with the Beloved through your sacred imagination. Grow the wisdom of your spiritual practices. Be the alchemist as you explore, express, and imagine endless forms of connection with your Highest Self.
VI. ***Share***: Contribute your wisdom, creativity, imagination, prayers, and spiritual ingenuity as you co-create and collaborate with your

family, community, or co-workers. Share your intellectual, spiritual, and material gifts and embrace the gifts that others offer to you.

The Chamber of Devotion

*Our devotion to follow prophetic obedience,
to be led by God rather than adhere
to the religious rules of men,
was the foundation stone of our order.*
(*I&H:* 140)

The myriad forms of devotion

The Practice of Devotion refers specifically to a sister or community's expression of affiliation and faithfulness to Christ, God, the Holy Spirit, Logos, as embodied within the center of Belle Cœur spirituality. Devotion is also held within the encompassing circle in celebration of the Sacred Feminine including: Wisdom Sophia, Creation (all forms of life within the natural world), The Mother, Mary Magdalene and the early Christian Feminine Mystics.

The spiritual practice of devotion is unique for each woman. Practicing devotion requires intentional commitment. Devotion is the interior reflection of personal spiritual expression: your praises, petitions, questions, lamentations, and spiritual fervor through your relationship with the Beloved. Devotion should be experienced in a way that is meaningful for you, and/or your community through shared common spiritual and creative practices.

Within the practice of interior devotion there are countless forms for prayer and the exterior creative expression of sacred/spiritual revelation. The following list is intended for your inspiration. You are invited to expand or edit this list according to personal resonance and specific need. Spend time in prayer and reflection with the forms that hold particular resonance for you. This exercise is also valuable as a community experience.

Suggested forms of devotion

- Contemplative prayer
- The practice of silence
- Prayers of petition
- Intercessory prayer
- A Prayer journal as a sacred form of personal journaling where daily prayers are scribed. A sisterhood's "Keeper of the Prayers" may also record the community's prayer requests within a community prayer journal.
- Rosary or prayer bead prayers and meditation
- A mantra journal where there is repetitive scribing of a personal or community's mantra in a small journal.

Book II The Four Chambers The Alchemy of Sacred Practice

- ❖ Meditation
- ❖ Yoga or body prayer
- ❖ Dance
- ❖ Chant or vocalization
- ❖ Gazing and beholding a candle flame, icon, or other sacred symbol for a period of time as a form of prayerful meditation.
- ❖ Scripture reading
- ❖ Lectio Divina as the practice of sacred reading and reflection.
- ❖ Visio Divina as meditation and reflection with a sacred image, icon, or photograph.
- ❖ Audio Divina as meditation and reflection while listening to sacred or inspirational music.
- ❖ Labyrinth walking
- ❖ Walking in nature
- ❖ Writing sacred poetry
- ❖ Gathering in nature as the practice of collecting found natural objects.
- ❖ Shrine or altar building

Reflect

- ❖ How do I experience my resonance or dissonance in relationship with the above practices?
- ❖ What are the sacred practices that currently feed my spirit?
- ❖ Is there a past practice that I'm called to revisit?
- ❖ What are the particular personal sacred practices I might share or introduce to my community?

❖ How is the Spirit inviting me/my community to co-create a new practice or reinvent an existing one?

A Belle Cœur Sister shares her wisdom

"When I first began the practice of daily devotion, it involved reading the Bible and prayer. It evolved to writing my prayers, which led to journaling. It took place early in the morning before my family was awake and it prepared me for what lay ahead in my job as a high school special education teacher. Now in my early seventies my daily devotion is not always in the early morning. It happens later in the day. It still includes Bible reading and prayer.

Prayer takes different forms. Sometimes I pray out loud, sometimes I write or journal it, and sometimes I move or dance my prayer to sacred music. My devotion time includes expressing my feelings to God. Even if I'm angry, disappointed or sad I usually end with gratitude and awareness of where God is in my circumstances.

There are several places where my devotion takes place. The first is in my living room where my special centering prayer chair is. The second is my kitchen table or outside, deck table where I journal. The next is in an open space between my kitchen and dining room where I dance and do body prayer. The daily devotion keeps me be aware of God's presence."

Evelyn Pope
Sister of Belle Cœur

Book II The Four Chambers The Alchemy of Sacred Practice

Reflect

The following list is provided for your contemplation. Spend some time journaling about the feelings, ideas, and inspirations that arise as you reflect upon each quality as a sacred practice. Notice when you feel resonance or dissonance. Explore the possibilities for the creation of a particular sacred practice in response to two or more of the qualities (practices) listed here. Describe and/or illustrate your practice in your codex. Create a visual prayer collage to illuminate your intention to integrate the new practice(s) into your life.

- Silence
- Adaptability
- Orderliness
- Contemplation
- Simplicity
- Time (the daily hours, the seasons)
- Contentment
- Acceptance
- Invocation
- Intention
- Creativity
- Enthusiasm
- Discernment
- Mercy
- Patience
- Reverence
- Perseverance
- Tranquility
- Wonderment
- Hopefulness

The Way of Belle Cœur

- Forgiveness
- Appreciation
- Generosity
- Beauty
- Courage
- Self Discipline
- Tolerance
- Non-judgment
- Awe
- Awareness
- Reflection
- Solitude
- Playfulness
- Love
- Listening

Create

Meditate upon the following words. What personal feelings do they evoke? Where do they lead you? You may choose to look for images to represent these words in your codex. What are other words you might imagine to evoke feelings of place, purpose, spiritual anchoring, beauty, sacredness? Allow a drawing, painting, collage, poem, dance, assemblage or altar to be inspired by your contemplation of, and associations with, one or more of the following words or words of your own creation.

- Stone
- Labyrinth
- Portal

Book II The Four Chambers The Alchemy of Sacred Practice

- ❖ Window
- ❖ Cathedral
- ❖ Alchemy
- ❖ Hearth
- ❖ Earth
- ❖ Plants
- ❖ Mystery
- ❖ Fire
- ❖ Saint
- ❖ Rain
- ❖ Light
- ❖ Darkness
- ❖ Silence
- ❖ Pilgrim
- ❖ Bone
- ❖ Litany
- ❖ Angel
- ❖ Contemplative
- ❖ Reliquary

The Chamber of Craft

*Each of us does her best
to bring her prayers,
wisdom, and sacred life art
to each day.
(I&H: 349)*

The Chamber of Craft is where creativity and Belle Cœur spirituality are expressed through the sacred life-arts. The sacred life-arts are realized through the prayerful and intentional creation of beauty. As a sacred life-artisan you are a craftswoman and beacon of creative inspiration for others.

The sacred life-arts include all forms of creative expression infused with prayer and intentional awareness to fully demonstrate an aesthetic of beauty and sacredness. The practice of craft is revealed and invigorated by the sacred life-artisan according to her creative passions and interests. The same is true collectively when a community practices a co-creative craft as a form of prayer or as a community service-oriented ministry of service. The choices for practicing the sacred life-arts are infinite.

When we invent something new or bake a loaf of bread, or craft an illumination to represent the sun or the moon, we express the Dominion of Spirit.
(*I&H*: 62)

Examples of the Sacred Life-Arts

The intentional prayerful practice of...

- ❖ Weaving
- ❖ Knitting prayer shawls
- ❖ Quilt-making
- ❖ Book-making
- ❖ Gardening

Book II The Four Chambers The Alchemy of Sacred Practice

- Cooking/Cuisine
- Eucharistic bread baking
- Wine-making
- Cheese-making
- Collage-making as visual prayer
- Floral arranging
- Beekeeping
- Hearth-keeping as an expression of intentional hospitality.
- Journaling in visual and written form
- Personal wisdom keeping within the pages of a Sacred Wisdom Codex.
- Creative writing
- Poetry writing
- Drawing, sketching
- Painting
- Icon writing/painting
- Rosary or prayer bead-making
- Shrine building and altar-making
- Jewelry and sacred adornment-making
- Dancing and body prayer
- Singing and chanting
- Playing an instrument and music-making
- Photography
- Film-making
- Papier mâché
- Sculpture
- Arranging as the prayerful and intentional sorting, archiving, organizing, and placement of things.
- Gathering as the intentional collection of things from nature, photographs, objects of interest, etc.

- Bundling known in Belle Cœur vernacular as portundae-making. The sacred ritual and craft of gathering and arranging personal, meaningful, sacred purposed objects into a small cloth package or bundle. This craft will be fully explored later in the section, The Chamber of Story: Portundae.
- Assemblage crafted as an array of assorted objects configured with sacred intention as an intentional structure.
- Crafting "*les cadeaux de vôtre cœur*" (the gifts of your heart).

Reflect

- The various ways I express my creative heart are…
- When I imagine my community co-creating a creative representation of our charism, I envision…
- The sacred life-art I can offer (as an expression of outreach) to benefit a charity or a particular community need is…
- The practice of craft and sacred life-arts could support and nourish my spiritual experience and understanding if I…

My mother has always been a sacred life-artisan. Before her eyesight diminished she was a quilt maker.

Book II The Four Chambers The Alchemy of Sacred Practice

I observed her at work at her craft as she carefully placed a template on fabric to sketch the pattern for her stitches. The design created by the template was merely a guide, an inspiration, for her particular push and pull of the needle. Even though she used a template for the quilting, it was her choice of fabrics and colors that made each quilt an expression of her unique and creative heart.

Templates, in the form of role models, are helpful when one makes the conscious awareness to live authentically and purposefully. Emulating the behavior and approach to life exemplified by a person or persons you admire, provides a map or a guide as you create and shape *your* authentic life.

Over the centuries artists have copied the famous works and creations of the great master painters and sculptors. This is how new techniques and methods have come into being over time. Through the process of studying and exploring the brushstrokes of Rembrandt, Van Gogh, Warhol or Rauschenberg, the artist discovers her authentic way of applying paint to the canvas.

Who would you choose for your role model as a sacred life-artisan?

The authentic life is multi-faceted. To live fully, with a sense of purpose, requires the engagement of body, mind, and soul. Bring your sacred awareness to each day. Enliven your spiritual and creative palette as you paint your life in the outer world, the way you visualize it to be within your inner world.

The Way of Belle Cœur

Here are a few suggestions to express and contain the forms of inspiration you will discover for the enrichment of your authentic and purpose-full life. I invite you to make a journey through your sacred imagination in search of human templates (role models and mentors) to quicken your creative heart and spirit. Engage your creativity to bring color and spontaneity to the greatest adventure you can have, the encounter with your creative Self as a "sacred life-artisan."

Reflection

- ❖ Select three teachers to design your imaginary curriculum to creatively, spiritually, and energetically inspire your body, mind, and spirit. These persons may be living or deceased, from history/*her*story, or people you currently know or have known during your life.
- ❖ Name two people from your childhood who impacted your life in a memorable and positive way. What characteristics did these individuals have in common? How did they differ?
- ❖ Who are the artists, musicians, writers, or specialists in your field of work or interest that you admire? What is the common thread regarding your appreciation of their gifts? In your journal list these various persons and their inspirational traits that you would like to emulate.

Book II The Four Chambers The Alchemy of Sacred Practice

Create

- ❖ Create a collage from images cut from magazines that represent (either figuratively or symbolically) your role model template. You may also incorporate clippings from copies of personal photographs. Cut and glue the images onto a piece of cardboard or poster board. Place your collage in a prominent place to remind you of your role model's desirable traits while you excavate new aspects of your intellect, creativity, and radiant spirit.
- ❖ Keep an inspiration bulletin board as a sacred container for images of those things that influence and stimulate your vision of your authentic Self. Clip pictures from magazines to serve as symbols for the realization and fulfillment of the qualities, actions, and personal visions you wish to attain.
- ❖ Once a week as a meditation practice, make a collage to focus on one personal characteristic and/or goal-oriented outcome that you intend to create for your life. Keep your inspiration board where you will see it frequently throughout the day. Allow it to evolve over time. Refer to it as you embrace the parts of yourself that are finding new voice and form.
- ❖ Print words, phrases, and affirmations to express the values, characteristics, and creative endeavors that support and interest your inner process of Self-discovery. Keep these in a clear

The Way of Belle Cœur

glass jar on your desk. Once a day reach in and choose one at random. Read it aloud and copy it ten times in your journal as a way of integrating ideas and concepts into your psyche and spirit.

❖ Most of all engage all your senses to enlarge your inner and outer worlds. Look at art and nature for inspiration. Listen to music and recordings of poetry and literature or foreign languages to stimulate your creativity. Taste new foods and make unfamiliar recipes, explore other cultures, rent a foreign film or documentary to stretch beyond your everyday boundaries.

❖ Create a patchwork of images as another form of representation of the people that inspire you. Use photos of friends, colleagues, relatives and images of *her*storical figures, which through their example call you to your highest self. Cut these images into small squares. Glue each image onto slightly larger squares of card stock. Blank, unlined, index cards work nicely for this. Sew the individual photo squares together and hang your creation in your workspace. An alternative method is to glue the various small images together on a large piece of cardboard to create a patchwork pattern. You may wish to add paint, colored pen, or crayon to complete your patchwork, photomontage. Make a copy of the finished piece to add to your codex.

Raise the bar for your life. Draw forth from your soul the gifts that are waiting to be born through the sacred practice of craft. Be inspired by others' contributions and creativity.

Design your inspiration template sketched from the aspirations and desires of your heart.

A Belle Cœur Sister shares her wisdom

We created a safe place, a sacred container, in which to share our own unique sacred wisdom and sacred life arts. Felting, printing, journaling, painting, ancient encounters, shalom-making, creation energy, orbs, healings...we shared in a way that broadened and expanded each woman's wisdom and we became Sisters.

Mary Ann Matthys
Sister of Belle Coeur

Saint Hildegard of Bingen's Inspiration

On my desk I have an icon of Saint Hildegard of Bingen, a 12th century abbess, visionary, writer, founder of monasteries, Christian mystic, herbalist, and composer. She was most definitely a sacred life-artisan. Her spiritual strength and creativity are a source of unending inspiration. She is also a beloved saint and spiritual role model for Belle Cœur sisters. (*I&H*: 207, 209, 210)

I have studied her writings and many stories about her life and when I find myself creatively blocked I

The Way of Belle Cœur

turn to her icon and ask, "*How would Hildegard approach this problem?*"

You're invited to study Saint Hildegard to contemplate her creative process, her prayer life, and her courage to express her visions. She is inspirational for those seeking to draw fearlessly from the well of creativity.

Hildegard's spirit also teaches the importance and spiritual relevance of the six senses as conduits to the Divine Presence. Our senses (taste, touch, sight, sound, smell, and discernment/intuition) inform our recognition of beauty and inspire our creative hearts and minds. Our crafts and our lives as sacred life-artisans are enriched through the conscious awareness of our senses as our link with Creation and the sacred imagination. Saint Hildegard's sensual, spiritual, and creative wisdom offers sustenance from the ancient well.

The Sacred Life-Artisan and Her Senses

...what do you feel?
What do your senses tell you?
(*I&H:* 48)

The senses provide insight and inspiration about our environments, daily experiences, and life's layers of complexity. When our senses are engaged portals open to realms of inner discovery and the possibility for co-creation with God.

Unlike Hildegard's medieval world, our contemporary life often doesn't provide obvious opportunities to engage our senses. Consider how many times a day you touch something made of synthetic materials. In contrast, how often do you touch an object from the realm of nature?

Our senses, rather than the senses of our medieval sisters, are rarely used to gather necessary information for our survival and wellbeing. The Internet or cellphone app provides the daily weather forecast. Sniffing the breeze for the smell of oncoming rain is not our usual instrument for thunderstorm predictions. We have digital thermometers to check for fever rather than the reliance upon a warm or cool touch of the forehead by the hand. Milk is packaged with an expiration date printed on the container. There's no need to taste it for freshness.

There are countless other ways our senses no longer connect us with our surroundings or with nature and Creation. In fact, it's quite possible that our current way of life has atrophied our senses, not unlike the way muscles go flaccid without exercise.

Contemplation of the blessing of your senses

- ❖ Imagine how you might reactivate your senses to deepen the experience of feeling a sacred connection to life.

The Way of Belle Cœur

- ❖ How would it feel to become a full participant with all of Creation?
- ❖ What does the concept of *living through the senses* evoke for you?

You're invited to make an internal shift to see the world through a renewed lens as you go about your life, to *behold* the person, thing, or situation that's on the path there before you. Look with the eyes of your heart and your other senses will follow the example. See, listen, touch, taste, smell, and discern passionately and reverently as you live each day. Become a sacred life-artisan *and* co-creator with the Beloved.

We are sensate creatures. We move through life guided by the messages our senses relay to our brains. It's too hot, no it's too cold. The light is just right, the music is loud, the toast must be burning. We interpret these needs and urges and make the necessary adjustments through our perfunctory responses, while forgetful that our divinely designed senses are so much more than biological informants for our brains.

A key to the door of a sensual life lies within the remembrance of a time before the invention of electricity and all the conveniences of our modern era. Imagine for a moment what it was like to live in Goscelin's world without cell-phones, automobiles, computers, fast food, running water, indoor plumbing, and microwave ovens.

The *old* world was a time and place where the senses were in a continual heightened state of awareness. Life itself was immersed in an ongoing series of sensual

Book II The Four Chambers The Alchemy of Sacred Practice

experiences. The senses were relied upon for survival, for intuitive guidance, and direction.

Hands kneaded the soft dough to make the daily bread. The dense, smooth, and *just right* touch was the goal. Only then was the loaf ready to be baked. The wood for the fire was tested for temperature to ensure a clean hearth. Dry wood burned nicely while the cool to the touch, damp log could cause a room to fill with smoke. The sacred life-art of hearth-keeping required full activation of the senses.

Vegetables were carefully harvested when a woman's senses told her, through sight, touch, taste, and smell that it was the right moment for ripeness. Only then could she be assured that the cabbage and carrots were at their peak. Planting was accomplished through the intuitive reading of the weather and the changing seasons. The stars and planets were also observed for guidance. This was mastered through the attunement of a woman's vision to read and interpret the encrypted messages that appeared to be etched in the realms of the heavens. These were a sacred life-artisan's meditative sensory rituals of the day.

Butter was churned. The chicken was plucked and cleaned. When one sat down to a meal the taste and the fragrance of the food was fully appreciated for the work of the hands and heart that had planted, cultivated, harvested, and prepared it. All the senses were piqued and present.

In earlier centuries (and primitive cultures today) the sixth sense of intuition fed the sacred imagination. Circles of moss and mushrooms were believed to be homes for the earth spirits, the faerie folk. In medieval times many believed that even the morning dew was touched by the life of the Fey.

In autumn when the hogs were butchered for meat, their fat was collected along with wood ash to make the family's soap. Later the same hands that made the soap scrubbed each article of clothing. This ritual allowed time to contemplate those who wore the clothes. Prayers were offered with each pass across the scrub board. The sense of touch and the soul were inextricably connected.

Imagine Helvide at work in the Belle Cœur olitory, a kitchen garden and miniature grove filled with edible flowers and herbs. In late summer these delectables were gathered and bound together to hang from the ceiling to dry. The fragrance of lavender, rosemary, and sage filled the house with a pleasant and soothing aroma that lifted the spirits of the occupants. (*I&H:* 165)

We recall how important the sense of smell was to the Belle Cœur sisters that worked in the infirmary. It was a primary tool used to diagnose illness. Every form of stench held a meaning. Aromatic oils and salves were often used as treatment and more often, to mask the odor of sickness.

When night approached and the light grew dim candles were lit to soften the vision and bathe the room with a golden glow. The eye adjusted from the natural light of day to the flickering shadowy realm of evening. The rhythm of life slowed as the lyre was strummed, stories were shared, and sugared ginger was passed round to sweeten one's dreams.

Book II The Four Chambers The Alchemy of Sacred Practice

Today, many of the daily tasks I have just described would be considered tedious, back breaking, and a waste of time. One thing is for certain; our technology has taken us far away from the life I've just described. Current daily routine moves at a very different cadence from the time of Goscelin, Beatrice, and their sisterhood. Our way of interacting with our senses is more automatic. We receive the sensory message that we are hungry and we grab a readymade sandwich from the corner deli or drive thru. When we're uncomfortably warm we flip a switch and the air conditioning comes on. Modern life certainly has its advantages. Yet, questions arise…

- ❖ Is it possible that in the midst of our technologically addicted lives we have forgotten how to make connection with nature and with one another through our senses?
- ❖ Could it be that our magnificently designed senses of touch, taste, smell, hearing, seeing, and intuition, have experienced spiritual and physical atrophy from lack of use?
- ❖ How do we, as sensate sacred life-artisans, reconnect with the wonder and blessing that emerges from conscious engagement with our senses and the sensual world?

At the heart of these questions rests a core issue. What is the difference between a response to sensory messages to meet a physical or emotional need, versus the engagement with the senses, to access the soul's guidance, to receive spiritual/sensual enrichment of a given experience? Is it possible that our senses are actually the Beloved's gift to us as a way to receive inspiration and guidance from Spirit?

Rather than a biological survey of how the senses and sensory system work as functions of the body, Belle Cœur spirituality looks to the past to incorporate the wisdom of the medieval woman. She instructs us to experience each of the six senses as conduits to inform our creative hearts and spirits. When we choose to live life as attuned, sensate, and sensual beings, we become fluent in the language of the soul.

The senses feed and nurture the soul, just as the soul inspires and enlivens the senses. Like two tango dancers, each is magnificent independently but when paired together their combined dancing becomes a transcendent experience.

You are invited to the sensual dance of life. Taste, touch, look, listen, see, hear, and intuit to engage the language of your soul.

The Sacred Life-Artisan's map for the senses

Here's an exercise to help you identify how you interpret the world through your senses. It will also indicate your personal definition of *beauty*. You might think of this practice as the creation of a map for discovering the colors, texture, and creative elements that enrich your feelings of peace and wellbeing. After you complete your map for your senses, contemplate

Book II The Four Chambers The Alchemy of Sacred Practice

how to incorporate its guidance into your sacred life-arts as you craft your prayers in co-creation with the Beloved.

Materials

A piece of cardboard or foam core board 36" x 36"
Pencil
Magazines to cut up
Glue stick
Your favorite paints
Crayons or colored pencils

Optional Materials

Rubber stamps
Charms
Touchstones
Shells
Feathers
Stones
Things collected from nature
Color copies of favorite photos
Glitter
Metallic pens

The Way of Belle Cœur

Process

Enter into this process with prayer and reverence. Light a candle. Play music you find comforting or choose to work in silence. Offer your prayer of intention.

- Using the paper or foam core board and a pencil, create a map of your senses. Begin by marking a 3" border on all sides.
- Draw a square inside the boundaries of the border that measures 30" x 30".
- Within the square divide the space into 6 segments. This can be done in whatever way you choose. Each segment can be a different size and shape or you may choose to divide the space evenly. You may want to color each segment as you prepare the background for collage. Allow your intuitive sense to guide you.
- Label each segment for the six senses: sight, sound, taste, touch, smell, and inner sight (intuition).
- Within each segment create a collage using images, photos, torn paper, words, etc. as your personal interpretation of how each specific sense speaks to you of beauty.
- Embellish the border with text from your favorite poems, sacred texts, quotations, your own thoughts, etc. or fill the border with random drawn or painted patterns.
- Fill the entire map with color, texture, sparkle, words, etc. Paint can be added as

enhancement. Imagine your map of the senses as your personal and creative interpretation of sensory experience and sustenance for your soul.
- ❖ Place your map flat upon a table. On the surface or around the border, arrange stones, flowers, fruit, shells, and other treasures to engage and represent each sense. Meditate upon the importance of welcoming sensual experience and beauty into your daily experience.
- ❖ Over time add additional sensory objects and images. Think of your map of the senses as a work in progress.

The Chamber of Story

*On these pages I will record
the stories of our community,
the stories of Belle Cœur,
and my observations of
the formidable events that befell us.
(I&H: 2)*

The value and power of women's stories

The story of a woman's spiritual journey is the declaration of her truth, a portrait of the landscape of her life, and her legacy of inspiration. A woman's story is encoded with spiritual guidance and mystical wisdom. When authentically and prayerfully recorded, her story becomes an integral, luminous, organic tapestry of feminine wisdom. It becomes an illumination of *her* story and also a legacy for her family and her sisterhood or community.

The story of a community's journey is a bountiful treasure of feminine sacred understanding and knowledge. It bears repeating that each sister's story is a piece of a larger tapestry traversing centuries of women's circles and communities. Sacred wisdom lives, thrives, and stands the test of time through our stories, individually and collectively.

A Belle Cœur Sister shares her wisdom

"I hold the belief that it is through story that we are able to connect with ourselves and also with others. I think it is crucial to our truth to spend time reflecting on our stories and recognize if we are holding on to stories that are no longer true, but may instead be habit or just created in our brains. I am fortunate that my work allows me to hear many women's stories from joy to pain and grief. Each one is an offering of love that beckons to be heard and felt in my heart. It is then that I see the connection of women's stories woven together through time."

Book II The Four Chambers The Alchemy of Sacred Practice

Rev. Terri Lynn Hubbard,
Mind, Body, Spirit-Life Coach & Healer
Sister of Belle Cœur

The Keeper of the Codex

The practice of story is a major foundational precept of the way of Belle Cœur. Through the examination, honoring, and sharing of our stories we mirror to one another the universality of woman's experience within the context of the uniqueness of our personal circumstances.

The invitation cocooned within the alchemical chamber of Story is two-fold. First, you're invited to create your legacy through the archiving and curating of your life's journey within the pages of your sacred codex. Secondly, you're invited to contemplate service as one of the weavers of the collective story of the journey of your community.

With regard to sisterhood, it's suggested that the call for the charism of *Herstorian* and/or *Keeper of the Codex* be named. This may be either a rotating or permanent position. It is suggested that a specific journal (for note taking, programming details, and planning) be designated. A codex should also be created as the sacred reliquary for the sisterhood's wisdom, photos, and as a record of various celebratory moments and sharing.

Reflectively, each sister is invited to archive and curate the story of her journey as the *Her*storian of her spiritual and creative life. The Belle Cœur codex provides the container for a sister's journey as a reflection of her particular charism and wisdom.

Like each of the sisters of Belle Cœur in the story of *Ink and Honey*, you carry and express a particular feminine wisdom that is uniquely iconotypal (archetypal) to you. The process of excavating *your* unique brand of wisdom through the discovery of the metaphors and symbols within your life's journey is the sacred practice of Story.

Belle Cœur Sisters share their wisdom

"When I arrived at my first Belle Cœur gathering, I had the rough draft of a memoir in hand. I was terrified to share my story with others, because there was much in it (and in my life) that caused me shame. To share parts of my story with my Belle Cœur sisters and see their eyes shine with love, support, and compassion, gave me the courage to offer my story to a wider audience. The sharing of my story changed me, and I believe, helped other women as well."

Mary Montayne
Author of *Above Tree Line: A Memoir*
Sister of Belle Cœur

Book II The Four Chambers The Alchemy of Sacred Practice

A story expressed as a poem, inspired by Mark 5:21-43
Life Giving Faith

Desperate father, dying daughter
 Come Lord Jesus
  Widows wailing proclaiming her death
Woman bleeding
 Pushes through the crowd to touch his garment
  Who touched me?
Little girl arise. Woman be healed.
 Your faith has made you well.

The Reverend Mary Anne Dorner,
Episcopal Priest
Sister of Belle Cœur

The Portundae

"In the vision, we were each making a small bundle. I understood these to be called portundae. That's the name I was given. Each bundle held a particular collection of sacred offerings, our relics… All of us have things we use each day, humble possessions necessary for our work or personal needs. Consider how two or more of these things might reflect the sacred wisdom you carry. What objects would you choose to express the story…the essence of who you are?"
(*I&H*: 456)

Inspired by Petronilla's instructions, the portundae (plural for portunda) is another form to represent your life story. The portunda (a small bundle of personal sacred relics) is a curated form to express a tangible representation of your charism and life's story. The creation of your portunda is a sacrament by virtue of your prayerful intention to bear witness to your story through the representation of your sacred possessions. The portunda contains your carefully selected touchstones and objects to reflect and represent your *her*story, your spiritual and creative heart, and life's calling and purpose.

Imagine…a thousand years from now an archaeologist searches for clues to know the people from the time you currently inhabit. To the scientist's surprise, she uncovers your portunda during an excavation. With reverence and awe she lifts the curious bundle from where you hid or buried it a millennia ago. She unwraps it slowly, object, by object as your story comes to life, and your wisdom spills forth from her discovery. In this way, the lineage of sisterhood continues. Once again, the past informs the present through your portunda that you so carefully and prayerfully prepared as your legacy for the future.

What relics would describe the essence of who you once were, how you lived, and what truly mattered to you?

Contemplate the particular objects, mementos, touchstones, and images that hold sacred and reverential meaning for you. What are the objects you think of as reflections of your personality and story? How might you create a small bundle of things to tangibly portray your spiritual beliefs, your work, and/or calling? What symbolic personal treasures would you choose to demonstrate and visually express your creativity, your unique wisdom, and charism?

You might find it helpful to write a list of the various qualities of your personality and then contemplate the particular objects, photographs, and touchstones you possess to represent each facet of your persona and life's story. Begin to gather these things. Store them in a reliquary, a basket, or a box that you decorate or embellish such as: a wooden trunk, clay vessel, or a curiosity cupboard.

A curiosity cupboard is a glass front cupboard, tabletop style, or freestanding that is filled to the brim with personal treasures, oddities, curiosities, ephemera and memorabilia. A curiosity cupboard can serve as a reliquary (a sacred stronghold) to store and display those things that hold spiritual, and/or creative inspiration, and purpose.

The portunda is a very personal creation to honor the energetic implements, mementos, tools and other physical representations of a woman's life. The size of this beautifully fashioned bundle should be no larger than a small loaf of bread.

"Make the covering from fur or linen, hide or sackcloth. Prayerfully choose your relics then place them in the center of the covering. Fold the corners inward to make a bundle, and bind it with strips of linen, wool or thong....Remember, Sisters, you're preserving your wisdom for the ages."
(*I&H*: 459)

Engage your creative heart and sacred imagination as you craft your portunda. With prayer, sacred intention, and contemplative preparation you will express your essence as a tangible gift of legacy. If you prefer, your objects may be scanned and printed. The printed copies of the objects may then be carefully wrapped to serve as a facsimile of the actual objects, until you're ready to create your portunda with the genuine articles.

A Belle Cœur sister shares her story

"I follow in the footsteps of the anchoress and nuns who protected the first treasury of Belle Cœur relics. I am the Keeper of the Portundae for my Belle Cœur Circle, in addition to being a Belle Cœur Sister myself.

The portundae abide in a special box by my personal altar. On top of the box is a photograph of all the women of our Circle along with our formational Sisters gathered underneath the raised arms of an autumn tree. There is a feathered effigy of Crow, the Belle Cœur guardian, which mysteriously appeared on our altar during the second day of our formation retreat. There is also a signed copy of Ink and Honey, a replica of the encircled Belle Cœur cross, a small jar of Belle Cœur honey, and a bar of honey soap wrapped in moss that adds sweet fragrance to this hidden treasure of Sisters. The reliquary is our Belle Cœur home while we live in diaspora.

I tend the portundae. On the day of each new moon, I open the box to the freshness of air and sun, while in deep darkness I cleanse the sacred bundles with sage. Daily I pray by the reliquary, in the company of my Sisters, as smoke

Book II The Four Chambers The Alchemy of Sacred Practice

streams from rose incense. Sometimes I sit and simply witness the mystery.

With the eyes of my heart, I see the Sisters' faces and behold this epiphany of our incarnated presence, our communicated participation in the life of Belle Cœur. Each bundle is a sacrament of unique identity and call—an outward and visible sign of the inward and invisible grace of each woman, her authentic life and purpose. The reliquary itself is a sacrament of our connection, community, and commission. Portundae are vestigia Dei, likenesses of the Divine—traces, mirrors, footprints, and fingerprints of our Beloved.

Each relic bears a woman's "yes" to Christ, to herself and her wisdom, and to all of creation. Each bundle is a woman's "alleluia." Each portunda is a sermo sapientiae, each woman's sermon on wisdom, her message conveying the goodness and good news of God. The portundae are icons, windows looking onto eternity, manifesting each Sister's "thisness," her particular form of the universal incarnation of the Christ Mystery. Every bundle is a love letter expressing for whom and how a Sister pours out her heart, mind, soul, and strength. Each one shows the giving of a Sister's flesh for the life of the world (John 6:51), how power went out from her (Luke 8:46) for healing and wholeness.

Every relic also bears a woman's "goodbye" to this life. The root of the word "relic" is relinquere, to leave behind, to relinquish. Portundae reflect present gifts as well as what each woman leaves behind as her legacy. In the assembling of her relics, each woman faces her own ending and, at the same time, a new beginning, as her wisdom is remembered and carried forward. A Sister's portundae welcomes Sister Death with a sacrifice of praise and thanksgiving. And in this joyful Belle Cœur relinquishing, each woman touches the mystery of something thoroughly old and yet startling ever new: ancient Wisdom in Her ten thousand forms: I love those who love Me, and show Myself to all who seek Me. I am true abundance, enduring prosperity…I bless My Lovers with wealth and fill their treasuries with timeless things" (Proverbs 8: 17-18, 21).

The Reverend Anne Ellen Fuquay
Sister of Belle Cœur

Reflect

- When I contemplate each decade of my life, I can identify pivotal moments and themes. The titles I choose for each decade of my earthly journey are…
- When I imagine creating a portunda for each decade of my life, I recall the following objects that have been important symbols for me…
- Throughout the remaining years of my life, how might I create a written and visual library of as my personal legacy? How would I present this and to whom?
- When I have created my portunda to represent my life's story I will place it…
- When I imagine the collaborative co-creation of a sacred codex as the community's documentation of our community's shared journey, the wisdom (sacred, creative, inspirational, intellectual) I would personally include can be described as…
- What would it feel like, and how could I benefit from a visit to a women's *her*storical library.

Book II The Four Chambers The Alchemy of Sacred Practice

When I imagine a place dedicated to the archiving and curating of women's journals, photographs, women's stories, and their portundae, I envision…

Create

Consider your codex, your portundae, and the sacred practice of Story, as expressions of your personal legacy. Encourage your community to co-create a collaborative codex. Incorporate the wisdom of your sisters as documentation of the individual and collective journeys within the context of your community. Perhaps you or one of your sisters will carry the name, *Guardian of the Codex*, as the one who will gather the stories and wisdom of your circle and record it in your community's codex. Think of your collective codex as a *her*storical document, a work in progress.

The Chamber of Study

*We implore you to gather
a circle of kin for shared study
of this sacred manuscript.
(I&H: 5)*

The Way of Belle Cœur

The process of the cultivation of personal sacred knowledge is a continual and evolutionary process throughout a woman's life. The practice of study is far more than the intellectual engagement of the mind. Study is also an inspirational process to inform the creative heart and spirit.

The concept of study, as it pertains to the Way of Belle Cœur, is engaged through the faculties of intuition and the sacred imagination. The discovery of wisdom heralded by a sweet "aha" moment is a natural and organic experience. Revelation occurs when the eyes and ears are attuned to respond to the Spirit's guidance or inspiration. Wisdom is always awaiting our discovery within ordinary everyday moments and also through the extraordinary and unexpected.

The following alchemical/spiritual practices are tools for transforming life's experiences into wisdom. Each practice is explored in depth in the following section.

I. Attentive listening, conversation/dialogue, and relationship with others (***oracular***)
II. The observance and witnessing of Creation (***natural***)
III. Art-making and creative, inventive forms of self-expression (***expressive***)
IV. Numinous understanding received in myriad unexplainable ways (***mystical***)
V. Responsive knowing and guidance through "gut feeling" (***intuitive***)

Book II The Four Chambers The Alchemy of Sacred Practice

VI. The exploration of books, films/television/online, workshops, classes (*intellectual*)

Six Responsive Practices for Study and Enrichment

Information and wisdom are acquired through various practices of awareness with regard to experiential understanding and intuitive response. Bring your conscious awareness to the practice that will best serve your particular need and circumstances. Six practices are offered for your exploration. Additional practices for enrichment may be added to the list, as your process unfolds.

I. Oracular

An oracle is a person with a clear voice for wisdom and guidance. While you wait to see the dentist or when you are in the checkout line at the market, listen attentively to the snippets of conversations around you. Is there a word or phrase that catches your attention? Receive this indirect information and ask yourself if the message holds meaning for you at this particular moment in time. Be attentive to receive the synchronistic wisdom that may arrive for you in unexpected ways through ordinary circumstances.

The Way of Belle Cœur

II. Natural

Arise before dawn to see and hear the subtle changes within your environment, as the night gives way to day. The same practice may be experienced at day's end as the dusk gives way to night. What are the differences between the beginning and ending of the day with regard to your environmental surroundings?

Make a practice of keeping a sketchbook to record drawings or written impressions of your ever-changing landscape. Make notations of what occurs in your own backyard throughout the year.

Choose a nearby place in nature for a yearlong study. Take a weekly photo of your chosen spot throughout the seasons. Create a visual record of Creation to increase your awareness of Wisdom Sophia's miraculous handiwork.

III. Expressive

You're invited to commit to the following practice for one week. Take a plum size ball of soft clay into your hands. Close your eyes and simply allow the clay to take form in whatever way your hands feel guided to shape it, without editing or forcing of any kind.

Over seven days, create an evolutionary series of spontaneous, expressive, molded impressions (one per day) as outward reflections of your inner world. This practice can also be done weekly, or monthly. Keep a journal where you title, date and record your creative process and reflections pertaining to your creations. You may also wish to photograph and title each piece and add the images to your journal.

IV. Mystical

Choose or create a sacred container. A small basket or box works nicely for this practice. Imagine your container to be your reliquary for meaningful notations, found objects, images, and photographs that express the synchronicities, revelations, and mysterious connections that unexplainably show up as inspiration and guidance. Become the curator and archivist of your journey.

Pay attention to the symbols and messages within your dreams and to the subtle and profound movements, illumination, and changes within nature and the weather. The mystical realm is also experienced through interaction with and the observance of your pet(s) and the animal kingdom. Birds are especially important as nature's feathered bridges. They have been said to carry messages from heaven to earth. Study birds in your area and become familiar with their songs. Creation is God's living language and affirming visible presence.

V. Intuitive

Consciously check-in with your body when you must discern a decision, or seek direction for your inner/outer journey.

Often our minds, our egos, and self-will give an affirmative to an action or response and all the while there is a "gut feeling" to the contrary. Notice how your belly and heart respond when you pose an important question to your self. Do you feel a knot in your stomach or ache in your heart as an unmistakable, "NO!" Or do you feel an overall sense of peace and softening of your body as a resounding, "YES!" The sixth sense of intuition has a direct correlation with physical response. Engage the practice of attentiveness to the wisdom of your body as the interpreter for your intuitive guidance.

VI. Intellectual

Make a list of your favorite books, films, teachers, and classes and workshops that you've attended. Contemplate how you might combine and blend the wisdom you've gleaned from these various sources to create an offering that is unique to you…in the form of a book, photo or film representation, or workshop/class.

Visit museums and art galleries, listen to various genres of music, and explore topics you've previously touched upon but been hesitant to pursue. Is there a subject you have always longed to know more about? Seek sources, teachers, and opportunities to grow your wisdom through intellectual pursuits as a lifelong learner.

Book II The Four Chambers The Alchemy of Sacred Practice

Reflect

- ❖ When I review the various forms of acquiring/receiving wisdom, listed above, I most resonate with the alchemical practice(s) of #...
- ❖ I would like to try...as I explore my selected alchemical practice(s).
- ❖ The form of alchemical practice that I'm most unfamiliar with is #... When I imagine exploring this practice I feel...
- ❖ An additional form/practice that I've experienced for the acquisition of wisdom is...
- ❖ Our community could benefit through the practice of #...

Book III
The Compass
True North and Wisdom Sophia

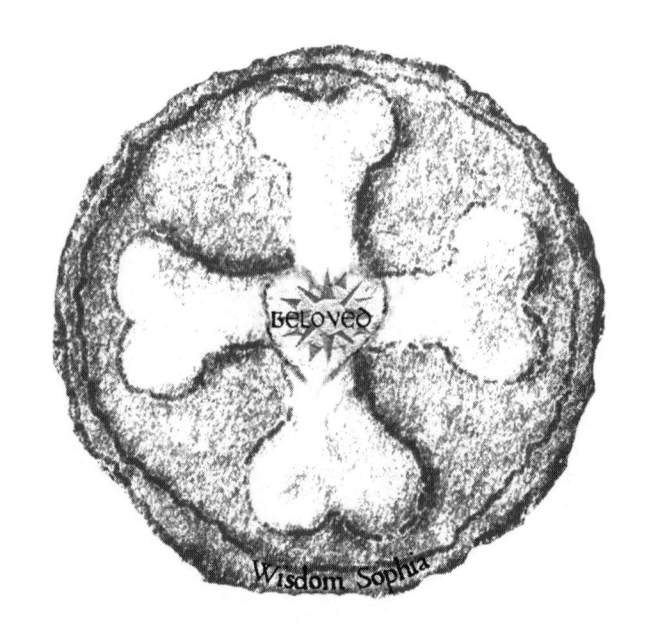

Wisdom Sophia

Book III The Compass True North and Wisdom Sophia

The Center: Jesus the Christ, the Beloved True North

The heart of Belle Cœur is Jesus the Christ. Christ (meaning the Anointed One) within the all-encompassing sense as the Logos, the Word, and the One that existed as the preamble and overture to every creation within the Universe. Christ, the Alpha and Omega, the heartbeat and rhythm keeper of our days and nights. Christ, our True North, the ever constant and enduring Light in all things, beyond the boundaries of religion, doctrine, and dogma.

Jesus is the Beloved, the full realization of Spirit in human form. He is our brother, teacher, life's and after life companion, physician and healer, guardian and mentor, consoler, counselor, friend and inspiration.

Jesus is Logos, the Word existing before time began. The pivotal spiritual concept of logos, frequently expressed by mystics, philosophers, and visionaries began in the classical world centuries ago. The concepts of intelligence, creativity, order, harmony, and sacred geometry, are represented within logos, the all-encompassing intelligence and loving flow of the universe.

"*In the beginning was the Word...*" according to the Gospel of St. John. The "Word," as used here, translated to the original Greek is logos. Logos, in this context, is the Word that holds the vibration, cadence, logic, and pattern of Creation.

Jesus *is* the Way of Belle Cœur and the center of Belle Cœur spirituality. He is our model for a balanced pattern of living and being that is paradoxically selfless and prophetic, ordinary and extraordinary, evolutionary and revolutionary, authentic and radical. To walk with

The Way of Belle Cœur

Christ is to journey inward. It is a journey to learn and embrace your truth. The ultimate goal is to understand the purpose of why you are here, and to realize what you and you alone were born to deliver through your living.

Jesus opens an inner portal to reveal the gift bestowed to your soul before birth. He leads you to experience the beauty of your true nature. To know Christ deeply and dearly is a continuous, life giving, unending sacrament, and spiritual quest. Belle Cœur spirituality relies on the center, on Jesus the Christ, and on the guidance of the Holy Spirit foremost and always.

The growth of the soul is inextricably woven into the fabric and template of the Way of Belle Cœur. For those called to become sisters of Belle Cœur, the leadership of sisterhood circles rotate in accordance with the needs and wisdom necessary within a given moment, Christ is eternally at the center. He is the constant and unchanging Sacred Heart of Belle Cœur spirituality.

When Belle Cœur sisters gather, we place a candle on the altar at the center of our circle to represent the Beloved's presence. In moments of doubt, challenge, celebration, prayer, discernment and questioning the Spirit of Jesus is present in the flame. He is our leader and teacher.

While we make personal and community decisions and choices, we slow down to reverently and prayerfully witness the Divine Presence. Through prayer and periods of silence we contemplate and await Christ's guidance while we focus on the holy flame of Love upon the altar.

Through our central devotion for the Beloved we are continually restored and fuelled with resilience and hope. We find sustenance, strength, healing, inspiration, and purpose at the center of the symbol for Belle Cœur. We also find these qualities at the center of the circle within the candle flame, and within our hearts where the indwelling Christ resides. For in all of these places the Spirit of our Beloved is present as expressed through the words of St. Patrick.

"Christ with me,
Christ before me,
Christ behind me,
Christ in me,
Christ beneath me,
Christ above me,
Christ on my right,
Christ on my left,
Christ when I lie down,
Christ when I sit down,
Christ when I arise,
Christ in the heart of every
(wo)man who thinks of me,
Christ in the mouth of everyone
who speaks of me,
Christ in every eye that sees me,
Christ in every ear that hears me."

Reflection

- ❖ When I contemplate my personal relationship with Jesus I imagine and feel…
- ❖ The Beloved modeled a way of living and being that is selfless and prophetic, ordinary and

extraordinary, evolutionary and revolutionary, authentic and just. Of all these qualities the one(s) I most resonate with and express in my life is/are…
- The quality/qualities I most need to cultivate include…
- At this time in my life I feel Jesus calling me to…
- The person that has been my greatest teacher and role model with regard to Christ is…
- What do I experience in my heart and spirit when I surrender my attachment to a desired outcome with the simple and profound prayer, "*Thy will be done?*"
- The greatest question for the Beloved that rests on my heart today is…
- My prayer in this moment is…

The Seasons of Life's Journey With The Beloved

You are blessed with the teachings of Jesus, our Beloved.
(*I&H:* 184)

Our Beloved's life from his conception throughout his ministry, crucifixion, resurrection, and beyond, provides a sacred map with reference points for specific seasons throughout life's journey. When you traverse a particular set of circumstances, whether the situation is uplifting, challenging, devastating, or miraculous it is helpful (for orientation) to refer to the following outline of experiences and events in Jesus' life.

We have learned that the Beloved is our compass and through reference to the various seasons of his journey you can become attuned and orientated through the recognition that you are experiencing a time of birth, healing, or crucifixion, etc. During the course of lifetime it's important to realize you may find you revisit these various spiritual seasons, time and again in random order. The Beloved is your guide no matter the twists and turns during your life's pilgrimage.

Jesus lived the full potential, extent, and measure of human experience. He is our True North and whatever circumstances you may be living through at any given moment, the Beloved is with you as you navigate your way to find your center once again.

It is helpful to align with the guideposts provided below and to know that Jesus has walked before you through all life's valleys, mountaintops, and deserts. He knows the way to ultimate peace and transformation and no matter what season you are traversing…take comfort in the knowledge that you are not alone as you journey.

Jesus' earthly journey

Below you will find the seasons of the Beloved's earthly journey and accompanying Scripture references. You are encouraged to research additional passages for personal resonance and enrichment. This section invites lectio divina practice with Scripture as the inspiration. A reflective word follows the description of each season.

Annunciation Luke 1:26-38

A call to step into unfamiliar terrain is received. It may also be a season of gestation for an idea, vision or new project. *Discernment*

Advent Isaiah 11:1-10

This is a hopeful season of promise and preparation as you await a new beginning. *Patience*

Birth Luke 2:1-20

A season of new life, work, place, or relationship, a fresh start. *Transition*

Teaching/Ministry Matthew 4:23

This is a season to mentor or be mentored. It is also a time to share or receive wisdom with/from others. *Growth*

Miracles Matthew 9:18-26

A numinous and grace filled season that delivers healing, blessing, and/or revelation. *Gratitude*

Book III The Compass True North and Wisdom Sophia

Healing Matthew 8:5-17

A season for self-healing (extreme self-care) or the participation (caregiving) and support for another's healing process. *Restoration*

Community Acts 1:14

An active season for co-creative and collaborative experiences. *Celebration*

Solitude Luke 6:12

This season calls for self-enclosure to allow uninterrupted spaciousness for prayer, reflection, spiritual replenishment, and renewal. *Reflection*

Transfiguration Luke 9:28-36

Transformation and change arrive in this season accompanied by radiant revelation. *Alchemy*

Desert Matthew 4:1-11

A season of spiritual aridity and feeling lost or abandoned. It is often a period of wandering, searching, and yearning for God's presence. There may be also be the experience of temptation. *Longing*

Gethsemane Matthew 26:36-46

A season to acknowledge the need for surrender and acceptance… "Thy will be done." *Abidance*

Crucifixion John 19

Great suffering occurs and there is grief and profound challenge. There may be the experience of death of a part of the Self. *Desolation*

The Tomb

Matthew 27:60

Physical and spiritual transition occurs during a period of deep rest and unknowing between the death of the old and eventual rebirth of what will be. *Void*

Resurrection

1 Corinthians 15: 35-58

Rebirth, renewal, and the re-emergence from a dark night of the soul arrive with the season of resurrection. *Renewal*

Reflect

Ecclesiastes 3:1-22
There is a time for everything, a season for every purpose under heaven: a season to be born and a season to die; a season to plant and a season to harvest; a season to hurt and a season to heal; a season to tear down and a season to build up; a season to cry and a season to laugh; a season to mourn and a season to dance; a season to scatter stones

and a season to gather them; a season for holding close and a season for holding back; a season to seek and a season to lose; a season to keep and a season to throw away; a season to tear and a season to mend; a season to be silent and a season to speak; a season to love and a season to hate; a season for hostilities and a season for peace.

- ❖ As you reflect upon the seasons of Jesus' life and the seasons described in the Scripture passage from Ecclesiastes, what season do you find yourself living in at this present moment?
- ❖ Does a prayer emerge from your heart as you reflect upon this current season of your life?
- ❖ Is there a correlation between the qualities of the seasons of nature in relationship to the circumstances of your current, personal, and spiritual season?

The Circle

Wisdom Sophia

*In my dream a bright golden light
shines around the circle's rim.
(I&H: 12)*

The Way of Belle Cœur

The circle that encompasses the Belle Cœur cross provides a sacred container that is symbolic of wholeness. The circle represents the compassionate and fierce love of our Mother, the Sacred Feminine. She is life-giver and nurturer. She is generative and ever birthing. Wisdom Sophia is represented in many forms through Mary (the mother of Jesus) as Our Lady of Guadalupe, Our Lady of Lourdes, Our Lady of Fatima, the Queen of Heaven, the Queen of the Angels, and in countless additional ways. Our Mother also embodies the entirety of Creation. She is alive within the elements of earth, air, fire, and water and present within the spirit of Mary Magdalene, the Apostle to the Apostles.

The spirit of Wisdom Sophia courses through our blood and bones as holy passion for all that lives and breathes. We express her creative energy through our crafts and sacred artmaking. Her spirit illuminates our sacraments whenever we anoint with oil and prayer. We live within her generative circle of compassion and strength while the Spirit of the Beloved radiates eternal Love from the center. We are held and sustained by Jesus and Mary, and our hearts beat in syncopation with the heartbeat of Wisdom Sophia and Christ's Sacred Heart of the Cosmos.

Jesus and Mary. Logos and Wisdom, the Flesh, the Spirit, the Word, the Masculine and Feminine are combined as the life-giving power of Creation…this is the way of life and the Way of Belle Cœur.

Book III The Compass True North and Wisdom Sophia

A Belle Cœur Sister shares her wisdom

"When I envision the Sacred Feminine, I see the Holy Mother – in the moon, the ocean, the stars, the flowers, the trees, the babies, our tears, our joys. I see her in earthquakes and volcanoes, tornadoes and hurricanes, as the earth trembles in response to our ignorance. I see her in tenderness and fierce protection. I feel devotion in response to her wisdom, her loving power, and her powerful love. She is everywhere."

Regina Bogle
Sister of Belle Cœur

The world turns

A small globe on a bookshelf in my workspace catches my eye. I pick it up and feel connected with the realization that all of humankind is fastened to the earth, a whirling sphere, suspended in the inky black universe.

We are tethered to our world composed of forests and deserts, mountains and plains, water and ice. We are souls alive at this time in history and *her*story through God's grace. We are star stuff, space travelers, and pilgrims on an evolutionary journey leading to transformation. We are the unborn, rocking in the waters of our mothers' womb. We are dependent, suckling infants, energetic teens, mellowing middle-agers, wise elders, and we are the dead…our bodies at last returned to dust. We are sick, healthy, wealthy, and destitute. We are Christians, Muslims, Jews, Hindus,

Buddhists, and Atheists. We love, laugh, cry, create, destroy, eat, sleep, age, and die.

We live out our lives in myriad ways through varying stages of...hunger and abundance, suffering and elation, confusion and clarity. We are a tribe of believers and unbelievers, saints and murderers, and each of us is capable of expressing generosity and greed, forgiveness and revenge. We are on a planetary voyage...together...here and now. Our commonalities are that we come from One Creator, we are human, and we are mortal.

The collective soup, that is humanity, is stirred by the hand of fear, seasoned with the salt of our tears and over peppered with war and suffering. This unsavory mélange has been cooking for millennia and has reached the boiling point. We whirl round and round in our cosmic soup-pot, while day becomes night and night returns to day. Like the nursery rhyme forecasts... *"Round and round we go and where we'll stop nobody knows."*

A reassuring fact is that our home, this blessed earth, is suspended exactly the right distance from the sun and the moon. The seasons come and go and all the while we keep turning, like an entranced whirling dervish, we twirl, each one of us tethered in our particular place in time and space. Species disappear, the icecap melts, and the revolving door (the eternal portal) for birthing and dying goes round and round from here to eternity and back again.

Images taken by the Hubble telescope reveal our world as a planet without boundaries. From a "God's eye" view we are indistinguishable as black or white,

Book III The Compass True North and Wisdom Sophia

male or female, rich or poor, Christian or Muslim. From a distance, we blend into the landscape. Viewed from space, we merge with the giant redwoods, the Atlantic and Pacific, the earthworm and the gazelle. From afar we blend together with all living things, with the earth herself as one living and breathing being.

After all, we humans are simply one thread in the tapestry of Creation. Each thread is dependent upon the next and the next in order for the weave to hold. Lately, it feels as if the warp needs mending. The threads are frayed and worn. They are coming undone and the tapestry is in urgent need of repair. We are filaments of every variety. Each strand is precious, unique, and purposeful. Each fiber is intrinsically beautiful as a separate entity.

However, when we are woven together, when we discover ways to co-exist and co-create within community, when we reach out to one another for compassionate connection to share our resources, wisdom, and creative gifts, then the weave of our human tapestry grows strong and resilient.

I turn the little globe in my hand and kiss her wounded places. If only it were this simple. Kiss it and make it better. I return the world to its place on the bookshelf while questions arise…

- ❖ How might you begin in even the smallest way to repair the weave of Creation's tapestry?
- ❖ What necessary ingredients will it take to re-season the rancid fear based soup that's boiling over?

- What is God's universal invitation for each of us in the midst of the chaos of this time of transformation?
- Where should we commence the search for the lost key to Eden?

A Belle Cœur Sister shares her wisdom

"I have always thought of the feminine when I think of God, the Beloved or the Greater Power. Mother Earth, the Mother God and the Caring Mother are all significant to me and have become even more so since my Belle Cœur experience. I believe the Sacred Feminine is indeed growing in the awareness of people in these times. We are returning to our roots in so many ways and the Sacred Feminine or Mother God is a broad base of that return. What a joyful way to celebrate the Sacred – to be wrapped in the arms of the Feminine Mother."

Millie Park Mellgren
Sister of Belle Cœur

Reflect

- When I envision the concept of the Sacred Feminine I feel…
- The particular name for the Sacred Feminine I most resonate with is: Wisdom Sophia, The Mother, Mary, Our Lady, Magdalene, Creation, etc.

Book III The Compass True North and Wisdom Sophia

- ❖ When I contemplate how the relationship between the Beloved and Wisdom Sophia balances the scales of masculine and feminine, spirit and matter, birth and death, I...
- ❖ I long to deeply and prayerfully connect with the Sacred Feminine to...
- ❖ The question I carry for the Sacred Feminine in my heart at this moment is...
- ❖ My prayer right now is...

Book IV
The Wisdom Keepers of Belle Cœur

*As their community grew,
each woman's gifts bloomed
into loving action,
an offering to God
and the sisterhood.
(I&H: 107)*

The sisterhood of Belle Cœur, as depicted in the story of *Ink and Honey*, features feminine iconotypes (archetypes) referred to in this section as *The Wisdom Keepers of Belle Cœur*. Additional iconotypal wisdom keepers from the story include, Myrtle and Henriette.

Book IV The Wisdom Keepers of Belle Cœur

Archetypal classification of personalities has proved to be a useful tool to identify patterns of behavior and certain human characteristics. Anthropologists, Jungian analysts, and others have used this method of classification throughout the years. Psychiatrist and psychotherapist, Carl Jung, was the first to use the term *archetype* with reference to literature. Jung believed there were motifs within mythologies and stories that revealed universal constructs. These archetypes shared a commonality, despite a varied historical timeline or diverse culture. Through his research and studies, Jung came to believe that a corner of the human psyche held a collective unconscious shared by all humanity as a form of communal memory.

Readers have expressed resonance and heartfelt connections with the various characters and events depicted in the pages of *Ink and Honey*. Perhaps in part, this is due to the phenomena of the collective unconscious. Some have shared how they glimpse fleeting memories from a past life, not unlike the one lived by the sisters of Belle Cœur in the story.

Are these feelings rooted in the phenomenon of the collective unconscious or past life memories? No one can say for certain. However, I do know with certainty there is something curious and unexplainable in the fact that large numbers of women are hungering for the sacred and for women's community. Women are seeking creative and spiritual enrichment to deepen their relationships with the Beloved. This shared feminine longing is specific in nature. It is full with potential for the birth of new forms of sacred study, the sharing of personal stories, community prayer, and creative expression within the context of a spiritual circle of sisterhood.

For our purposes in relationship to our study of the Way of Belle Cœur, we will explore a form of codification for the Wisdom Keepers I have named, *iconotypal portraiture*. For twenty years I have been a student of the sacred art of iconography. Religious icons are hand painted images of transfigured saints, Christ, Mary, and other religious subjects. An icon represents a visual and meditative portal leading the viewer to the Divine Presence. The iconographer is said to *write* an icon rather than paint it. Icons, in this way are a form of visual Scripture.

While I discerned the content for this book I contemplated the characters of *Ink and Honey* as archetypes. The thought occurred that rather than labeling the characters as archetypes it would be more appropriate to consider them as *iconotypes*. An iconotype is a particular form of classification often used for scientific labeling and study.

The word iconotype, for our purposes, holds a sacred connotation. There is a particular invitation within the iconotypal portraiture of the Wisdom Keepers. You're invited to contemplate not only the creative and psychological characteristics of each iconotype, but the spiritual and sacred attributes, as well.

Iconotypal portraiture offers a set of universal criteria for each Wisdom Keeper. You will discover how the individual characters embody specific, creative, and spiritual gifts that combine to form her unique iconotypal portrait. The layering of personal story, characters' individual qualities, values, and personality traits blend to create each unique iconotypal portrait. This layered process is similar to the way an iconographer writes an icon or sacred portrait. Numerous sheer layers of paint are applied atop one another until the image appears luminous, as if it is illuminated from within.

As you explore each individual iconotypal portrait pay attention to your interior responses. Notice the places where you relate (expand your imagining) and where you experience resistance or ambivalence (contract your imagination) to a particular Wisdom Keeper's message, characteristics, etc.

A Meditation

Before you begin to work with the material included in this section, it's important to shift from ordinary Kronos time (clock time) to a more relaxed and expansive state of Kairos time. The following meditation is offered to engage your sacred imagination and to invite you to cross the threshold of mystery to enter the world of Belle Cœur.

Read the following guided journey slowly, pausing frequently to enter deeply within the experience. Make yourself comfortable. Take several deep breaths. Inhale and exhale slowly. With soft focus, you're invited to enter into a waking dream as you enter into the following visualization.

You are traveling back in time.

The Way of Belle Cœur

You are walking through a green meadow, deep in the heart of the French countryside. Notice what you see. Notice what you hear.

You are on your way to visit the sisters who live in the house named Belle Cœur.

Breathe in the scent of fresh grass and lavender as you make your way up the rise to the path that leads through a garden.

You arrive at the house. A worn sign with the symbol of a rusted cross, enclosed by a blue painted circle hangs beside the front door.

You see the sisters in the nearby garden and inside the house busily going about their work.

A sister comes to the door to greet you. She wears a blue linen dress and plain linen apron. Her head is covered with a shoulder length linen veil.

You enter the house.

Your senses take in the beauty of the place.

Breathe in the scent of fresh bread baking on the hearthstone.

What other fragrances do you notice?

The earthen floor is soft and yielding beneath your feet.

A sister places a soft, blue shawl around your shoulders.

Several sisters are seated in a circle around the table near the stone hearth.

One of them rises to show you to your place on the rim.

Notice the sisters seated on either side of you.

Who is directly across from you?

A simple prayer is offered.

Book IV The Wisdom Keepers of Belle Cœur

You are given a burning taper and invited to light the candle at the center of the table.

You light the candle and extinguish the taper.

You and the sisters sit silently together for a time.

A sister offers a prayer.

Another sister holding a smooth white stone poses the question to everyone…"*Who are you?*"

She places the stone on the table in the center beside the candle. Again, everyone is silent.

A sister reaches for the stone.

She rubs the smooth surface with her thumb before responding to the question.

Notice how she responds.

One by one, each member of the community passes the stone 'round the circle.

They provide their answers in the form of stories, painting portraits of themselves with words.

You behold their faces as you become acquainted with each sister's uniqueness, her gifts, passions, challenges, and most importantly… her story.

Finally, the stone is passed into your hands and you share your wisdom story in response to the question, "Who are you?"

You feel safe and at peace in the good company of the sisters of Belle Cœur.

How do you express what's resting upon your heart?

When all have spoken there is silence for a time.

A sister offers a closing prayer.

The candle at the center is extinguished.

Honey cake and mead wine are served with lively conversation.

You listen to the sisters' conversation and breathe in the beauty and love within this place.

They are grateful for your presence.

You thank them for their hospitality and as you say goodbye, a sister stands in the doorway to offer you her blessing.

"Hope and wisdom, dear friend. Remember us. Our spirits will always remain here to offer you counsel and the door to Belle Cœur is forever open. Now…go and find *your* sisters."

She touches your forehead with two fingers and draws an equidistant cross within a circle.

You turn to leave while a large black crow caws out from overhead.

Take several deep breaths and allow yourself to slowly return from your waking dream state to the present moment.

Respond to the following reflection questions in your journal. Resist editing.

Reflect

- ❖ Contemplate the metaphor of your walk through the meadow in relationship to your spiritual journey. Name the spiritual and/or creative longings that have called you to explore the Way of Belle Cœur?
- ❖ What feelings arose for you when you first entered the house at Belle Cœur? Sketch what appeared to you on a blank page of your journal.

Book IV The Wisdom Keepers of Belle Cœur

- Who greeted you? Why do you think she's the particular sister who appeared to you?
- How did it feel to be vested with the blue shawl?
- What feelings arose as you were shown your place on the rim of the circle?
- What are the various significances of the shawl, the circle of women, and the candle flame?
- If you were called to offer the opening or closing prayer for the circle, how would you pray?
- When the stone arrived into your hands, what thoughts and feelings arose for you? How did you respond to the question, "Who are you?"
- What thoughts, inspirations, and feelings arise as you reflect upon the sister's parting commission to you? *"Hope and wisdom, dear friend. Remember us. Our spirits will always remain here to offer you counsel and the door to Belle Cœur is forever open. Now...go and find your sisters."*

Express

The following exercise is intended to deepen your experience and understanding of iconotypal portraiture.

Find magazine images to visually represent each Wisdom Keeper. Glue each image onto a page of your codex. You may also choose to sketch your impressions of each Wisdom Keeper or add personal photos of yourself, and/or your friends and family members that remind you of a particular iconotype. Make

The Way of Belle Cœur

your reflective notes in the margins surrounding the various images.

Explore

As you study the following iconotypal portraits of the Belle Cœur Wisdom Keepers you're invited to imagine each spirit is speaking directly to you from beyond the veil. Work through this section slowly. Savor each Wisdom Keeper's message as a meditation. Contemplate the iconotypal wisdom to make it your own according to your understanding and interpretation.

Become acquainted with the characters' challenges, secrets, charisms, passions, and other facets of their sacred wisdom as revealed through their iconotypal portraits. Each portrait concludes with topical reflective questions to explore in your journal for further revelation and inspiration, as well as, an invitation to creatively express your response to the Wisdom Keeper.

At the completion of your study of this section you will find an invitation and an outline to create your personal iconotypal self-portrait. Ultimately you may wish to synthesize your notes and journal reflections as sacred wisdom to be added to your codex.

Book IV The Wisdom Keepers of Belle Cœur

The Belle Cœur Iconotypal Portraits

*Our spirits arrive
through these stories
bearing flint and wood
to kindle your creative fires.
(I&H: 4)*

Beatrice

The Cook and Soothie

Iconotype: The Hearth-keeper
Qualities: Nurturer and Caregiver
Wisdom Keeper of the Hearth

Beatrice's spirit delivers her wisdom...

"Throughout my lifetime my heart overflowed with passion for the pleasures of hearth keeping. When I tended an infant at my breast while I stirred a simmering kettle of soup, I was a happy woman. Scrubbing and cooking completed with prayer became offerings of devotion to God.

My invitation to any tired and weary soul is this... 'Come sit at my table and I will feed you the truths I hold dear. Taste the wisdom I offer like sweet honey from the hive. You are welcomed here.'

What are the truths I hold dear, you ask?

The Way of Belle Cœur

I believe you must stoke your soul's hearth-fire ignited by God's angels deep within your spirit before you were born. Trust that you know what needs to be done. A woman who distrusts her wisdom lacks the wherewithal to nurture others, just as a woman with false humility belittles the gifts God has given her to share.

With regard to tending a home, dear sister, keep order and cleanliness in your living space, for these are the spiritual practices of the Hearth-keeper. Claim the various rooms of your home as reflections of your spirit. The bedchamber should be a sanctuary, unencumbered by distraction, a place of rest. The kitchen is the heart of the home. It should be lively and well tended to ensure a steady and healthy pulse. Bless all rooms with sacred meaning and beauty.

Welcome those who cross your threshold with genuine hospitality and lend your listening ear to hear the deeper story within the conversation. Help others to thrive in all situations according to their needs. Learn to recognize the nature of another's hunger. Offer food for the body for this is polite and a gesture of kindness. Yet, be prepared to also offer food for the spirit through compassion, prayer, or your listening heart.

Pay attention to the nourishment and needs of <u>your</u> body and soul, as well, dear sister. A well-tended body ensures a quick mind. Replenish yourself according to your particular rhythm and requirements. If you neglect your creative spirit and personal needs how will you feed others from your table, from your wisdom, or from your heart? Be conscious of your motives for nurturing others.

Be aware of the dangers of martyrdom. I know this lesson well from my lifetime in service to others. My sisters told me time and again to care for myself. This was good counsel that I seldom heeded.

Book IV The Wisdom Keepers of Belle Cœur

Become wise about the human condition and the importance of herbs for a good constitution. Helvide, our herbalist, taught me well. Find a teacher and study these things.

Fasting blesses the spirit in countless ways. Fast, not only from food, more importantly fast from gossip, judgment, and criticism of others. I regrettably often ignored this wisdom from our counselor, Sabine. However, I eventually learned to dedicate my fasting as my prayer for the healing of others.

Express unending gratitude to God for the abundance upon your table and within your life. Let your service through daily tasks become a river of prayer. Harmony, my sister, create harmony and a steady cadence within your home. Become a Hearth-keeper and offer a nurturing sanctuary where God may dwell among you and your beloveds, and those who find their way to your door."

༺༻

Beatrice's charism: The miraculous gift of her bountiful supply of mother's milk in her later years. Beatrice also carried the ability to intuitively discern a person's needs for physical, emotional, and spiritual nurturing. She imbued the hearth and home with love and beauty.

Her challenge: How to maintain order within the home without becoming bossy, controlling, judgmental or critical.

Her elements: Earth and fire.

The Way of Belle Cœur

Her secret: The burning desire to learn to read and write.

Her shadow: Her overriding tendency to serve others to the point of exhaustion. This caused her to have feelings of resentment that often manifested inappropriately through her snap judgments and sharp words to others. She lived in a state of self-denial to the point of martyrdom, *"I have so many to take care of and so much to do that I never have a moment for myself."*

Her passion: Nursing and tending hungry infants at her breast and maintaining an orderly, peaceful environment.

Her sacred practice: Beatrice kneaded her prayers and blessings into the daily bread dough.

Her wisdom phrase: *"Make your home a haven of peace as a welcoming sanctuary."*

Her gifts to her community and others: Her nurturing heart.

Her relics: A small wooden spoon crafted by Gertrude, a little wooden honey pot containing two remaining spoonfuls of honey from Belle Cœur, and her mortar and pestle.

Her symbol: The breast

Her birth sign: Cancer

Her sacred life-arts: Hearth-keeping, cooking

Book IV The Wisdom Keepers of Belle Cœur

Her invitation: *"Take care of your body, mind, and spirit to assure you are healthy to complete the work God puts before you."*

Suggested active service: Prepare and deliver a meal to someone who is homebound. Invite someone who is alone to your home for tea or a meal. Volunteer at the nursery of your local hospital.

Her petit cadeaux: Ses recettes préférées. Her favorite recipes.

Her earthly prayer: *Beloved, I pray to serve You through my ready hearth and open hospitality. May my home be a place of welcoming and may my table always have a place set for the stranger, the broken hearted, the pilgrim, the one who is lost. I give thanks for the blessing of mother's milk and pray for Your nourishment to flow through me to the suckling infants in my care. I ask for the spirit of Belle Cœur to live within the home that is a sanctuary of peace, beauty, and safe haven. May all who enter there feel Your presence and receive Your grace.* Amen

Beatrice's identity passage from Scripture: Proverbs 31:15, 20

She rises before dawn to put into motions the working of the household.

She holds out a hand to the hungry, and opens her arms to the homeless.

Selected *Ink and Honey* passages pertaining to Beatrice: (*I&H:* 90, 95, 158-159, 161, 184-185, 191-192, 267, 312-313, 367, 385, 421).

Reflect

- What activities, material possessions, or opportunities do I presently deny myself because of feelings of unworthiness or selfishness?
- Are there ways I tend to act out the role of martyr in my life?
- What would it feel like to nurture my Self?
- In what way(s) do I most enjoy nurturing others?
- How do I embody the iconotype of the *Hearthkeeper*?
- Are there specific changes I could make to bring order and harmony to my home or workplace?
- If Beatrice joined me at my kitchen table for a cup of tea, what would I ask her? How would she respond? What would she ask me?
- Where (within my environment) do I fully experience the heartbeat of my home?
- When I imagine fasting, what kind of fast would be beneficial for me (fasting from food, gossip, judgment, shopping, alcohol, criticism, technology, etc.)
- If I am called to begin fasting, to what cause, person, or social justice issue would I prayerfully dedicate my fast?
- What additional personal observations and revelations are inspired by Beatrice's iconotypal portrait?

Book IV The Wisdom Keepers of Belle Cœur

Express

- ❖ Spend some time in your kitchen rearranging, sorting, clearing, and cleaning. Imagine Beatrice's spirit is present with you. How does she inspire you to enrich the "hearth" of your home?
- ❖ Evoke Beatrice's spirit as you prepare a meal for friends or family. Incorporate ritual and prayer into the entire process including: planning the menu, shopping for the food, setting the table, all aspects of preparing the food, blessing and serving the meal, the conversation while eating, and the cleanup afterwards. Refer to *The Feast of Life* in Book IX to find Beatrice's Communion bread recipe.
- ❖ Plan a day to immerse in Self-care. What does your body, mind, spirit need? How will your prepare?

Cibylle

The Waif

Iconotype: The Misfit
Qualities: Beloved and Misunderstood
Wisdom Keeper of Hidden Knowledge

The Way of Belle Cœur

Cibylle's spirit delivers her wisdom…

"Here, in the realm of Spirit I am healed and free. I have a voice for the voiceless. At last, I long to share the wisdom I was unable to express when I lived in my seeming imperfect body. A body that was wholly perfect to God's eyes.

When I lived in the world, I was seen as different from others. I spoke an unearthly language given to me by God and understood only by the angels and the few precious souls that took the time to know me.

Most found me to be homely and frightening. I made others uncomfortable. They looked away when I came near without taking the time to truly know me. My awkward appearance caused most to believe I was a woman-child possessed by madness and demons. These were souls blind to the knowledge that a person deemed ignorant is not without a relationship with God, or capable of divine understanding.

If holy madness is the result of one's unbridled love for God and all of Creation, then surely I succumbed. My spirit was untethered to earthly existence. Rather, the landscape I inhabited was colorful and playful with God's presence within all things. I saw God within the wind. God was also present at the mysterious moment of sweet in-between before dawn, when it is neither night nor day.

God instructed me to build shrines, nests, and hiding places crafted from twig and frond, stone and mud. It was not for me to understand why I was to do these things. Without question, I followed the divine instructions that angels with wings made of fire sang into my heart.

I was blessed to cherish all that lived and even more, blessed to carry life within me. Soon after my child was conceived, in a way that must remain a sacred secret forever, God told me in a dream… 'The infant in your womb is alive

Book IV The Wisdom Keepers of Belle Cœur

with purpose. She is woman's wisdom incarnate. She will illuminate the vision of those blind to sacred understanding. She will inspire them to recognize the Holy in their midst.'

My beloved sisters named my child, Grace, and though I touched her but an instant before a river of blood carried emptied me of life, I tell you this... Grace's spirit lives within you. She is present each time you respond to another with compassion. The spirit of Grace shimmers in your bones when rather than turning away, you take the time to recognize Christ's presence there before you... within the stranger, the homely one, and within the broken and broken-hearted.

I was the one perceived as witless and mad. I am the unlikely mother of Grace, the blessed return of the Sacred Feminine. Remember, dear sister, seeming ignorance does not mean a person is less than perfect. The one who appears simple minded and homely to the eye, may be the very soul God has chosen to carry and deliver a holy purpose and miracle of perfection."

Cibylle's charism: Her innocent and childlike ways.

Her challenge: Unjustifiable projections and judgment were thrust upon her, based upon her unconventional outward appearance. These injustices caused Cibylle's overall diminishment and withdrawal into her inner world as her means of self-protection.

Her elements: Earth, air, mother's milk, honey.

Her secret: The way in which she conceived Grace.

The Way of Belle Cœur

Her shadow: Cibylle's shadow is indeterminable due to the innocence of her spirit.

Her passion: All forms of playfulness as sacred expression and praise for the Beloved.

Her sacred practice: The creation of nature shrines.

Her wisdom phrase: *"Follow me in the search for the lost key to the garden."*

Her gift to her community and others: Her child, Grace.

Her relics: A walnut shell and moss collected from one of Cibylle's shrines, a perfect stork feather, and her apron.

Her symbol: A twig

Her birth sign: Unknown

Her sacred life-arts: Candle-making and the gathering of natural treasures for the assemblage of her nature shrines.

Her invitation: *"Seek the wisdom and beauty in whatever or whomever you believe to be unbeautiful."*

Suggested active service: Ask permission from a local school and the appropriate authorities to invite a classroom of children to help you to design and create a nature offering for your local park, playground, or elder housing.

Her petit cadeau: Une nature sanctuaire minuscule. A tiny nature shrine.

Her earthly prayer: *Beloved, You inspire my creative heart to nest, burrow, forage and gather. Like the robin and mouse, fox and mole I, too, am the work of your Creation. Help me to remember my animal ways. Help me to birth the Sacred Feminine through the sacred life-arts. When others ridicule me or do not recognize the gift within my offerings, make me strong and help me to forgive them. Banish my discouragement so I may radiate love and joy through your grace.* Amen

Cibylle's identity passage from Scripture: Luke 1:38
Mary said, "I am the servant of God. Let it be done to me as you say." With that, the angel left her.

Selected *Ink and Honey* passages pertaining to Cibylle: (*I&H:* 260-268, 292, 316, 321-327, 363-367, 386, 412-441, 471-472).

Reflect

- ❖ How do I acknowledge those who are considered to be different or other?
- ❖ When I cross paths with someone (a Misfit) on the margins of society, the homeless, disabled, or mentally challenged, what feelings arise? How do I respond to my feelings?

- How does the human tendency to judge others play out in my life?
- Has there been a time in my life when I've felt like a misfit? What did I learn from that experience?
- Who are the misfits that I know and love? What special wisdom do they carry?
- What are my beliefs pertaining to life's most mysterious and numinous moments? Namely those events that have no explanation other than to be deemed as *miraculous.*
- What do I feel God has placed within my creative heart and spirit to deliver and birth into fruition?
- How does inspiration take hold in me? How do I express it?
- What is my relationship with the natural world?
- If I were inspired to build a shrine in nature, what would it look like? Where would I choose to build it?

Express

- Make a sketch of your vision for a nature shrine in your journal.
- Invite Cibylle's spirit to accompany you on a walk in your neighborhood or local park. Take along a plastic bag or basket to contain the things you will gather. Inspired by the spirit of Cibylle, collect gifts from nature and found objects (pennies, bottle caps, bits of paper,

string, etc.) that you will incorporate as you create your nature shrine.
- ❖ Spend time with someone that you consider to be a *Misfit*. Share your wisdom with one another.

Comtesse

The Needle-worker

Iconotype: The Iconoclast
Qualities: Secretive and Envious
Wisdom Keeper of Shadows

Comtesse's spirit delivers her wisdom…
 "*Feelings of jealously were weeds in the garden of my life. I was uncomfortable in my own skin. I saw my less than perfect reflection illumined in the gaze of others.*
 In my girlhood, I journeyed to Belle Cœur seeking my starlit place in the world. More and more I looked to others for their approval, for their adoration. In desperation I became a fearless seeker for attention. The thread throughout the tapestry of my life was the color of need. I became a needle worker and mender of cloth but always it seemed as though I was trying to stitch myself together into something other than what I was.

The Way of Belle Cœur

I longed to be important, learned, and beloved like Goscelin. Cibylle, despite her awkward and unseemly ways, was cherished by the sisters...cherished in a way that I would never know. Always longing to be someone else, I never discovered my own true nature.

Strangely, as much as I desired to be loved whenever love was offered, whenever someone came close, I pushed them and their efforts to love me far, far away. To my ultimate regret, I did all manner of hurtful and harmful things to be noticed.

My demons inspired my fits and tirades. I learned, to my wicked delight, that my seemingly holy sisters were susceptible to rage and rancor. My shameless ranting invited them to the frenzied dance, and so they bantered with me in my darkest moments. I received momentary pleasure during our confrontations, but at the last I was left with only my guilt and regret.

I believe each of us is capable of monstrous behavior. It all depends on the strength of one's faith in God's merciful love to keep the demons at bay. The devil seeks the weakest place within the human heart and tenaciously sets out to ruin the soul. Only prayer and faith fortify us to deter the evil one.

When Brother Gilles showed his favor for me and began to use me for his pleasure, I was at first exhilarated but as his demands increased so did my shame. I knew he was diabolical from the start but I sought love wherever I believed it could be hiding. I claimed justice when I took his life for his vile trespasses. In the end, I paid with my life for the murder I committed.

Sister Marguerite lured me with her insincere compliments and special favors. I did all that she asked of me to remain in her good graces...to become her favored one. I learned too late that she befriended me to gain favor in the bishop's sight

Book IV The Wisdom Keepers of Belle Cœur

through her attempts to add me to her fold. In the end it was she who betrayed me and handed me over to the inquisitors.

Mocked by those who came to watch me burn, this was my final humiliation. Yet, in those choking moments as I cried my confession, begging God to be merciful, only then as my soul was mercifully released did I recognize and understand the sweet irony. Love had always been mine. It was present within me from my birth. God's Love abides still and I am held in that Love for all eternity.

My earthly life was opprobrium at best and a disaster of my own creation. Remember, dear sister, Love is the indwelling Presence and your birthright. You have only to place your hand upon your heart to know you are loved for evermore."

༄༅༅

Comtesse's charism: In her best moments she was loyal and forthright.

Her challenge: Her inability to allow herself to receive love from those closest to her and her unwillingness to harness her egocentric desires and fervent need to be the continual focus of others' attention.

Her elements: Water, fire, thunder and lightening.

Her secret: She wanted to *be* Goscelin.

Her shadow: Her calculated ability to inflict emotional pain upon those who loved her as the result of her self-loathing.

The Way of Belle Cœur

Her passion: Her creation of fine tapestries worthy of praise and adulation.

Her sacred practice: She struggled without success to find a sacred practice to enrich her spirit.

Her wisdom phrase: *"Do not look outside yourself for others' approval. You must love yourself before your heart will be made ready to receive the love you long for. God's Love is your birthright and eternally yours."*

Her gift to her community and others: Comtesse's unbridled and challenging behavior offered the opportunity to those around her to grow their wisdom through the practices of patience, compassion, and forgiveness.

Her relics: A small tapestry, her needle, and wool.

Her symbol: A shard of broken pottery.

Her birth sign: Leo

Her sacred life-art: Needlework

Her invitation: *"Rather than feeling jealous of someone… choose to feel inspired by her."*

Suggested active service: Reach out and make amends with someone you have offended or hurt.

Her petit cadeau: Un chiffon signet, a cloth bookmark.

Her earthly prayer: *Save me from myself, my torment overtakes me. Quiet my tongue and calm my vengeful heart. Give me peace. Help me to resist temptation and turn to You though I am vexed and drowning in a dark sea of my own making. I am lost. My judgment of others brings me shame and fills me with desperation. I am on my knees. Help me to redeem myself and repair my life through Your merciful forgiveness and love.* Amen

Comtesse's identity passage from Scripture: Proverbs 27:4

Anger is fierce as a fire, wrath relentless as a flood—but jealousy is a feeling the soul cannot withstand.

Selected *Ink and Honey* passages pertaining to Comtesse: (*I&H:* 8-13, 84-89, 170-171, 226-227, 230-232, 263-265, 309-310, 355-357, 413-416, 449-453, 478).

Reflect

- ❖ How do I nurture my psyche to maintain and ensure my emotional wellbeing and spiritual centeredness?
- ❖ What are the various direct and indirect ways I express anger?
- ❖ The iconotype of the Iconoclast refers to one who denigrates or lashes out at ideas, institutions, and sacred imagery. When have I been an attacker of someone's personal concepts, beliefs, or convictions?

The Way of Belle Cœur

- *Remember that Love lives within you, eternally.* How does this statement resonate with me in this present moment?
- When I imagine offering my spiritual and creative gifts to the world without need or desire for acknowledgement the following feelings arise...
- How would I feel if I anonymously donated money to a person or cause, performed a random act of kindness, or created a work of art to be given away?
- What does the concept of humility mean for my life?
- Where in my life and relationships do I experience envy?
- Could my envious feelings be repurposed (with prayer and God's help) and transformed from thoughts of *jealously* to regard for another's gifts as *inspiration*? How might an "enviable" person become a muse for me?
- Comtesse inspires me to acknowledge the following about my Self...
- How have I been betrayed? When have I acted as the betrayer?
- Where in my life do I need to forgive someone and/or myself?

Book IV The Wisdom Keepers of Belle Cœur

Express

- ❖ Call together a circle of knitters to knit prayer shawls or lap blankets for those in hospitals or eldercare facilities.
- ❖ Stitch a crazy quilt of memories. Transfer photographs to fabric and blend with color and pattern to make a wall hanging to represent your life's story.
- ❖ Sew printed messages of hope and healing (made from paper or fabric) onto the pages of your journal.
- ❖ Create a ritual of Self-forgiveness for whatever troubles your heart and spirit.

Gertrude

The Carpenter

Iconotype: The Survivor
Qualities: Creative and Resilient
Wisdom Keeper of Courage

Gertrude's spirit delivers her wisdom...

Mein desire on earth vas to please God with de vurk of mein hands. I am a builder. Ven I vent to join de men at Chartres to build de cathedral for Our Lady, I heard God speak to mein heart. God's teaching I share wit you now. I pray it vil bless you as it blessed me. God spoke to me des vords...

The Way of Belle Cœur

"Become like a stone, Gertrude. Be firm in your purpose. Receive the mantle of courage. Trust. Learn from the stone. Be still and rooted in place. I will pick you up and carry you to where you will best serve. I will set you amongst the other stones as I build the New Jerusalem. I will etch your purpose and make it real.

You are a singular stone. Your true nature is revealed and your service begins when you are joined with others. Contemplate the stone. Contemplate the ages required for its formation. Sun and ice, wind and pelting rain hone the stone and shape it. Imagine the stone's particular placement upon the earth and its unending patience until the moment when the stonemason chooses it, for its unique shape, and potential to serve its purpose.

You, like the stone, have been chosen. You will be held fast until the time arrives when you will be delivered to where you will best serve. You must have the patience of the stone."

I did not know I vould fall from de cathedral. Ven I lost mein arm I understood dat God told me I need patience.

Courage is your best friend, dear sister. You must find your courage to do vhatever God calls you to do. Courage is ein fierce teacher. You vill learn how truly strong you are ven you act bravely.

I had no choice, only courage. I vonted to build like de men and I had to hide my truth to climb de height of de cathedral. Den de terrible fall happened und months of pain und suffering but God fed me courage und I healed and grew stronger. I survived wit de help of mein beloved Imene and after vee run for our lives de night of de fire, vee find Goscelin and together vee go to rebuild our home, Belle Cœur. God blessed us wit courage to do vhat veee did not know vee could do and God vill do de same for you, sister, but you must believe it vill be so.

Book IV The Wisdom Keepers of Belle Cœur

Ven tragedy und challenge come, be faithful wit prayer und keep going. Dis is vie I say to mein sisters, "Hope und visdom!" Time und again I had to endure und use mein vits to push thru from de difficult places with hope to come to de otter side, vere I find peace. Each time I do dis I grow in visdom.

I couldn't speak de language when I arrived from mein country. I had so much to learn und it vas a struggle. I lost mein arm and suffered pain and hard days of not being able to vurk or help anyone. I had to rely on God to give me strength of heart. In time, wit hard vork und de help of others I learned how to speak und understand de language.

Den I fell in love wit Imene. I kept my love secret from all but her, und prayed to God to keep us safe within de shadows vere vee lived. Ven de sisters came into our lives, dey loved and accepted us. Our life at Belle Cœur vas blessed and a blessing for us all.

Never give up, dear sister, und never stop believing dat God is wit you even in de darkest of times. Do one ting each day to velcome courage. One ting, just like building a cathedral, one ting, one stone, den another, und another. Soon, ven you place stone by stone wit courage, you vill build de life you dream of.

༺༻

Gertrude's charism: Her courage and profound resilience of spirit and character in the face of challenge and adversity and her creative abilities.

The Way of Belle Cœur

Her challenge: How to maintain her focus upon only one creation at a time, from inception to completion.

Her elements: Earth, air, bone, blood, stone.

Her secret: Her desire to be an architect of a great cathedral and inability to publicly declare her love for Imene.

Her shadow: Her procrastination of routine duties in favor of her dedication as a craftswoman and sacred life-artisan.

Her passion: The crafting of beautiful useful furnishings and objects with her hands as her devotional practice of thanksgiving to God.

Her sacred practice: Communion with God through the work of her hands.

Her wisdom phrase: "*Hope und visdom.*"

Her gift to the community and others: Her creation of furnishings and objects important to the needs of the sisterhood, including Grace's cradle and the box for the sisters' relics, as well as, their pilgrimage amulets and the sign of Belle Cœur.

Her relics: Her wooden mallet and pouch of nails, a pilgrimage amulet with the sign of Belle Cœur on a leather thong, her knife used for whittling, and a small jagged stone from Chartres Cathedral.

Book IV The Wisdom Keepers of Belle Cœur

Her symbol: A stone.

Her birth sign: Capricorn

Her sacred life-arts: Carpentry, cathedral building, and handcrafts.

Her invitation: *"Be creative und brave!"*

Suggested active service: Volunteer for Habitat for Humanity or offer to help paint or repair a shut-in's home.

Her petit cadeau: Hoffnung und Weisheit Steine. Hope and wisdom stones.

Her earthly prayer: *You gif me courage, Beloved, und I grow strong. Even in de face of injury, danger, und certain death you are always dare as mein strength. You show me time und time again how courage is de certain path to freedom. You gif me hope und teach me how to grow mein visdom. Fear cannot stand nor overtake me ven I rely on You. I feed my courage fierce belief und I am steady like a stone.* Amen

Gertrude's identity passage from Scripture: Luke 20:17-18

But Jesus stared at them and said, "Then tell me what the Scripture means when it says, 'The stone which the builders rejected became the cornerstone.' All who fall on that stone will be dashed to pieces, and all those upon whom it falls will be scattered like powder."

The Way of Belle Cœur

Selected *Ink and Honey* passages pertaining to Gertrude: (*I&'H:* 94, 107, 129-132, 154-155, 224-225, 230, 248, 253, 265-266, 350, 388, 398, 405-408, 422, 424, 443-446, 462, 467-469, 473, 479).

Reflect

- How might I stretch my abilities to find the courage to explore a place, a craft, or a calling that has always been of interest to me but that I've been timid/afraid to explore?
- What would it feel like to achieve or master something that I believe I can't possibly attain?
- How it would feel to study and learn a language I have always wanted to speak?
- How could baskets, boxes, and bowls be creatively used as containers for my sacred objects? What in my life needs to be contained, literally and metaphorically?
- When I contemplate my hands as holy instruments capable of creatively manifesting whatever I envision, I imagine creating...
- When I contemplate my life in the context of the iconotype of the Survivor, the following comes to mind...
- In what ways could my body and spirit benefit through the exercise of physical labor such as: gardening, polishing windows and furniture, painting walls?

- ❖ When I imagine my environment and workspace as blank canvasses for my creative spirit, I am inspired to create…
- ❖ Some new ways to add prayer and intention to my art and craft-making include….
- ❖ If I were to have a conversation with Gertrude, I would ask her…
  I imagine her response to me would be…

Express

- ❖ Gather small stones from the woods or the beach. If you don't have access to a forest or seashore, you may purchase a bag of stones in the floral department at your local craft store. Use the stones to:

  I. Build miniature stone cairns (carefully arranged piles of tiny stones) as part of a dish garden.
  II. Write words or affirmations upon an assortment stones with a permanent marker. Keep them in a container to draw at random for inspiration.
  III. Fill a series of glass containers with stones of varying sizes and colors. Use these as meditation objects. Arrange and rearrange your stones as a meditative process.

The Way of Belle Cœur

Goscelin

The Scribe

Iconotype: The Witness
Qualities: Dedicated and Trustworthy
Wisdom Keeper of Sacred Texts

Goscelin's spirit delivers her wisdom…

My days on earth were numbered by God, and enriched through the love shared among my sisters. While you continue your life's journey my spirit offers the following counsel, dear sister on the path.

Be a brave pilgrim and adventurer. Trust God in all circumstances and know there are no boundaries to your spirit's wisdom and power. Remember that angels accompany you as you journey towards the truth of your radiant and illuminated nature.

Henriette, my ever faithful cloth companion held my secrets, listened to my fears, and shared her wisdom. Some would say she was only a tattered remainder from my childhood. Doubters would tell you that a doll is not capable of offering counsel or comfort in the way I experienced her presence. You and I know differently, don't we?

Claim a sacred object, a small stone, a doll, or some such beloved thing and bless it with purpose and meaning. Keep it close and use it the way a voyager would use a compass to find her way.

Embrace the Beloved, through prayer and devotion, dear sister. Listen intently with compassion to those who cross your path. Oracles are everywhere. Pay attention to the messages that come your way. Become a collector of stories and an observer and gatherer of nature. Observe the subtleties within Creation. The changing light that accompanies the dawn and dusk, the turning of the leaves from green to gold, and the gathering clouds of the oncoming storm.

Also observe the nuance of movement and timbre of those around you: the faraway gaze, the flushed cheek, and the trembling hand. The human body is a living, breathing storyteller. Pay attention to the story beyond the words that are spoken and watch for the quiet one, the voiceless, and forgotten. For she, too, holds a gift to be shared.

Scribe your poetry and portray your visions and illuminated pictures in the margins of your journal's pages. Add your wisdom from your discoveries to your codex. Name your experiences for the lessons you receive. Title your stories and dedicate your work as an offering of blessing for another.

Our beloved sister, Grace, eventually became the scribe for those of us who survived the enforced diaspora of our sisterhood. She was my eager student even to the last of my days, when I turned my gaze away from teaching and scribing to look towards heaven.

Grace's hand was steady and her heart was open. These are necessary qualities for the scribe. Gather your students, sister, and share your wisdom, your crafts, and your heart. Grow the wisdom in others, as you cultivate it for yourself.

Our Belle Cœur manuscript is hidden away with our portundae awaiting discovery at a future time. Contemplate your relics as your treasure. Prepare and offer them as the tangible evidence of your essence and life's journey. Create your portunda and write your message to those you will leave behind and for those not yet born. You must ensure that our lineage of sisterhood will continue after your bones have become dust.

The Way of Belle Cœur

You are alive in the world, while your soul yearns for the peace and freedom of your true home. Honor your earthly body as the reliquary of your spirit.

Be compassionate and forgiving with those who challenge you. If a beloved betrays or turns away from you, set aside time for discernment and reflection. This is a lesson I learned from Comtesse. The difficult ones we meet on life's journey often deliver the most important teachings. Honor your spirit and compassionately bless and release those relationships that no longer serve you.

Heal your bruised and broken places, for all who are born into life receive their share of wounds and scars, both visible and invisible. Release your memories of unrighteous trespasses that have been made against you with forgiveness for the perpetrator and yourself. Embrace healing and victory over darkness to ensure the realization of the gifts of wisdom that emerge from the riches of your womanhood and full humanity.

Feed and nurture your sacred imagination. Study all manner of things that stir your passion and interest. Learn from the bees. Study the form of the honeycomb. Learn the parts of the hive and the mysterious dance of the scout bee. Transform bee wisdom and the metaphors that they offer into purpose and meaning for your life.

Record your dreams to discover the deeper meaning of your experiences. Remember Our Lady when you pray, for she is the Queen Bee and her honey is the Christ.

Be conscious of the symbols in your life. Live your days fully and completely to become pages of your Book of Life, your sacred codex, so when bound together they will portray the story of your soul and earthly journey.

You are in my prayers. Yes, my spirit prays for you.

Book IV The Wisdom Keepers of Belle Cœur

May your heart remain open. May love and blessings flow to you and through you. Amen

Love is everlasting. Love is all you will carry with you when at last God calls you home to Heaven's threshold. Live your life with fervent love and your spirit will thrive, while day upon day the story of your life will be scribed upon your soul by the hand of the Beloved.

⁂

Goscelin's charism: The ability to transform her soulful observations into story through the sacred life-art of scribing and her active, prayerful dedication to live into the fullness of God's highest purpose for her life.

Her challenge: Her allowance to be pulled away from her sacred scribing by life's distractions.

Her elements: Earth, fire, ink and honey.

Her secret: Her deep longing for reunion with her mother.

Her shadow: Her fearful suppression of the full expression of her truth when in disagreement with another, thus, creating feelings of bitterness and resentment within her.

Her passions: To keep an ongoing record of her life's observations through words and images. Walking the labyrinth as a form of prayer, and taking advantage

The Way of Belle Cœur

of every opportunity to make an inner or outer pilgrimage to grow her wisdom.

Her sacred practice: A special devotion to the Blessed Mother and the practice of making a sacred invocation to God and the angels before scribing.

Her wisdom phrase: *"She (Mary) is like a holy beehive, and her Son is the honey that flows from her heart."* (*I&H:* 189)

Her gift to the community and others: The gathering and recording of the individual stories of her sisters and her written and sketched detailed observations of the daily life of the sisterhood. Her abilities for teaching scribing and illumination.

Her relics: A brown goose-feather quill, a glass vessel of ochre stopped with red wax. A round black box containing a queen bee and a small piece of parchment with the inscription: *May the one who finds these things discover their meaning and make wise use of them again. Goscelin, Scribe of Belle Cœur*

Her symbol: A Queen honeybee

Her birth sign: Virgo

Her sacred life arts: Scribing and illumination of manuscripts.

Her invitation: *"Create your sacred wisdom codex and grow your wisdom."*

Suggested active service: Volunteer as a scribe for an elder or sightless person. Create a blog to inspire others through your stories.

Her petit cadeau: A scribe's ritual in preparation for scribing.

Her earthly prayer: *Beloved, lead me. Guide me to new depths of spiritual understanding. I pray to serve you as a Keeper of Stories. Grow my wisdom so I may create all that you have inspired within my heart. My spirit feels the pull of life's adventure. You are my compass. Please show me the way so I may fulfill my destiny according to your will, without hesitation, with my whole heart.* Amen

Goscelin's identity passage from Scripture: Proverbs 16:24
Pleasant words are like the honeycomb: sweet for the soul and healthy for the body.

Selected *Ink and Honey* passages pertaining to Goscelin: (*I&H*: 2, 4-6, 33, 84, 94, 98, 135, 172, 174, 271, 329, 345, 381-384).

Reflect

- ❖ My greatest teacher(s) in life has been? From my teacher(s) I learned...
- ❖ I mentor, companion, or teach others when I...
- ❖ When I reflect on my life from the perspective of the Witness, I recall...

The Way of Belle Cœur

- The first sentence of the story I carry within me that I have yet to scribe is...
- If I were to begin a new chapter of my life, I would title it...
- The places in my spirit that are in need of fortification are...
- The inspirational places I have visited that feed my soul include...
- The sacred object, doll, touchstone that brings me comfort and helps me to access my intuition is my...
- When I think about the honeybee I imagine...?
- A time when I spoke my truth was... A time when I withheld my truth was... My life is informed today by these experiences in the following way(s)...

Express

- Take your journal to various places (the park, a coffee shop, your backyard, another room in your house, the library) to experience writing in different kinds of environments. Notice where you feel the most resonance and also the most dissonance.
- Try the following as a spiritual/creative practice: Create a journal that is solely for images. Take photos or use imagery from books and magazines. Choose one image each day for a month (or longer) and paste it on a page in

your journal with a date and title. Incorporate the images as symbolic representations for whatever your creative heart and spirit long to express.

Grace

The Child

Iconotype: The Harbinger
Qualities: Ancient and New
Wisdom Keeper of Sacred Feminine Knowledge

The spirit of Grace delivers her wisdom…

I always lived in the company of women. My body and soul were delivered into life wearing an invisible cloak of mystery. When I was twelve my appointed mother, Ravenissa, told me the story of Cibylle, my true mother, the one who gave me life. The name of my father came to me in a dream and through the dream I understood it to be a secret, known only to me and to Cibylle.

I learned that she conceived and carried me in her womb and God imbued my bones and blood with sacred gifts of understanding. From earliest memory I recall how I effortlessly grasped the rules of nature, the purpose and blessing of silence, and the value of being in the world, but not of it. We are at last together Cibylle and me, in the world of Spirit. Our dwelling place changes in accordance with our thoughts and eternity is our landscape.

The Way of Belle Cœur

The Divine Mother claimed me as her earthly vessel while I lived and she is within me now in the afterlife. She has established her spirit within others throughout time. I was Her. I am Her, and Her spirit is alive today within particular women of your realm.

When I was a young girl my spiritual sister and tutor, Goscelin, taught me to use the quill to scribe my codex. I filled the pages with holy wisdom harvested from my dreams and visions. Perhaps the time will arrive soon when women will discover my codex's hiding place and reclaim the beauty I was guided to record upon the pages.

When I reached my elder years God called me to serve as the anchoress of Belle Cœur. Enclosed in my cell with Goscelin's faceless doll, Henriette, and my three-legged cat, I lived the remainder of my life enraptured within my ever-deepening devotion to the Beloved, while Our Lady spilled her wisdom into my quill.

In my solitude I continued the tradition of Dominions and Graces, carefully scribing my inspired interpretations in the margins. Often there were visitors from the nearby village. They came to the little grated window of my cell seeking counsel, comfort, and healing.

I was conceived in mystery and born of Cibylle, the waif. In my infancy I suckled at Beatrice's breast and later Ravenissa became my adopted mother. My maidenhood was spent with my tutor and mentor, Goscelin. God's purpose for my life unfolded year upon year. I served as the Mother's bodily presence so others might fully experience her brief return.

The world of Spirit, where I now dwell, is separated from your earthly home by a simple portal. The threshold is welcoming. One day, according to God's plan for your return, the door will open and you, too, will step through.

For now, dear Sister, open your heart in the early morning hour betwixt darkness and dawn. Listen for the whisper within the birdsong. You just might hear the angels' morning prayers as they welcome the day.

Pray without ceasing. For your world is spinning towards the Great Awakening and within the dizzying chaos of your Dark Age transformation for good is occurring. The Sacred Feminine is returning while the key to the garden remains lost. Gather with your sisters and recommence the search, for it will take many of you to find it. Share your stories, reclaim your symbols, renew your senses, and craft your sacred tools. Forge a new pathway leading the way towards home. Soon it will be the season of illumination and wonder. Be ready!

༺☙༻

Grace's charism: She carries Sacred Feminine intuitive wisdom and holy presence.

Her challenge: How to best share the alchemical wisdom that God placed upon her heart.

Her elements: Air, spirit, light, water.

Her secret: Her knowledge of her father's name.

Her shadow: As the Mother's voice for holy wisdom, Grace lived without shadow.

Her passion(s): Listening for the Beloved and Wisdom Sophia's guidance in silence.

Her sacred practice: Solitude.

Her spirit's wisdom phrase: *"We awake each morning to faithfully carry on the work the Beloved has placed in the tender but fierce heart that is Belle Cœur."*

Her gift to the community and others: Her earthly, bodily presence as an instrument of Sophia Wisdom.

Her relics: A remnant of her birthing cord and her sacred codex.

Her symbol: A stork feather.

Her birth sign: Aries

Her sacred-life arts: Scribing and lacemaking.

Her invitation: *"Contemplate how you may reclaim the Sacred Feminine through your daily encounters with others and your acts of compassionate service to restore balance in the world."*

Suggested active service: Explore how you might discover a small way to help care for Creation.

Grace's petit cadeau: A wax figure of Mary.

Her prayer: *In the silence, Beloved, You are there. I hear Your guidance with the ears of my heart. I see Your handwork* *within the symbols of my dreams. In sleep, You are there. My senses are piqued. You bless my bones with sweet vibration and I become a living prayer. You inhabit my being the way a hand fits into a glove and I am held fast by Your Love.* Amen

Grace's identity passage from Scripture: Psalm 22:10
You cradled me in your lap from my birth, from my mother's womb you have been my God.

Selected *Ink and Honey* passages pertaining to Grace: (*I&H:* 421-424, 430-431, 438-439, 442, 451-452, 471-472, 476-477, Epilogue).

Reflect

- ❖ I experience the presence of the Sacred Feminine in my life in the following ways…
- ❖ My spiritual sisters are…
- ❖ If I were to write a one-page story of my birth, it would begin…
- ❖ When I imagine crafting my "sacred tools" I envision the creation of…
- ❖ I become the Harbinger when I embody and express the Sacred Feminine, the Mother's presence, and Wisdom Sophia through my…
- ❖ When I reflect upon the concept of the Great Awakening, I imagine and I'm inspired to…
- ❖ When I listen within the sound of silence, I hear…

Express

- ❖ Create a visual prayer collage representing the Sacred Feminine, Sophia Wisdom.
- ❖ Draw a horizontal line on a blank journal page to represent a timeline for your life's journey to the present day. Contemplate your life incrementally by decades. Make notations for each decade on the timeline. Above the timeline write in the names of women that have been a strong influence for you as: mentors, teachers, or muses. Below the line of each decade write the names of the women in your life that *you* have personally influenced, mentored, taught, or inspired.

Helvide

The Herbalist

Iconotype: The Earth Steward
Qualities: Calm and Confident
Wisdom Keeper of Plants and Minerals

Helvide's spirit delivers her wisdom...

Good Sister, learn to comprehend nature in the way Goscelin deciphered meaning from her study of Dominions and Graces, through observation and devotion. Everything one needs to know about life is waiting to be revealed to you through nature's cycles and stories...gestation, birth,

Book IV The Wisdom Keepers of Belle Cœur

blossom, fruition, harvest, death, and resurrection. Creation offers herself as the great teacher when one takes the time to behold and grasp her lessons.

I learned from my mother, Myrtle, when I was young that all of nature is an alchemical chamber. She taught me that within Creation there are elements, as many as the stars in the heavens, that are fomented to provide your body, mind, and soul with healing and radiant health. You must seek nature's counsel for your personal prescription and remedies. Remember that you are made of stardust, bone, blood, earth, air, fire and water. Cultivate a variety of sacred practices to engage your senses…for your senses are the gateways to Divine guidance.

What can you learn from the song within the wind, the patterns of the ever-changing clouds, the temperature of the damp earth, or the sweet scent of rain carried upon the afternoon breeze? How do these moments inspire you or guide your choices for your day?

Do not forget that everything in nature is alive with the spirit of the Mother. Creation is the constant and generative life force and source of the Divine Plan for us all. Notice the living breathing prayer held within the hollow of the ancient Grandmother tree and radiance of the glistening stones upon the garden path. Observe the graceful swan gliding upon the pond, the fat dappled plum dropped in the basket and syrupy golden honey spilling from the comb. Even your salty tears and gilded laughter…all these are forms of prayer uttering praise to Wisdom Sophia.

The language of nature is also prayer. Malachite and moon-shadow, lapis lazuli, tortoise, and sycamore. Yarrow and pholcidae, muskrat, alumroot, and antler.

The Way of Belle Cœur

Befriend the plants and animals that live in your garden. These are your earthly companions. For you are as One with all, according to God's infinite design.

Feel how the moon's changing face alters your mood and state of being. Study shinorage to learn to read the language of the stars and heavens. Gather nature's gifts from upon the path. Acorn, snail shell, mossy stone, crimson leaf and tuft of rabbit fur. Make an altar to honor Creation. Write your prayer to the Mother with thanksgiving.

Live in union with her and care for Creation. For within the fecund and tumultuous, and the greening and decaying there is the eternal heartbeat of all that is and ever will be. Attune to the sacred pulse and know that you are one with all life. You are a living cell within the body of the Mother and it is time to rediscover her garden.

Helvide's charism: Her interpretation of the language of plants and minerals.

Her challenge: Her personal physical care and medicinal needs.

Her elements: Earth, water, lavender and seeds.

Her secret: She longed to become a hermit, living in the forest like her mother, Myrtle.

Her shadow: Her deep attachments and connections to nature caused her to become sullen when forced to be indoors for an extended time.

Her passion(s): Lying naked on the ground to align her pulse with the heartbeat of the earth. Time spent in the herbarium, to create her medicines, and provide healing for the sick.

Her sacred practice: Bundling plants and herbs in preparation for drying as a form of prayer.

Her wisdom phrase: *"Find those green, unripe places within your soul and nourish them so in time you will be ripe to God's touch and ready for His use."*

Her gift(s) to the community and others: Her deep awareness and understanding of how our bodies mirror the condition of the world around us. Her inventive wisdom used to create medicines, teas, unguents, and tinctures for healing.

Her relics: The Vade Mecum concertina belonging to Abbess Hildegard, Myrtle's small box of XII sacred elixirs. A tiny glass vial stopped with red wax, containing rainwater gathered at Belle Cœur and her golden earring, a gift from Myrtle.

Her symbol: A sprig of rosemary

Her birth sign: Sagittarius

Her sacred life-art: Crafting amulets and talismans from acorns, animal bones, rocks and shells to complement her medicines and herbal remedies.

The Way of Belle Cœur

Her invitation: *"Become intimately acquainted with nature where you live, right in your own backyard. Study of the healing properties of plants, minerals, and gems."*

Suggested active service: Become part of a vegetable co-op or volunteer to help with a community garden. Contemplate the possibility of studying astrology.

Her petit cadeau: A bundle of dried rosemary and lavender.

Her earthly prayer: *Creator of all life, You bless each day with Your miracles...the changing seasons, strange creatures that fly, swim, and creep, and all that grows to sustain and nourish life itself. You hung a map in the night sky to guide the planting of the crops and steer the course of each earthly journey. So great are Your mysteries. So vast is Your wisdom. I pray to be a good steward of all you provide. Open my eyes and heart so I may always recognize and cherish this earth, this sky, this holy wondrous life.* Amen

Helvide's identity passage from Scripture: Song of Songs 4:12-13
You are a garden behind walls, my sister and bride, a spring running clear that no one can drink from; a fountain that flows behind a locked gate. You are an orchard, planted with fine flowers and fruit: with pomegranates, saffron, henna, and nard, and with trees of spice: cinnamon and calamus, with aloes and myrrh.

Book IV The Wisdom Keepers of Belle Cœur

Selected *Ink and Honey* passages pertaining to Helvide: (*I&H*: 86, 95, 150, 165-167, 204-205, 209-210, 230, 232, 243, 259, 269-291, 300-301, 363, 373, 375, 416-418, 469)

Reflect

- ❖ When I was a child my experience of nature was…
- ❖ As an adult, I experience nature in this way…
- ❖ When I contemplate what it means to be an Earth Steward I feel inspired to…
- ❖ I become aware of the Divine Presence when I…
- ❖ When I imagine myself at One with all of Creation I feel…
- ❖ My greatest life lesson from Creation happened when…
- ❖ A symbol that speaks to me from the natural world is… (Examples: acorns, honeybees, trees, stones, etc.)
- ❖ My feelings about astrology are…
- ❖ When I look at the stars I…

Express

- ❖ Create personal recipes for herbal teas, lotions, tinctures, and oils as your version of XII Sacred Oracles/Elixirs for healing and comfort.

- ❖ Study the healing properties of minerals and gemstones.
- ❖ Keep a chart your emotional moods and your peaks and valleys of creative expression with the changing seasons and the cycles of the moon. Notice the patterns.
- ❖ Take a walk in nature and record what inspires you, such as: the trees, clouds, weather, light, birdsong, rain, etc.
- ❖ Arrange seasonal altars within your environment from things you find on your walks or in the garden.
- ❖ Integrate clay into your spiritual practice. While praying or meditating hold a ball of clay in your hands. Work with the clay without thinking about. Allow the clay to become an outer manifestation of your prayer. Create a series of clay prayers over a week's time. Embellish your creations with things found in nature. What do you notice from this practice?

Henriette

The Sacred Object

Iconotype: The Comforter
Qualities: Blessing and Consolation
Wisdom Keeper of Secrets

Book IV The Wisdom Keepers of Belle Cœur

The spirit of Henriette delivers her wisdom…

My spirit came alive through Goscelin's imagination and her love for me. I first felt stirrings of awareness and meaning when Goscelin's Maman created me from scraps of cloth as a gift for her little daughter. I was pieced together, stuffed with sheep's wool, and stitched into form. Faceless, and nameless, I was placed in Goscelin's tiny hand that autumn day so very long ago with her mother's prayer for my purpose. It was Goscelin who gave me my name.

We were companions for one another. I was her comforter. We shared many adventures. My understanding of all that happened during her life, throughout those years when I lived in her apron pocket, is not that of human understanding. Rather, my journey with Goscelin was guided by her constant faith and abiding trust in our friendship.

She relied upon my ever-constant presence and always looked after me. She assigned her aspirations for my existence and her prayerful intentions animated my form with purpose. I was given the charge to be the key to the door of her natural wisdom and intuition. There was no answer I could provide for her, rather my presence brought her comfort and she believed I was wise, when all along it was her own wisdom she relied upon.

How can it be, you may be asking, that an object made of cloth, stitched with yarn, and stuffed with sheep's wool, has a spirit? I can only say that love and purpose are what made me come alive, love and purpose and Goscelin's belief that I was real.

When a human loves an object, treasures it, assigns it with meaning and cares for it deeply, believing that it is capable of offering comfort and blessing, the object responds. This is not magic nor is it sorcery. Rather, it's a law of

The Way of Belle Cœur

Creation. Love begets love, purpose begets devotion, and belief begets wisdom.

My given name, chosen by Goscelin, was Henriette. Naming your beloved objects is as important as the purpose you assign to them. Guard your amulets, dolls, stones, and charms with care. Keep them safe. If a treasured object becomes lost, trust that whoever finds it will return it if possible. If your treasure doesn't find its way home to you, be at peace and accept that it has gone to where it is needed, for no thing is ever truly lost.

When you rely upon an object for guidance or comfort and that guidance or comfort remain elusive and out of reach, it may be that your belief in yourself is wavering and your purpose for your amulet has outworn its meaning. Bless the thing and pass it on to another. For all treasures under heaven have their season, even a doll.

What became of me, you wonder? Goscelin passed me on to Grace before she died. I went to Grace without regret nor joy, for I have no vocabulary or language for the feelings of my existence. I became Grace's comforter and companion while she assumed her duties as the new scribe of Belle Cœur and later as the Anchoress. I lived with her throughout her wisdom years. Her presence and prayers were needed by many, and like Goscelin, she kept me near her for consolation.

When her life was over her sisters placed me in her apron pocket. We were buried together on a snowy winter's morning. A blessed ending for a sainted woman and a doll stuffed with sheep's wool, women's secrets and prayers, and the stories of Belle Cœur.

Her charism: Her soft touch.

Her challenge: To not become lost.

Her elements: Air, snow, linen and lamb's wool.

Her secret: The secrets whispered to her in the dark of night by Goscelin.

Her shadow: She was innocent of shadow.

Her passion(s): Service to the one who loved her and gave her purpose.

Her sacred practice: Waiting in apron pockets until she was needed.

Her wisdom phrase: *"Believe."*

Her gift to the community and others: Her constant readiness and service as comforter, consoler, and companion for Goscelin and Grace.

Her relics: She (herself) is a buried relic and a sacred mystery awaiting rediscovery.

Her symbol: An apron pocket.

Her sacred life-arts: The sacred art of presence.

The Way of Belle Cœur

Her invitation: *"Craft your treasured objects with your prayerful intention for their purpose, and meaning."*

Her suggested active service: Craft a doll or amulet for yourself or a child.

Her petit cadeau: Her comforting and continual presence.

Her prayer: *Let me serve.* Amen

Henriette's identity passage from Scripture: Proverbs 19:24
It is God who guides our steps. How can we know the road by ourselves?

Selected *Ink and Honey* passages pertaining to Henriette: (*I&H:* 1, 3, 35, 76, 97, 245, 300, 387, 396, 435, 436, 455, 464, 465, 482).

Reflect

- ❖ My sacred object that is a companion for life's journey is…
- ❖ If I were inspired to craft a talisman or amulet it would appear like this… Draw a picture of your design or describe it in words in your journal.
- ❖ The prayerful intention and sacred purpose I would give to my creation would be…

Book IV The Wisdom Keepers of Belle Cœur

- ❖ The most treasured sacred belonging I have lost during my life was... When I imagine the one who found it, I like to think he/she repurposed it in the following way...
- ❖ The "things" that bring me comfort and consolation include...

Express

- ❖ Select four sacred objects. Choose one to companion you during each season.
- ❖ Each solstice or equinox, select a new sacred object. Set your seasonal intention for the object with prayer.
- ❖ Carry your object with you as a reminder of your intention and as a conduit for your intuitive wisdom.
- ❖ Create a reliquary as a sacred place to store your sacred objects.
- ❖ Using scrap fabrics, needle, and thread and cotton balls or cotton batting...create your personal version of a hand sewn and stuffed *pocket doll.* Give your doll a name, a prayerful purpose and intention, and sew a pocket for her to live in.

Imene

The Midwife

Iconotype: The Healer
Qualities: Steadfast and Intelligent
Wisdom Keeper of Birth

Imene's spirit delivers her wisdom…

Dear One, my message to you is urgent and simple. The time you are living in requires you to reverence your body as a holy creation. Your flesh and bones compose the ark that carries your soul throughout the decades while you are on the earth.

Honor the cadence and rhythm that your body prefers to follow. Find moments for rest and renewal.

Fasting is encouraged as a sacred practice. Make a prayer of fasting. Fast from foods that are void of nourishment. Fast from distraction that pulls you away from the Beloved. When you break your fast, return to what you know to be life giving and sustaining for you.

Sacred moments should be recognized and celebrated. Celebrate not only the day of your physical birth, but also the seasons of your life when you experience unexpected spiritual awareness. Honor those blessed times when you birth new understanding and wisdom within your spirit and heart.

In life, through my vocation as a midwife, I came to witness that the pain of childbirth rather than God's punishment is woman's privilege. Embrace your spiritual birthing pains as the body's song of holy transformation at that moment when Spirit becomes new wisdom within your body and bones.

My work as a healer also taught me that death is a process that begins with the first breath. While bound to earth before the soul takes flight to return to Paradise, embrace the latter years of life.

Aging, if you allow it, will cover you with increasing grace, year upon year. Dimming eyesight and diminished hearing are steps on the path that lead to new terrain within your spirit and a deeper relationship and reliance upon God.

Meditate upon these truths: Your heartbeat is in rhythm with the pulse of the Beloved. Your spirit is a conduit for light. Shine brightly. Know your body and care for it with self-compassion and sacred attention.

Dear sister, I invite you to consider yourself a spiritual midwife. It is the season for death and rebirth on the earth. Midwives are needed to tend the birth of the coming transformation. Find your sister midwives and make ready to minister at the delivery. I call to you with urgency from beyond the veil. Believe me when I tell you that the world and humankind are experiencing the death of the old ways. This is the hour of laboring and the time for crowning grows near!

༄

Imene's charism: Her intuitive touch for diagnosing illness and her healing wisdom and midwifery skills.

Her challenge: How to balance her time to care for others *and* herself.

The Way of Belle Cœur

Her elements: Water, blood, earth, and bone.

Her secret: Her fear of the dark.

Her shadow: Endless hours of work to bring healing to others to the point of Imene's physical, emotional and spiritual depletion.

Her passion(s): Midwifing new life into the world and comforting her patients.

Her sacred practice: A secret silent prayer for each newborn at the moment of birth, *May this child remember and deliver the commission You placed in her soul. May she grow in grace and peace as a child of God.* Amen

Her wisdom phrase: *"Many who arrive at our door are in need of spiritual counsel that no doubt you could offer."*

Her gift to the community and others: Her knowledge of the physical body and her intuitive way of delivering comfort for human suffering.

Her relics: Herbs of blessed thistle and black cohosh. A little forch tool made from a branch of the willow tree at Belle Cœur. Her biting bar used by Cibylle when she was in labor and a vial of her special serum for healing broken hearts.

Her symbol: A lead spoon

Her birth sign: Libra

Book IV The Wisdom Keepers of Belle Cœur

Her sacred life-art: The craft of making medicines for bodily and spiritual needs.

Her invitation: "*Become a spiritual midwife for the great planetary transformation.*"

Imene's suggested active service: Consider registering for Red Cross disaster training. Learn CPR and First Aid.

Her petit cadeau: Little vessels of healing oil for anointing.

Her earthly prayer: *Beloved, you are our Great Physician. Guide my hands in loving service as your faithful midwife. Help me to fully birth my gifts so I may in turn help others realize their gifts that come from You. I long to be a conduit for Your healing love and grace. Use my hands and caring nature for good as the world spins round towards a brighter tomorrow. Use me, Beloved, as you deliver us from evil.* Amen

Imene's identity passage from Scripture: James 5:14-15
Are any of you sick? Then call for the elders of the church, and have them pray over those who are sick and anoint them with oil in the name of Christ.

Selected *Ink and Honey* passages pertaining to Imene: (*I&H:* 94, 100, 102-103, 130-132, 143-144, 156-158, 221-225, 234-239, 363-364, 371-372, 407-408, 416-425, 429, 437, 470-474, 479)

Reflect

- When I contemplate what it means to live with the awareness of a midwife at this time of global paradigm shifts, I feel...
- When I think of my physical body as the ark of my soul the following thoughts arise...
- If all of nature is an alchemical chamber, I find the most transformative place(s) for my spirit to be: the forest, beach (sea), mountains, desert, prairie, or garden, etc.
- My practice for daily self-care for my body, mind, and creative heart and spirit is...
- If we are truly living in a time of paradigm shift and transformation, one small way I might assist the birthing process is...
- What gift am I carrying that I must midwife to make it real...

Express

- Put your hands into the earth and plant something in the ground or in a pot.
- Create a visual prayer collage to honor the creative and spiritual gifts you have birthed during your life.
- Create a page in your codex to express the theme of shifting paradigms and global transformation.

Book IV The Wisdom Keepers of Belle Cœur

Mabille

The Chanteuse

Iconotype: The Virtuoso
Qualities: Talented and Aware
Wisdom Keeper of the Voice

Mabille's spirit delivers her wisdom…

Dear Sister, use your voice. Speak the truth that God inspires your heart to express. Sing your prayers. Study the angelic realms and invite the angels into your life. Find an instrument and make a song for your life.

Music is the conduit that connects us to the mystical realms, to the angels. Notice the different properties of sound, music, and noise. Contemplate how to weave music into your daily life. Imagine the music or sound you would choose to inspire you while you pray, go about your work, tend your garden, or prepare a meal. Imagine the music or sound you would choose to comfort you at the hour of your death.

I have always considered my music and songs to be gifts of grace. Perhaps there are other symbols and signs I have been blessed to receive and embody that I have never appreciated as God's markings. I must contemplate these things in my heart and give thanks for that which I assume to be ordinary. There are always new songs waiting to be sung.

Use your voice to speak your truth with compassion. Find your instrument, voice, and song, dear Sister. Sing your praises for God, for life, for Creation.

The Way of Belle Cœur

Mabille's charism: Her talents and abilities to receive intuitive guidance regarding the tempo and rhythm of music to offer for mothers giving birth and for those who are dying.

Her challenge: How to find the courage to use her voice clearly and compassionately to speak her truth.

Her elements: Air, song, bone and whisper.

Her secret: Her desire to compose a choral play accompanied by instruments made from things found in nature.

Her shadow: The withholding of the truths of her heart. The fear of speaking her truth when it might cause conflict or possibly create hurtful feelings for someone.

Her passion: Making music and singing to comfort the dying and welcome the newborn into the world.

Her sacred practice: Song as her prayer at the beginning and ending of each day.

Her wisdom phrase: *"We all have songs sleeping in our bones."*

Her gift to the community and others: Her offering of peace and sharing of her wisdom of the angelic realm through her music, in the midst of chaos.

Book IV The Wisdom Keepers of Belle Cœur

Her relics: A parchment of musical notes representing her favorite Psalm given to her by Sister Lunetta. A tiny wooden flute carved by her brother. A yellow snail shell found in the garden at Belle Cœur the day before the pilgrimage began.

Her symbol: A lyre

Her birth sign: Taurus

Her sacred life-art: Singing and music making.

Her invitation: "*Sing the song of your deepest truth.*"

Mabille's suggested active service: Contemplate how you might give the gift of music to someone you know that is making a healing journey.

Her petit cadeau: Small carved wooden flute.

Her earthly prayer: *Beloved, you fill the morning air with birdsong and the Mother's whispered prayer upon the wind. I pray today to use my voice as an instrument of peace. Inspire my song to deliver a message of love, hope, and healing.* Amen

Mabille's identity passage from Scripture: Psalm 100: 1-2
Acclaim Our God with joy, all the earth! Serve Our God with gladness! Enter into God's presence with a joyful song!

Selected *Ink and Honey* passages pertaining to Mabille: (*I&H:* 95, 138-139, 147, 162, 213, 217, 224, 237, 238,

252, 256, 293-296, 312-314, 354, 416-421, 424-428, 453-455, 461-464, 470, 482)

Reflect

- ❖ Write about the various ways that music affects your spirit.
- ❖ The genres of music that soothe, inspire, agitate and/or calm me are…
- ❖ My list of favorite songs, singers/artists/composers and works of music includes…
- ❖ The instrument I've always wanted to play is the… I have never pursued my interest for this instrument because…
- ❖ My creative heart longs to reflect my inner *Virtuoso* in the following way…
- ❖ The truth I withhold from myself is… The truth I withhold from…is…
- ❖ For me to speak my truth I need…
- ❖ There are many ways to express my inner wisdom. I give voice to my spiritual and creative gifts when I…

Express

- ❖ Evoke Mabille's spirit and sing your prayerful praise to God while in nature.
- ❖ Listen to the world around you throughout the day. Notice the difference between the quality

and value of sound, music, and noise. Notice how each of these affects your body, mind, and spirit.
- ❖ Sing softly to an infant or small child, or to your pet. Notice what happens for you and for the one you sing to.
- ❖ Write a poem or song. Create an audio recording while reading or singing it. Share your recorded gift as a vocal or musical prayer with someone you love.
- ❖ If you used to play an instrument imagine picking it up to see what new song awaits you.

Marie

The Helpmate

Iconotype: The Playmate
Qualities: Wise and Tenderhearted
Wisdom Keeper of Curiosity

Marie's spirit delivers her wisdom…

Take time to play, Sister. Make use of ordinary things in extraordinary ways. Be curious about your life and remember to play. Find the beauty hidden inside whatever is called "strange or ugly." Keep your eyes and heart open to be helpful and kind. Make charitable and thoughtful gifts through the crafting of your petits cadeaux.

The Way of Belle Cœur

Recall a dream from your childhood. Give it new meaning to fit who you are today. Be careful when you share your dreams and visions. Choose trustworthy friends to listen to your deepest secrets. Be mindful that many may not understand or hold enthusiasm for your playful spirit. Beware of the dream stealers and robbers of joy.

Playmates are important companions. Cibylle was my dearest friend. She was different and often feared by others because of her strange appearance. I was her protector. She taught me how to see the beauty and gift within the strange and mysterious world of nature and within humans, too.

Who is need of your friendship? How can you bless someone who is forgotten, lost, or odd to the eyes of others?

Most of all, dear sister, look for ways to be helpful and hopeful. Hope is good medicine for broken hearts. A smile and hopeful word carry God's Love where it is needed most. Be love in the world, the way a child is love. Be innocent, playful, imaginative, and curious. Be love.

Marie's charism: Her expressive sense of wonderment and play and loving kindness for others.

Her challenge: Frequent chastisement from adults for Marie's generous enthusiasm and exuberance.

Her elements: Earth, air, twig, and stone.

Her secret: She could see spirits.

Book IV The Wisdom Keepers of Belle Cœur

Her shadow: Fits of laziness and rebellion against authority.

Her passion: Her imaginative games and hiding where no one could find her.

Her sacred practice: Sitting under a tree to say her prayers.

Her wisdom phrase: *"Grace is a miracle. A miracle of Holy Love for the World."*

Her gift to the community and others: Her ability to recognize beauty and truth within a person's soul, regardless of one's outer appearance.

Her relics: Her pouch of sticks and stones.

Her symbol: A kitten.

Her birth sign: Gemini

Her sacred life-art: The creation of games inspired by things found in nature.

Her invitation: *"Remember to take time for play."*

Marie's suggested active service: Spend time to explore the world of nature with a small child.

Her petit cadeau: A set of "Bâtons et des Pierres (Sticks and Stones).

The Way of Belle Cœur

Her earthly prayer: *Beloved, I pray to be joy in the world. I pray to be the reason people smile. I pray to bring laughter where there are tears. I pray to be a good friend to others, the way the Jesus is a friend to me.* Amen

Marie's identity passage from Scripture: Matthew 19: 13-14

Then small children were brought to Jesus so he could lay hands on them and pray for them. The disciples began to scold the parents, but Jesus said, "Let the children alone—let them come to me. The kindom of heaven belongs to such as these."

Selected *Ink and Honey* references pertaining to Marie: (*I&H:* 95, 182, 200, 202, 244, 248, 258, 260-261, 265, 267, 292, 297, 314, 317, 321-323, 327, 356, 366-367, 386, 400, 414, 418, 424-425, 430, 433, 440-442, 469, 471, 478, 482)

Reflect

- My list of favorite games and creative pastimes I enjoyed during my childhood includes...
- The person I can imagine reaching out to in a playful way is...
- Marie's girlhood spirit and wisdom calls me to remember...
- When I imagine myself as playful, I envision...
- Some ways I might demonstrate playfulness with a friend are...
- My curiosity inspires me to explore...

Book IV The Wisdom Keepers of Belle Cœur

- If my ten-year-old Self could share her wisdom with me she would say…
- If I were to create a board game it would be called… Sketch the game and playing pieces in your journal

Express

- Treat yourself to box of crayons and a coloring book or a book of paper dolls.
- Create a visual prayer collage to express the intention of a playful, imaginative, and curious heart.
- Do you know someone who others find "different or odd?" How might you reach out as a friend or companion? How might you share your wisdom with one another?
- Observe a child at play. What can she help you remember with regard to spontaneity, self-expression, and the courage to try something new?
- Imagine how you might express a childlike sense of wonderment as a spiritual practice.
- Visit a toy store. What toy would you choose for yourself? How would playing with the toy make you feel?
- Make a "play date" with friend. Share your memories of favorite pastimes from your childhood or maidenhood. Go to the beach and build sandcastles. Play jacks. Watch a favorite

film from your younger years. Reconnect with your playful heart.
- ❖ Re-read a favorite book from your childhood.

Myrtle

The Crone

Iconotype: The Empath
Qualities: Protective and Inventive
Wisdom Keeper of Forest Secrets

Myrtle's spirit shares her wisdom…

Curled frond and still blue pond. Musty forest and damp cave, these are places I called my home. My mother left me in the woods soon after I learned to walk. She gave me a gift that day. From that time on I could recognize the suffering child, the broken hearted, and abandoned.

My heart had room for all of these, though my mind would sometimes rail with opposition. Magic was my way. No charlatan's trickery or sham but true sorcery from the bosom of the Mother's garden. Nature was my teacher and her ways are wonder filled and many.

Creation's plan was for me to become mother to Ravenissa and Helvide. Two blessed daughters I was given. They grew their wisdom during their time with me through their curiosity and wild imagining. One fair, one dark, their magic was deemed holy by some and witchcraft by many. Our days

Book IV The Wisdom Keepers of Belle Cœur

together were blessed with unbridled freedom, the telling of stories, and the crafting of beauty. This is my prescription for you who read these words.

Be fearless. Look to the Mother, to nature, for the medicine to heal you. You will find what your heart is seeking in the language of the clouds and the sunlight as it moves across your floor from dawn to noon. What message are you seeking? Do you have the eyes to read the stars or the water in the gazing bowl, or the wisdom within the story of the one standing next to you?

Be patient. Follow the caterpillar and study her cremaster, the place where she attaches her chrysalis. She knows how to anchor herself to prepare for the great transformation when she will one day break free and fly. Where is your cremaster? What is your anchor?

Make beauty your prayer. Know your symbols. Draw the acorn. Paint the bit of bark when it falls away from the branch to give it new meaning. Weave autumn grasses with sticks upon your loom. Could there be a more perfect tapestry? What colors catch your breath away? The verdant greens of summer or the waning rusty hue of autumn's splendor? Color your prayers with your blood and tears. This heavy palette is made from grief, ennui, and melancholy. These conditions, too, cast their own beauty and spell.

I am, Myrtle, the crone, the old one buried in the hollow of a hillside by Ravenissa and Helvide. I call to you from the place of all tomorrows. When you go walking in the woods you might see me.

When I died, Ravenissa and Helvide gave my body and bones to the earth. Over time my spirit was renewed and I grew to become a Grandmother Tree. My branches are wide and home to crow and owl, squirrel and jay. My shade is comforting and within my torso, my trunk, there are secrets hidden away…awaiting your discovery.

༺⚬༻

Myrtle's charism: Her intuitive understanding of the human condition. Her innate ability to offer healing through her creation of beauty and her forest wisdom made manifest in forms from Creation.

Her challenge: To be understood rather than feared for the great wisdom she carried.

Her elements: Earth, air, fire, and water.

Her secret: She could move objects with her thoughts.

Her shadow: Her hidden desires for constant change and for the freedom to go where the wind willed her to go. When she felt confined she was consumed by dark thoughts.

Her passion(s): Reading the stars, the clouds, and the stones for the messages they contained.

Her sacred practice: Saying prayers on her "mother-round." Communicating with Grandmother Tree.

Her spirit's wisdom phrase: *"Even when your day's work is done, you must continue to make beauty."*

Her gifts to Ravenissa, Helvide, and others: A spirit of fearlessness and the XII elixirs.

Her relics: Her mother-round prayer beads, a remnant of deer antler, a circle of wood vine upon a cross made of branches.

Her symbol: The Tree of Life (a Grandmother Tree)

Her birth sign: Virgo

Her sacred life-art: Weaving with things from nature and painting symbols as a form of symbolic protection.

Her invitation: "*Make an offering to the Mother and freely place it where your heart knows she will find it.*"

Myrtle's suggested active service: Leave offerings of beauty in unexpected places to be discovered by strangers.

Her petit cadeau: A knotted prayer cord.

Her earthly prayer: *Mother of all Creation, make me wise. Reveal pathways in your starlit sky to lead the way to the dream world where you store night's secrets. In the morning, cast the day's fortune with the sunlight's glinting script upon the dewy meadow. I pray to you, Mother of earth and sky, fire and water, carry me deep into your stream of sacred wisdom. Make me wise in the ways of nature so I may heal the broken hearted and make beauty from the gifts you scatter at my feet.* Turah, Turah

The Way of Belle Cœur

Myrtle's identity passage from Scripture: Psalm 96: 12
Let the fields exult all that is in them, let all the trees of the forest sing for joy!

Selected *Ink and Honey* references pertaining to Myrtle: (*I&H:* 273-292, 301, 416, 470).

Reflect

- My particular brand of beauty is…
- A person in my life who recognized when I was in pain and offered me comfort was…
  I was changed by this experience because…
- Nature teaches me about fearlessness, patience, beauty, and magic in the following ways…
- An Empath is someone that identifies with another's feelings and moods. She also has the intuitive ability to absorb global feelings and situations, as well as, understand the energies within nature and the creatures of the earth. I have experienced being an Empath when…
- If I suddenly met Myrtle on a pathway in the forest, I would ask her…
  I believe she would respond in this way…

Book IV The Wisdom Keepers of Belle Cœur

Express

- ❖ Create a visual prayer collage with images to represent your concept of aging. How do you want to look as you grow into your elder years? What will your interests be? How will you express your creativity, wisdom, and spirituality as you age?
- ❖ Look for images that speak of the concept of magic. Write a poem to accompany the images.

Petronilla

The Prophetess

Iconotype: Mystic
Qualities: Mysterious and Blessed
Wisdom Keeper of Prophecies

Petronilla's spirit shares her wisdom...

This is what I learned during my time on earth, dear Sister...
Mystery will plague you. It will follow you as surely as smoke follows fire. You must engage all your senses to reveal the answer to life's riddles. My sisters and I can only lead you so far down the path to understanding our lives, our rhythms, and our stories.

The Way of Belle Cœur

Make the connections. Find the treasure. We may bring you guidance through your dreams and through your pens, but only you may observe your world with new eyes to see the links in the chain from our story to your story.

Put your hands into the mud in search of the bone, the fragment of another time and place. Lift it from where it has been waiting for a thousand years. Wash it clean and hold it in your hand. Fix the bone of wisdom within the reliquary upon your altar.

When you grow weary, take your prayers to your oratory and draw sustenance from the gift within the bone. Ponder the deeper story within this instruction. You must reclaim our bones, the shards from our stories. They will form the foundation to rebuild the sanctuary, the sacred safe house, for the new wisdom that will be birthed through you and the eternal sisterhood.

Become the Mystic! Be the Prophetess and Poet! Grow your wisdom and express it through your creations of beauty and sacred offerings.

Belle Cœur, the Beautiful Heart, is yours to behold. Take what is offered to you each day (the dark and the light) and nourish each moment with love, prayer, and imagination. Witness the deep roots of your life as they grow stronger like the roots of Myrtle's Grandmother Tree.

There is wisdom to be discovered in the most unlikely places. God often plays hide and seek. You will never be abandoned in the game. God goes into hiding, to inspire your longing and to inspire you to renew your search for truth of who you are. When you begin your quest you will find the Beloved on the path, awaiting you, to show you the Mysteries, and to help you to remember what you have forgotten…you are worthy of love, healing, and the miraculous.

Book IV The Wisdom Keepers of Belle Cœur

Before I took my last breath, I received a fleeting moment of grace, a final prophecy to accompany my spirit to Heaven. God sent it like an arrow into my heart.

In the vision I saw the time you are living in and women polishing the world with your tears and stories, your magic and wisdom, your prayers and the beauty of your creations. Polish well. Your gifts are needed now, as our gifts were essential for our day. Polish your life and then polish the world with love.

The Beloved needs your prayers and presence on the earth, as there will soon be another turning in time. Love, beauty, and prayer will become the text for the new story for humankind. Know God, love one another, and pray without ceasing. We are at the edge of the veil to pray for you while time turns round again.

༄༅༅

Her charism: Her spiritual gifts of visions and prophecies.

Her challenge: Her struggle to stay grounded in her body while she maintained her open connection to the mystical realm.

Her elements: Air, water, spirit, and heart.

Her secret: She longed to be free of her body.

Her shadow: Her addiction to the mystical experience.

The Way of Belle Cœur

Her passion: To envision new ways to experience prayer, to discover the sacredness in everyday life, and to create rituals of intention.

Her sacred practice: Speaking in tongues before she went to sleep.

Her wisdom phrase: *"Make honey of your lives, my sisters. Make sweet, holy honey of your lives."*

Her gift to the community and others: Her vision to save the relics and stories of the Sisterhood of Belle Cœur as their legacy.

Her relics: A white, knotted prayer cord, a wedding gift from her husband. A coquille shell found while on pilgrimage to Chartres. Her little gazing bowl made of bone.

Her symbol: A dove's skull.

Her birth sign: Aquarius

Her sacred life-arts: Gazing and dreaming.

Her invitation: *"Seek the grace of humility as your spiritual gifts increase. Beware of the danger that accompanies fierce attachment to the mystical experience."*

Petronilla's suggested active service: Pray without ceasing.

Book IV The Wisdom Keepers of Belle Cœur

Her petit cadeau: A prophecy for the recipient's life.

Her earthly prayer: *Beloved, cleanse my heart of all that separates my spirit from your presence. Quicken my senses. Illuminate my seeing and inspire my understanding of my visions. Protect me, Jesus. Shield me from darkness and the onslaught of distraction, temptation, and malevolence. My bones ache for your indwelling presence. Do not hide from me. Come. Come, oh, blessed Keeper of my Dreams. I will be your instrument. Play me as the piper plays his flute. Fill me with prophecy so I may be your voice, your song, and your sacred mistress of Holy Wisdom all the days of my life.* Amen

Petronilla's identity passage from Scripture: Amos 3:7
YHWH does nothing without revealing those plans to the prophets.

Selected *Ink and Honey* references pertaining to Petronilla: (*I&H:* 4, 5, 95, 100, 101, 135, 160-164, 175, 176, 198, 240, 248, 260-264, 354, 355, 360-362, 376, 413, 422, 423, 427, 442, 456-458, 474, 482).

Reflect

- ❖ The most numinous experience I recall was… The experience changed me in the following way…
- ❖ I experienced a time when God seemed to be hiding from me when….

The Way of Belle Cœur

- ❖ For me, the words mystical and/or mysticism mean...
- ❖ The images and words that come to mind when I contemplate the concept of *the bone of wisdom* are...
- ❖ When I contemplate becoming a Poet or a Prophetess I feel and imagine...
- ❖ Dreams inform my life in this way...
- ❖ I have/have not experienced a prophetic dream...

Express

- ❖ Keep a designated journal as a place to record your revelations, visions, and mystical experiences.
- ❖ Collect sacred images to represent your spiritual discoveries and add them to a special designated section of your codex.
- ❖ Make a visual prayer to represent the concept of the bone of wisdom.
- ❖ Set a timer for five minutes. Write a poem to express your deepest longing.

Book IV The Wisdom Keepers of Belle Cœur

Ravenissa

Healer for God's Creatures

Iconotype: The Interpreter
Qualities: Reserved and Benevolent
Wisdom Keeper of Animal Understanding

Ravenissa's spirit shares her wisdom...

All living things, even the spider on the fence post, speaks a language. When one has the eyes and ears to learn from them, the animals, birds, and all creatures become teachers and guides. Study the creatures' symbolic meanings. Welcome them into your dreams. Listen for their sounds and observe their ways.

Watch for animals that appear to be lost, injured, or in need of assistance. Imagine living inside the skin of your pet or a creature in nature to experience the animal's world and condition.

All living things are threads in the weave of Creation. Take one animal, plant, fish, bird, or human away and the weave ripples with change. Nourish and reverence nature and she will respond one hundred fold.

My mother, Myrtle, taught me to respect all of Creation as life's miraculous field of wonderment, beauty, and wisdom. The creatures are our teachers. They offer us lessons of compassion, caring, and companionship.

The Way of Belle Cœur

At my birth I was given the gift of understanding the languages of mouse, rabbit, crow, and deer. My relationships with the animals inspired and informed my life's journey.

When mother's milk filled my breasts as God's miraculous call to become Grace's mother, I was charged to also be her teacher. Wisdom Sophia's passion, presence, and prophecy flowed through me with mystical nourishment for beloved Grace. As I nursed her, the Mother fed the milk of holy wisdom to Grace, through me. She grew to become the embodiment of the Sacred Feminine and all who crossed her path were changed and inspired by her countenance.

Dear Sister, I implore you to nourish Creation. Seek ways to care for the earth and her creatures. Serve the Divine Mother as a ready helpmate. Within the birdsong, the whispers on the wind, and the cat's purring you will find blessing for your spirit. Become the interpreter of Creation's language and bear witness to the miracles that surround you.

༄

Her charism: Her seventh sense and the unique ability to speak and understand various languages of the birds and animals and her skills as an intuitive healer.

Her challenge: The avoidance of the experiences of ridicule, fear, and branding as a "witch" by those who could not accept her special gifts as holy and real.

Her elements: Earth, air, water, and feather.

Her secret: A desire to fly so she could see the world as Crow could see it.

Her shadow: Her frequent denial of human companionship and communication in deference to her animals.

Her passion: Feeding, caring for, and healing animals of all kinds.

Her sacred practice: Her orchestration of animal funerals.

Her wisdom phrase: *"The Mother speaks to us through the voices of all her creatures."*

Her gift to the community and others: Ravenissa's ability to educate others, through her loving example, of how to revere the animals as our kindred earthly companions.

Her relics: A single feather from crow. Her golden earring given her by Myrtle. A large tooth taken from the doe that died in the forest, an amulet given her by Goscelin. A perfect hummingbird's egg, cupped in a tiny nest.

Her symbol: A crow feather

Her birth sign: Pisces

Her sacred life-arts: Her natural and instinctual animal-speak and interpretation, and her intuitive healing practices for God's creatures.

The Way of Belle Cœur

Her invitation: *"Teach children and others in your life to tenderly revere all creatures."*

Ravenissa's suggested active service: Become educated about the many ways our culture mistreats and abuses animals for our dietary, cosmetic, fashion, and medicinal "needs." Respond accordingly.

Her petit cadeau: A shiny black feather from Crow.

Her earthly prayer: *Wisdom Sophia, Mother of all Creation, you call me to care for your creatures and your earth. Make me your steward in thought, action, and prayer. I pray to use my senses to recognize when an animal is in need. Help me to see, to hear, and to touch the helpless ones with compassionate care. I long to be a faithful protector and friend for dog and wren, bee and butterfly, tree and stream. I pray to be a guardian of the web of life.* Amen

Ravenissa's identity passage from Scripture: Job 12: 7-10

But turn to the animals, and let them teach you; the birds of the air will tell you the truth. Listen to the plants of the earth, and learn from them; let the fish of the sea become your teachers. Who among all these does not know that the hand of Our God has done this? In God's hand is the soul of every living thing; in God's hand is the breath of all humankind.

Selected *Ink and Honey* references pertaining to Ravenissa: (*I&H:* 168-170, 179, 203, 212-213, 242, 259-260, 279-294, 390-397, 438-439, 442, 476, 478, 482)

Book IV The Wisdom Keepers of Belle Cœur

Reflect

- When I think of Ravenissa's devotion to the earth's creatures I feel called to…
- Throughout my life my animal companions have been…
- The concept of the web of life as the relationship of one living thing to another inspires me to…
- The animal I relate to the most is the…
- The memory of a sacred moment I've experienced with an animal or bird that informs my life today is…

Express

- Choose a birdfeeder and seeds that are appropriate for where you live. Hang it where you can observe the various birds and their birdsongs. Record the sounds of the birds that arrive to feed there.
- Integrate clay into your spiritual practice. Create tiny animal figures and dry them in the sun.
- Plant herbs and flowers (oregano, fennel, lantana, lavender, sweet alyssum) to attract the bees and butterflies.
- Inspired by Ravenissa's ability to interpret the animal languages, spend time with your pet or in nature observing the birds, squirrels, rabbits, and other creatures. Listen. What do you imagine they're saying to one another… to you?

The Way of Belle Cœur

Sabine

The Counselor

Iconotype: Mentor
Qualities: Competent and Logical
Wisdom Keeper of Resourcefulness

Sabine's spirit delivers her wisdom…

Every woman, to her unknowing, carries mystical maps embedded within her heart and soul. These inner schemata, when realized, ensure a fully creative and authentic life rooted within a passion for beauty and truth and colored with purpose and meaning.

Inspiration is the pathway that leads to the maps that reveal a fertile landscape within your sacred imagination. Seek inspiration and you will have the key to portals of discovery placed deep inside your spirit before you were born.

As sisters of Belle Cœur, we believed God spoke to each of us according to her particular spiritual understanding. Our sisterhood's rituals and prayers unified our community. We lived as women in service to God and God's people. The Beloved inspired our practices and beliefs and held us in a steady place of mutual devotion and prayerful purpose.

We grew together as a sisterhood in ways that reflected our love for God, our fidelity with one another, and our compassionate, loving, service for God's people. Our individual, spiritual, and creative gifts, talents, wisdom, and spirits were unique according to God's plan for our lives.

Book IV The Wisdom Keepers of Belle Cœur

You and your sisters are carrying on our tradition. My spirit longs to share with you that each sister of Belle Cœur grows her soul through her intimate relationship with God, her commitment, camaraderie, and shared beliefs with the whole of her sisterhood, and her dedication to her sacred practices. Finally, the sisterhood creates a relationship with God, as a living body of service, to benefit and aid God's people and all of Creation.

Belle Cœur's pathways of Spirit, Sisterhood, Sacrament, and Service, became our sisterhood's Way of Belle Cœur. We relied upon, and we invite you to share our reliance for sacred practices and prayer, the sacred life-arts, the sensual nurturance of the seasons, the study of the Holy Mysteries, and the experience of community life for spiritual and creative inspiration. Our spirits also reach out from this side of the veil to inspire you to lean into one another for thoughtful counsel, honest accountability, and the joy of shared, sacred experience.

Lastly, always in all things, depend upon the guidance, grace, and mercy of God's Love. Our Beloved Jesus is your constant assurance that though you may live in disorienting times, you will never be lost.

༄

My sisters and I call out to you to share our timeless counsel. Grow our wisdom and make it your own...
Trust your visions.
Pray ceaselessly for guidance.
Pay attention to your dreams to recognize your guides and guardian spirits.

The Way of Belle Cœur

*Learn from the examples of Mary and Martha.
Become the embodiment of Wisdom Sophia and nurture Creation.
Be fearless as you make your life's pilgrimage.
Share your abundance in all ways, always.
Consciously appreciate your blessings.
Self-nurture to replenish your energy.
Become a co-creator with God.
Attune your wildness and passions for the highest good.
Pay attention to details, metaphors, signs and symbols.
Organize and create your daily life to reflect your inner world.
Seek to become part of a spiritual circle community,
to share life's journey and grow your wisdom.
Be conscious of the deeper meanings
within the tangible and intangible pleasures
of physical comfort and the material world.
Live as a conduit for God's Love.
Pray without ceasing.*

Sabine's charism: Her inventiveness and compassionate intuitive guidance for others.

Her challenge: How to achieve balance between her contemplative life and the demands of each day. How to continually renew her spirit while paying attention to the needs of others.

Her elements: Fire, lightening, earth, and velvet.

Her secret: Her frequent desire for material possessions.

Her shadow: Her attempt to control others and the outcome of certain situations, therefore interfering with the natural flow of God's unfolding plan. Her ego's fervent need to be regarded as being perfect in all ways.

Her passion: To provide counsel and guidance for her sisters.

Her sacred practice: Her prayerful devotion to Mary Magdalene.

Her spirit's wisdom phrase: *"The circle holds me in place."*

Her gift to the community and others: Her ability to build and sustain a spiritual community.

Her relics: One remaining golden coin stolen from her uncle. A fragment of yellow ribbon from the dress she wore when she first arrived at Belle Cœur. Her string of counting beads used for Belle Cœur's household accounting and her mother's ring reclaimed from the ashes.

Her symbol: A coquille shell

Her birth sign: Aries

Her sacred life-arts: Money-tending

Her invitation: *"Be generous. Share your resources with those in need. Be grateful for all forms of abundance in your life. Your abundance of riches: friends, health, home, and most importantly, your faith."*

The Way of Belle Cœur

Her petit cadeau: Ten bone "counting beads" on a knotted cord.

Her Belle Cœur prayer: *My heart is centered in love. My sacred imagination is blessed with the Spirit's inspiration. My mind is wrapped in peace. My being is illuminated by the Divine presence. In the name of Holy One, I pray for the healing and protection of human kind, all creatures of the forest and seas, the birds that fly through the heavens, and my beloved sisters, my spiritual companions on life's journey. Be near me, Beloved. Teach me to clear distraction from my path so that I may live in loving service to the creation of your Kin-dom on earth.* Amen

Sabine's identity passage from Scripture: Romans 12:6-8

We have gifts that differ according to the grace given to each of us. If your gift is prophecy, use it in proportion to your faith. If your gift is ministry, use it for service. If you're a teacher, use your gift for teaching. If you're good at preaching, then preach boldly. If you give to charity, do so generously; if you're a leader, exercise your authority with care; if you help others, do so cheerfully.

Selected *Ink and Honey* references pertaining to Sabine: (*I&H:* 34, 90, 106, 110-140, 178-187, 218-221, 248-251, 260-264, 308-310, 321-322, 356-359, 371-375, 402-408, 420-478)

Book IV The Wisdom Keepers of Belle Cœur

Reflect

- Sabine's spirit inspires me to attune my "wildness" for the highest good. My wildness manifests as...
- When I contemplate the abundance in my life, I am grateful for...
- Generosity is a quality I...
- When I imagine how I might create a spiritual practice dedicated to Mary Magdalene, I envision...
- Consumerism manifests in my life in the form of...
- With regard to managing my finances I feel I...
- My needs for pleasure, luxury, and material comforts can best be described as...

Express

- Share your abundance with someone in need, anonymously.
- Create a visual prayer to express your material needs and desires. In your journal, write about what you discover during this reflective process.
- For one week, make a notation each time you make a purchase to gain awareness of your expenditures.

The Way of Belle Cœur

Mary and Martha

Sacred Feminine Wisdom for Today

Mary and Martha of Bethany
Wisdom for our lives today

The ancient Scriptural story of the Beloved's visit with Mary and Martha offers an important teaching, as well as, a model to inspire balance for the contemplative and active lives of contemporary women. Mary and Martha provide wisdom to compliment the iconotypes of the Belle Cœur Wisdom Keepers. They are two sides of the same coin. Their Bethany story illustrates the conflict and contrast between the reflective needs of the inner *contemplative*, Mary, with her sister the inner *doer*, Martha, and her desires for productivity.

As we begin an in depth exploration of today's Mary and Martha iconotypes, it's important to refer to Luke's Gospel account of Jesus' visit with the two sisters at their home at Bethany.

Luke 10:38-42

As they traveled, Jesus entered a village where a woman named Martha welcomed him to her home. She had a sister named Mary, who seated herself at Jesus' feet and listened to his words.

Book IV The Wisdom Keepers of Belle Cœur

> *Martha who was busy with all the details of hospitality, came to Jesus and said, "Rabbi, don't you care that my sister has left me all alone to do the household tasks? Tell her to help me!"*
>
> *Jesus replied, "Martha, Martha! You're anxious and upset about so many things, but only a few things are necessary—really only one. Mary has chosen the better part, and she won't be deprived of it."*

This story reflects the inner struggle many women today seek to resolve. Mary and Martha's spirits live within us. However, it is often easier to identify with Martha's frenetic busyness and management of the endless details and tasks of everyday life.

Mary, on the other hand, is perceived by Martha to be somewhat lazy and unconcerned about what she "should be doing." Mary, unlike her busy sister, chooses to sit quietly at Jesus' feet in contemplation and reflection while he affirms her choice.

Luke's account depicts the inner struggle within the hearts and minds of many contemporary women. A question arises:

How do I maintain spiritual, emotional, creative, and physical balance in today's fast paced, technological, and demanding world?

Daily responsibilities definitely call for Martha's sense of duty, organizational skills, and intentional action in the outer world. Meanwhile, the soul yearns to join Mary at the feet of Christ for prayer and contemplation, to experience the still and grace-filled terrain of the inner world. Perhaps the way to lasting inner and outer harmony is through the conscious, sacred, indwelling partnership of Mary and Martha. Mary and Martha must make peace with one another and honor and respect their two distinct charisms: Mary, the introverted, reflective, and prayerful, contemplative, and Martha, the extroverted, diligent, and active, taskmaster.

Through sacred awareness and spiritual practice it's possible to encourage the spirits of your inner Mary and Martha to work together. Their collaboration increases the potential to bring balance to life's aspects of *being* and *doing*.

The weave of Mary's prayerful and reflective focus with Martha's task mastery, over time creates a blended harmonious tapestry. Mary's grounded and contemplative nature blends with Martha's energetic response to situations as they arise. The two aspects of the Self, the *contemplative* and the *doer* join together to complete the unending and diverse array of tasks that comprise contemporary life with prayerful commitment and sacred intention.

༄༅།

The world of the Scriptural Mary and Martha was fraught with challenge. Today, we also live in the midst of shifting paradigms and worldly chaos. Our creative spirits long to serve the planet, and tend the hearth and home. Simultaneously, we desire to be fully present for our families, co-workers, and friends. Each morning we awake to a seeming unending list of "to dos." We go to work, run endless errands, cook, clean, garden, tend the needs of our beloveds, care for aging parents and grandchildren, and manage a host of other tasks. Our busyness and "can do" perfectionism is fueled by the inner Martha as we navigate the daily list and schedule.

Meanwhile, inner Mary tugs at the heart. During the morning commute her spirit emerges to encourage a moment for prayer in the midst of a river of traffic. We pay attention to Mary's call to contemplation and also value Martha's need to be accountable. The blend of their voices creates balance and reveals the potential to live in rhythm with the heartbeat of God to temper the pace of everyday life.

༄༅།

Before we draw further sustenance from the Sisters of Bethany's wisdom it's important to assess the Western cultural messages women receive today. Messages that encourage unattainable perfectionism in all areas of life including: our relationships, our work and caring for the home, childrearing, and all aspects of physical perfection as well.

Activity and productivity are highly valued by the culture and encouraged at any cost. An over-scheduled and perfectionistic existence with rare periods of down time to care for the contemplative nature of the heart and soul is a life out of balance, captured within a state of chronic fatigue and frustration. Most importantly, this way of life erodes the soul and is detrimental to physical, mental, emotional, and spiritual wellbeing.

Belle Cœur spirituality values the importance of living holistically. Life from this vantage point honors active and vital participation combined with contemplative and creative practices. The balance of work and leisure and prayer and service ensure continual renewal and rejuvenation for the body, mind, and spirit.

The holistic pathway requires conscious awareness to embrace Mary and Martha's wisdom to foster internal centeredness and peace. Their qualities live within our hearts and spirits and each is a valuable spiritual and creative ally. However, it is the gift of their combined ways of being and doing that yields the greatest benefit.

The iconotypes of contemporary Mary and Martha

Belle Cœur spirituality is enriched and enlivened with the attributes of Mary and Martha. Not unlike the iconotypes of the Belle Cœur Wisdom Keepers, Mary and Martha hold particular strengths of character and charisms to inform our lives.

Mary, the Contemplative, is peaceful, centered, and prayerful. Her life and inner strength are rooted deep within her spiritual practices. She is a partner in prayer and a lifelong student of sacred wisdom. The practice of silence, and her full realization and understanding of the Beloved's presence within every moment are keys to her sustainable sense of inner peace. Her focused ability to listen to others with compassion and non-judgment is important to her charism. Mary is passionate and strong in her reserve. She is an attentive listener and follower of God's guidance and dedicated creator of sacred spaces.

Martha, the Doer, is an organized and productive activist. She tends her work, home, and familial responsibilities with a high attention to detail as she multi-tasks. She is also concerned about global affairs and her community. She is diligent, a dedicated friend, and someone to be counted upon. Martha speaks her truth and is often a voice for the voiceless. She embraces the values of inclusivity, diversity, and equality.

Once again, imagine the potential within Mary and Martha's combined spiritual and creative gifts. Consider the outcome of Mary's sacred awareness and prayerful countenance blended with Martha's abilities to complete whatever is necessary through her active and intentional service. Their shared wisdom and charisms create the possibility for a spiritually renewed and highly functional way of living and being.

How in the context of contemporary cultural messages do you honor your inner Mary (the contemplative) and inner Martha (the doer)?

Mary and Martha through their modeling, invite the opportunity for a new iconotype, the *Contemplative*

Doer. When our prayers are alive within our hearts throughout the day we are fueled with sacred awareness to complete the tasks before us through the indwelling Presence of God's grace, mercy and love. From this place of intentional commitment there is the potential for fulfillment, a peaceful countenance, and abiding joy.

Mary (Magdalene) of Bethany

(I&H: 123, 128, 141, 146*)*

Throughout the ages there has been theological discussion and debate with regard to Mary of Bethany and Mary Magdalene. Were they two different women or one in the same?

Belle Cœur spirituality embraces the tradition that Mary, sister to Martha and Lazarus, was Mary *Magdalene.*

Mary was the witness. She became Christ's companion as the *Apostle to the Apostles* and was the keeper of the holy oils and balms, guardian of rituals. Mary was the anointer. Mary calls us to create sacred practices and rituals to take us into the deepest recesses of our souls. Read John 12:1-8 to experience the story of the ancient ritual of anointing.

She held vigil at the crucifixion and Jesus appeared first to Mary after his resurrection. He sent her to tell the others of the greatest miracle the world has ever known. She spoke her truth to those who questioned her authority and her knowledge. Her contemplation paradoxically called her to social action and service. She saw the resurrected Cosmic Christ and responded, and her spirit continues to invite others to see him today.

She was the steadfast friend and patient student. Yes, she was a contemplative but she teaches us to temper our hermitic desires for solitude with thoughtful right action in all aspects of daily life and service for the greater good.

Mary invites us to spiritually and actively attune to our callings. She asks us to be courageous and to be way-showers for others. Her message is:

"Be steadfast and anchored in prayer within the Divine Presence. Be a conduit for hope and be fearlessly ready to serve when called."

Mary's spirit reaches out through the veil of time and space. She invites us to deepen our connection within the heart of God through our spiritual practices.

An invocation to Mary

Blessed Mary, beloved of the Beloved, teach me to embrace stillness, contemplation, and prayer as doorways to co-creation with the Divine.

Awaken my senses to illuminate the bridge that connects my mind with my soul. Inspire me to reclaim the ancient sacred practices of healing and anointing so I might share these blessings with others. Give me the grace to go into silence to listen for the voice of God, to learn my true calling. Help me to recognize when my spirit is depleted and to turn to Jesus for mercy, renewal, and replenishment.

Dear kindred sister in spirit, I welcome your ways into my heart. Amen

༄

Martha

Martha is our model for determination and perseverance through conscious social and spiritual action. Mary's sister recognizes the needs of others and responds. She invites us to embrace what Mary inspires to enliven Martha's wisdom with spiritual awareness as sacred action in the world. She calls us to serve God and humankind. Martha also teaches the practical sacred life-art of openhearted hospitality. She teaches to tend the hearth as though tending the soul of the world.

An invocation to Martha

Blessed Martha, sister of sacred action, guide my outreach in the world. Help me to be conscious in each moment to recognize and respond to the needs of those around me. Open my eyes to suffering, hunger, abuse, and neglect. Pray for me, that I will have the stamina to complete both the mundane and meaningful tasks of daily life.

Give me the courage to speak truth to the face of fear. I pray to encourage the creation of beauty as an antidote to

despair, and offer openhearted hospitality to those who arrive at my door.

Martha, I turn to your example for strength and physical empowerment. I pray to follow your model of active, creative, life-giving service. Amen

Martha and Mary offer wisdom and an invitation

Contemplation precedes action. Take time for prayer and sacred attunement within your spirit before there is engagement with the outer world. Follow Mary's model of attentive listening for the Beloved's guidance. Inhale Divine wisdom and guidance and exhale the illusion of separateness from your Source. Hold the sacred and prayerful intention for the highest outcome for all concerned as a precedent for daily, required responses and/or actions.

When the impulse to be reactive is held prayerfully within the contemplative heart... timely, sacred, appropriate action results. Carry your oratory within you where the next right deed or enterprise is held fast in the reliquary of consciousness. Visually construct through your sacred imagination, your personal inner sanctuary. Humbly return to your indwelling chapel throughout the day. Take momentary pauses to rest within the Beloved's Presence for guidance and peace. When your spirit is fortified return to the task or interaction at hand. This is the sacred co-creative work of Mary and Martha. They are navigators for the constant ebb and flow between the inner and outer world.

The Way of Belle Cœur

Reflect and Express
- Study translations of Jesus' teachings from his native language, Aramaic. Meditate with Aramaic words to deepen your spiritual understanding and connection to the Beloved. This area of study is manna for the soul. Enrich your spiritual practice with mystical understanding. Ecstatic vocalization, singing, chanting, and other spontaneous forms of prayer are natural expressions of praise and devotion.
- Reflect on the presence of Mary Magdalene and practice the Sacraments of anointing. This sacred ritual reflects devotion to Mary, the Anointer.
- Stay connected with your sister companions as you navigate your inner/outer journey. When possible, study, worship, pray, work, and create together. Support one another with Mary/Martha consciousness to encourage the weave of contemplation with busyness to ensure balance and equanimity.
- In the spirit of hospitality, practice inclusivity and respect other faith traditions. Welcome all to your table and learn from one another. Keep an open mind and open heart.
- Speak your truth with courage and reliance on God. Speak out when you witness social injustice. Speak your truth in the presence of those who may challenge you. Follow Jesus's teaching

for the disciples, "*I am sending you out like sheep among wolves. So you must be as clever as snakes, but innocent as doves.*" Matthew 10:16

❖ Follow Mary's example when she proclaimed to the disciples, *Mary of Magdala went to the disciples. "I have seen the Teacher!" she announced. Then she reported what the savior had said to her.* John 20:18 Call on the courage of Mary Magdalene when you must face your fears and speak what you know in your bones as your truth. Use the same courage to speak out against social injustice to serve as the voice for those who have been silenced by abuse, discrimination, and oppression.

Your Iconotypal Self Portrait

When you have completed your study of the iconotypes for *Ink and Honey's* Belle Cœur Wisdom Keepers and also become acquainted with the contrasting iconotypes, Mary and Martha, you are ready to contemplate *your* iconotypal self-portrait. Work through the process described here and record your discoveries in your journal. Later you may choose to synthesize your wisdom for the pages of your codex.

It's suggested that a time of prayer and inner preparation will enrich and deepen the experience as you discern your iconotype. Go to a quiet place for this work. Assure that you won't be disturbed. Light a

The Way of Belle Cœur

candle, become centered, and enter Kairos time. May blessings flow during this time of sacred reflection as you explore the beauty of your true nature, creative gifts, and luminous spirit.

Process

- Open your journal to a blank page. You're invited to create your personal iconotypal portrait through your responses to the outline provided below. Take your time and resist editing. Trust your first instinctual responses. Allow your creative heart and spirit to lead the way to the discovery of your most authentic choices.
- In addition to noting your responses to the various prompts, write a list of your spiritual and creative gifts. Give each of your gifts an appropriate title.
- Examples:
  I am an open-hearted listener = I carry the gift of Compassionate Listening
  I am capable of great Patience = I carry the gift of Attentive Waiting
  I enjoy entertaining and nurturing my houseguests = I carry the gift of Hospitality
- When you have completed your iconotypal portrait you may wish to copy it within your Sacred Codex and illuminate the pages with images, sketches, or photos or create a visual prayer to celebrate your iconotype.

Book IV The Wisdom Keepers of Belle Cœur

Outline for Your Inner Self Portrait

My wisdom story:

My birth name:

My various life roles (daughter, wife/partner, etc.) and chosen or given titles:

My chosen name:

My birth sign:

My charism (refer to your list of gifts and choose a collective title for your charism):

My nature (contemplative, doer, or unified)

My challenge:

The Way of Belle Cœur

My elements:

My secret:

My shadow:

My passion(s):

My sacred practice(s):

My wisdom phrase:

My gift to the community and others:

My relics:

My symbol:

My sacred life-arts:

Book IV The Wisdom Keepers of Belle Cœur

My invitation:

My suggested active service:

My petit cadeau:

My prayer:

My iconotype:

Reflect

- ❖ The sister(s) of Belle Cœur I most personally relate to is/are...
- ❖ She/they inspire me in the following ways...
- ❖ When I contemplate Mary, the *contemplative*, and Martha, the *doer*, I resonate most with...
- ❖ My inner Martha and/or Mary inspire and challenge me because...
- ❖ The greatest discovery I made when I created my iconotypal self-portrait was...
- ❖ The area of my life where I feel I am most centered is...
- ❖ When I contemplate my life's various roles, the role I most resonate with is...

The Way of Belle Cœur

- ❖ My wisdom phrase is inspired from my experience of...
- ❖ A sacred life-art I would like to explore is...
- ❖ The most difficult area of discernment for my iconotypal self-portrait is...
- ❖ When asked to name my personal charism I feel...
- ❖ My awareness of my challenge, secret, and shadow invite me to...

Express

- ❖ Create a series of visual prayer collages to express the particular facets of your iconotypal self-portrait.
- ❖ Print your wisdom phrase and chosen name and display these in your workspace.
- ❖ Each year on your birthday revisit your iconotypal self-portrait to notice if any of your preferences and/or details have evolved or changed. Make notes in your journal to indicate your ever transforming Self. Include a "Selfie" photograph or draw your outer self-portrait.

Book V
The Labyrinth and Chartres Cathedral

*The labyrinth was a living
river of life that flowed
to the center and out again
as one sacred stream.
(I&H: 334)*

Life, throughout the ages, has metaphorically been viewed as a pilgrimage. The labyrinth mirrors the seeker's inner journey or pilgrimage. We step onto the labyrinth's singular path and begin the walk.

The Way of Belle Cœur

The labyrinth as an archetypal symbol and spiritual tool is pertinent to Belle Cœur spirituality. This section will provide an overview of the labyrinth, in particular, the labyrinth at Chartres Cathedral in Chartres, France.

༺✤༻

The walk towards the labyrinth's center the may offer the walker the experience of *purgation*. This is the commencement of the journey where the burdens, experiences, and thoughts that no longer serve the Higher Self are let go. Purgation frees the human spirit so when one arrives at the center *illumination* may be received through the guidance and inspiration of the Divine Presence.

After a time of reflection and receptivity the walker leaves the center and follows the path to the place where she began. The walk from the center to the outer rim can be said to symbolize *union*. This portion of the walk may be experienced as an opportunity for the integration of the process of walking as living/breathing prayer. Through metaphor and reverie a labyrinth walk holds the potential for the mind and sacred imagination to glimpse the invisible world.

༺✤༻

Book V The Labyrinth and Chartres Cathedral

The Chartres Cathedral Labyrinth

There are mysterious, sacred, ancient portals upon the earth that lead, if one is open to being led, to the mystical transformation of the soul. The great medieval Chartres Cathedral (Nôtre Dame du Chartres) is such a place.

The current Chartres Cathedral emerged from the ashes of a previous ancient church that was built upon the ruins of a place of worship. The Druids made an annual pilgrimage to the area where the cathedral now stands.

There is a lineage of history and *her*story embedded within the stones of Chartres Cathedral. Her stained glass windows tell the stories of Creation and depict the stars and planets. There are also colored glass Scriptural stories of Christ's life and a host of other spiritual and cosmic portrayals within the windows.

Chartres Cathedral is frequently described as a living book. The stained glass windows are like the pages of the book. The windows were intended at the time when they were installed, to use images of colored glass to educate the illiterate country folk (pagans) and the pilgrims who found their way to the Royal Portal, the west entrance of the great church.

Like many medieval churches and cathedrals Chartres holds a relic, the Sancta Camisia (Mary's Veil). The relic is central to the cosmology and theology of Chartres Cathedral. Believed to be a portion of the tunic that Mary wore at the time of the annunciation or Christ's birth, "Mary's Veil" was delivered as a gift to the cathedral by Charles the Bald in 876. For centuries faithful pilgrims have made their way to Chartres to pay homage to Mary, as well as, for countless other spiritual and personal reasons. This is a cathedral that has always been about birthing new life through the Spirit.

The labyrinth at Chartres is also a call to the pilgrim's heart. Walking the ancient labyrinth on the floor of the nave of the cathedral can be a transformational experience. For the medieval pilgrim, some say, it became a symbolic representation for the New Jerusalem though there is no medieval documentation to substantiate this.

The labyrinth at Chartres Cathedral was laid between the devastating fires of 1194 and 1220 when the rebuilding of a particular section was completed at the west end of the nave, the central portion of the cathedral. It is approximately forty-two feet in diameter. The center appears to have a large scar where the centerpiece once was. It was made of copper, brass, and lead and was removed during the Napoleonic war to be used for cannon fodder. The Chartres labyrinth consists of eleven concentric circles with the twelfth being at the center of the labyrinth. The path overall represents Creation.

The Center is often called the rosette. The rose symbolizes the Holy Spirit in the ancient mystical tradition. It is also the symbol for Mary, the Mother of God.

Book V The Labyrinth and Chartres Cathedral

The various components that are foundational to the labyrinth include Creation, the Spirit, the Sacred Feminine, and the concept of a pathway leading to the center. It's interesting to note that the template and cartography of the Way of Belle Cœur are formed from similar elements.

The labyrinth rests within the womb of Chartres Cathedral where the Sacred Feminine is central to the heart of the place. The name of the great church, Chartres Cathedral Nôtre Dame (Chartres Cathedral of Our Lady or Our Lady of Chartres Cathedral) speaks to the importance of Mary. She was extremely meaningful during the Middle Ages as a goddess figure.

The medieval people of the countryside worshipped the Goddess of Creation as central to their nature-based religion. To facilitate their conversion to Christianity the Church ensured that Mary would become their new symbol as a divine goddess. Mary became a portal to Christian understanding for the pagans. Through the stories of the Mother goddess and her Son, the Church introduced the concepts of Christian belief.
(I&H: 235-236, 328-339)

A Sister of Belle Cœur shares her story

"I prepared for the pilgrimage to Chartres for months before leaving. My intention was to recapture my connection to feminine spirituality, and knock on the doors of sisterhood that I had read about in Ink and Honey. I knew that a pilgrimage is a journey into the sacred and the divine within and without. Yet, I was unprepared and continually caught by surprise by

the stories carved in stone and stained glass and the presence of Mary. To say that my experience with the cathedral changed me is an understatement, as it is still changing me."

Trish Morris
Sister of Belle Coeur

Sacred Geometry

Another symbolic form within the pattern of the Chartres labyrinth is the labrys. A labrys is a double ax design and ancient symbol for women's creativity. The ten labryses within the labyrinth form a cross if viewed from above. The labryses may also be described as chalices. The vessel shape of the labrys is yet another feminine image symbolic of the womb and birthing.

Sacred geometry is based on ancient sacred knowledge and articulated through and within architectural forms. This lost art held the knowledge to create a balanced and serene environment for the human psyche and soul. Gothic cathedrals all over Europe were built upon the principles of sacred geometry. Balance, appropriate materials, and proportion combined with a complementary system of numbers and angles create a space where the mind finds rest, harmony, and portals to other levels of awareness.

Little, regarding the labyrinth, has been recorded in medieval writings. You are invited to contemplate the possible meanings of the labyrinth for medieval walkers. I encourage you to imagine how the labyrinth was used in ancient times.

Book V The Labyrinth and Chartres Cathedral

Reflect

- ❖ Were there various rituals, prayers, and Sacraments associated with the labyrinth?
- ❖ What was the core sacred mystery held within the hearts and minds of pilgrims and others who experienced the labyrinth in medieval times?
- ❖ Meditate upon these questions as an opportunity for creative response.
- ❖ Draw what you imagine.

༺⚭༻

The best way to learn about the labyrinth is to walk it with an open heart and mind and allow your personal experience to guide you. There is neither a correct nor incorrect way to walk the labyrinth. Labyrinths differ from mazes. There are no dead ends or trick pathways. A labyrinth has one path leading to center and back out again.

People may feel inspired to dance, sing, sit, spin, and/or crawl while on the labyrinth. (*I&H:* 333) Your experience of walking a labyrinth will be unique for you. Bring your question to the labyrinth. Carry it within your heart as you walk and pray for guidance.

The labyrinth is a visible, sacred symbol for the Mystery. Once again if we look to the past to inform the present we create the opening for spiritual understanding, creative guidance, and the potential to experience awe. Within a peaceful moment or one of exceptional wonder, as you walk the labyrinth you will come to know that you are walking on Holy Ground.

The Way of Belle Cœur

The labyrinth inspired Belle Cœur Sister and pilgrim, Mary Montanye, during a recent Belle Cœur pilgrimage to Chartres.

A Belle Cœur Sister's story

I stood at the mouth of the labyrinth. Thousands of other pilgrims before me had traveled to this spot. Had they, too, come to find the Divine? The scent of incense, the hushed footfall of my spiritual sisters, and the flickering candlelight heightened my expectation and wonder.

My body, without thinking much about it, moved one foot and then the other forward along the path. Then, at some point, I noticed a small voice speaking to me from within. As I was not raised Catholic and had little knowledge of Mother Mary, the sudden thought that this was she speaking to me was a surprise. Her words resonated with great love. Over and over with each step forward she whispered, "You are mine. You have always been mine. You are my daughter and the sister of Jesus."

The mantra carried me to the center of the labyrinth, my throat thick with unshed tears. I realized I had come to this place not to find connection, but to renew the connection that had always been there. At the center of this labyrinth in Chartres Cathedral, I reaffirmed my place in the family of God. I affirmed especially my place with the women of God, a long line stretching for generations behind me and to continue on for generations beyond me.

Book V The Labyrinth and Chartres Cathedral

I had changed here in this temple of Mary. I now had the reassurance I had longed for—that I belonged in this holy family of women. That we all do. It is our heritage and our birthright and we can lay claim to it, knowing we are never forgotten.

Mary Montayne
Sister of Belle Cœur

The Sacred Made Visible

The era of the Middle Ages was a time when representations of the Sacred were visible everywhere. Icons were nailed to trees and coquille shells (a symbol for pilgrimage) were left along the roads throughout Europe so pilgrims could find their way to sacred sites.

Entire towns were engaged in myriad occupations and creative endeavors to build the glorious cathedrals throughout Europe. No signatures appear on the statues, windows, and edifices of the cathedrals. All that appears to have mattered to the artisans and stonemasons was that their creations glorified God and became true visual depictions of faith-filled stories and inspiration for a predominately illiterate population.

The Renaissance that began in Italy in the 14th century reflected how people of that time ached for beauty, new forms of creative expression, music, theater, poetry, and dance. We live in a world driven by technology, machines, and rapid-fire information. Perhaps there are those among us that once again yearn for new forms of worship and sacred arts to balance our 21st Century techno-based lives with opportunities for spiritual illumination.

Reflect

- ❖ I believe the creative invitation from the Spirit for contemporary sacred life-artisans and pilgrims on life's journey is…
- ❖ Where within today's culture and your everyday life do you witness sacred imagery and music for our spiritual inspiration?
- ❖ The forms of sacred visual and creative expression that I feel called to explore are…
- ❖ When I imagine the co-creation of a Creative and Spiritual Renaissance I feel and envision…

Express

Visual Prayer Tags

The following creative experience is a very simple way to spread handcrafted personal offerings of hope, inspiration, and beauty wherever you go.

- ❖ Purchase a box of 2"x 4" shipping tags at your local office supply or craft store.
- ❖ Tear images from magazines that represent the sacred to you. Images to reflect peace, harmony, nature, serenity and beauty.
- ❖ Glue an image to each tag.

Book V The Labyrinth and Chartres Cathedral

- On the back of the tag write a favorite inspirational quote or a prayer or a personal message such as: *May you be blessed today. May your heart feel hope and peace in this moment. Amen.* Sign it anonymously… *With love from a kindred-pilgrim on life's journey.*
- Create a variety of visual prayer tags with various uplifting messages.
- Place your completed tags in a plastic bag and carry them with you.
- Place them in random places and trust that those in need of prayer and encouragement will discover them. Leave them in public restrooms, or with your gratuity for a server after lunch. Place them on the bus seat or in the seat-back pocket on a plane. Hang them from trees in your neighborhood park. Let your imagination guide you.

Visual prayer tags are one small way to begin a movement to spread hope and inspiration. Imagine yourself as a co-creator of a Creative and Spiritual Renaissance. Help to bring blessing and hope to our world as you offer tangible, visible, and holy outrageous forms of sacred beauty.

Book VI
Seasonal Inspiration

The Belle Cœur Perpetual Calendar

*The seasons ever-changing
cycles circled round,
one following the next.
(I&H: 58)*

Our Belle Cœur pathways, practices, and prayers mark time as we traverse the seasons of the year. In this section you will find the Belle Cœur Perpetual calendar. The perpetual calendar marks the observation of particular dates that are meaningful for Belle Cœur spirituality, as well as, certain Christian liturgical celebrations and holy days.

Book VI Seasonal Inspiration

Please note: Ash Wednesday, the Lenten Season, Palm Sunday, Holy Week, Easter Sunday, and Pentecost are not specified on the Belle Cœur Perpetual Calendar, as the dates for these sacred days change annually.

Your Belle Cœur Perpetual Calendar

It will be helpful each year to designate a calendar to guide your Belle Cœur journey through the seasons. Begin by adding the year's specific dates for Ash Wednesday, the Lenten Season, Palm Sunday, Holy Week, Easter Sunday, and Pentecost. There are liturgical calendars online for your reference.

Make your calendar meaningful for you. Add images, sketches, prayers, quotes, and other creative touches to inspire your annual journey through the seasons. You're encouraged to make notations on your calendar to provide the opportunity for acknowledgement of our ever-evolving Belle Cœur traditions and practices. Record the perpetual dates listed below, month by month. Note important personal days of sacred significance. Include the birthdays of your sisters or community members and other important dates pertaining to your community on your calendar. Scripture and *Ink and Honey* references are provided and may be used for the practice of lectio divina.

The Belle Cœur perpetual calendar indicates specific dates for personal and unified prayer, spiritual reflection, artmaking, and celebration throughout the year. With the turn of each season we experience the sacred practice of anamnesis, as we recollect sacred celebrations from another place and time and imbue them with reimagined contemporary meaning for our lives today. Through the spirit of remembrance, our collective and individual seasonal journeys become grace-filled with intention, devotion, tradition, and unlimited forms of spiritual/creative expression.

A Belle Cœur Sacred Journey Through the Year Highlights of the Belle Cœur Perpetual Calendar

Intentions and Creative Expression

On the first day of each month you're encouraged to contemplate your monthly personal, spiritual, and creative intentions. These may be recorded in your journal or calendar. Also on the first of the month you're invited to create an intentional expression of beauty through the sacred life-arts. You may be inspired to arrange a bouquet of flowers, bake bread for the evening meal, create a visual prayer collage to reflect the particular month or season, or create a visual prayer tag to cheer someone's day.

These suggested Belle Cœur devotional practices invite the opportunity to slow down to enter Kairos time for reflection, and also provide space for you to become centered and focused as the new month begins. In this way, your intentions will be consciously honored in a sacred way.

Book VI Seasonal Inspiration

Companion Saints and Feast Days

Patron saints, by definition, are advocates, protectors, and intercessors. Rather than thinking of the various saints as *patrons*, Belle Cœur spirituality acknowledges them as spiritual *companion saints.*

Belle Cœur's companion saints are chosen and recognized specifically for their affinity for specific issues pertaining to women. Additional saints with relevance for the Way of Belle Cœur are also included. Celebratory days for Mary, the Mother of Jesus (Our Lady of Lourdes, Our Lady of Fatima, Our Lady of Guadalupe) and other Marian observances are noted. A "Feast Day" for a saint is traditionally celebrated on the date the saint died or it may be a date assigned by the Church.

Please note that St. Mary Magdalene, St. Joan of Arc, and St. Hildegard of Bingen are also considered Belle Cœur companion saints. The cross symbol (+) indicates Belle Cœur days of prayer, celebration, and special acknowledgement. You will find birthdays and memorials indicated on the perpetual calendar connected with the Belle Cœur sisters from *Ink and Honey*. You're encouraged to study the iconotypal portrait for the corresponding sister that is celebrated each month.

Connection and outreach

Posted on the calendar towards the end of each month you'll find a reminder to make a written connection with someone in your life. You're invited

The Way of Belle Cœur

to write a letter or a postcard to a person in need of your forgiveness or someone you wish to forgive. You may choose to write to someone who is ill, grieving or lonely, or perhaps a person you've lost touch with. You may also wish to write to one of your community's sisters on this day that is dedicated to prayerful written and illuminated communication and connection. Embellish your letter with sketches or drawings, quotations or include a visual prayer collage.

Email, online messaging, and texting are convenient and fast. However, taking time to thoughtfully handwrite a letter or note is a sacred form of expression and a valuable spiritual practice. A handwritten letter is also a gift and blessing for the one that will receive the benefit of your heartfelt and meaningful gesture.

The changing seasons and your altar

The seasonal "changing of the guard" refers to the summer and winter solstices and spring and autumn equinoxes. During these quarterly transitions, the perpetual calendar invites you to rearrange your personal altar to reflect the arrival of the new season.

The creation of a seasonal altar nourishes creative expression and spiritual awareness. Incorporate color, fragrance, texture, treasures from nature and cherished touchstones, and the four elements of Creation (fire, air, water, and earth). Engage your creative heart and spirit as you add candles, incense, imagery, and other sacred touches to represent and honor the season.

Book VI Seasonal Inspiration

Prayers are provided for your incorporation for your sacred seasonal practice of clearing and dressing your altar. In the months that follow continue to add beauty and meaningful seasonal offerings to your altar. Think of your altar as sacred work in progress. Revel in your creativity as you celebrate the blessings of winter, spring, summer, and fall.

Seasonal sharing

Belle Cœur spirituality encourages hearth-keeping to reduce clutter and ensure order. The concept of seasonal sharing invites you to look through your closets, drawers, and cupboards. Notice what articles of clothing, books, and household items you're ready to pass along to others.

Share what you no longer need or use with a local charity or someone you know that might benefit from the items. This is a thoughtful and meaningful spiritual practice to foster simplicity, gratitude, and sharing. Seasonal sharing helps to keep awareness of the acquisition, consumption, and flow of material possessions present in your consciousness.

Your blessing box

A Belle Cœur annual practice is the creation of your blessing box. Choose a box, basket, or other container of your choice no larger than a shoebox. Cut strips of paper, approximately 1" x 3." Place these in another smaller box or bowl near your container.

Beginning on January first and continuing throughout the year, periodically (daily or weekly) take a moment to jot your blessings on the strips of paper. Place these in the blessing box. At the end of the year on New Year's Eve, open your blessing box and slowly and prayerfully savor the blessings you received.

The Belle Cœur Perpetual Calendar

January
***
Sentry Moon

1 *A day for prayer, reflection, and expression of the sacred life-arts*

Write your monthly personal, spiritual, and creative intentions. Create and express beauty.

The Solemnity of Mary
Luke 2:16-21

A feast day in celebration of Mary as the mother of Jesus. Contemplate Mary as the Beloved's first teacher and the many ways she fed him her milk of Holy Wisdom.

Book VI Seasonal Inspiration

Prepare Your Annual Blessing Box +
Create your container for your blessings (refer to the previous instructions) and place it upon your altar with the prayer included here. Write your first blessing(s) of the year and place them in the container as the closing for this ritual. Continue to reflect on your blessings, daily, weekly, or monthly, and add them with the others.

Prayer of intention for blessing box
Beloved, I pray to open the eyes of my heart to recognize the blessings that will flow my way throughout the coming year. Help me to be ever grateful for the subtle and profound moments of grace, mercy, joy, and sharing that will anoint my life in the months ahead. I pray to be a blessing for others, as I am blessed. I begin today to fill this sacred container with my blessings. May every sunset, every turn of the earth, remind me of your Love, and Your precious gift of life. Amen

Epiphany
Ephesians 3:2-6
Celebrated on the first Sunday following January 1. A Feast Day celebrating the revelation of the Divinity of Jesus. A commemoration of the Magi's visitation with the infant Jesus.

The Baptism of Jesus
Matthew 3:13-17
The celebration of Jesus' Baptism by John follows Epiphany.

10 *Day of reflection upon the Holy Name of the Beloved +*

The Way of Belle Cœur

John 14:13-14
A day dedicated to adoration and reflection. Throughout the day call to mind and heart the many names of the Beloved: Jesus, Jesus the Christ, Yeshua, Alpha and Omega, The Christ, Cosmic Christ, Sacred Heart, and other names that spill into your reverie.

14 *Gertrude's Birthday* +
(*I&H:* 404-409)
Reflect upon the quality of courage and the healing power of love and faith. Study Gertrude's iconotypal portrait in Book IV.

21 *The Feast Day of St. Agnes* (291- 304) +
St. Agnes is the companion saint of girls and rape survivors.
Envision a world where girls and women are valued and honored for their creative and spiritual gifts and feminine wisdom. Envision healing between the genders and healing from patriarchal abuse. What do you imagine? What do you see?
Hold your vision for a time while you reflect upon and offer the following prayer.

Blessed St. Agnes, pray with me for (insert the name of one(s) in need) *and all young girls, women, and those who have suffered sexual abuse of any kind. May our merciful God deliver healing for their bodies, minds, and spirits. I ask your prayers for those contemplating crimes against women and children. May their hearts be opened and turned away from evil through God's grace. In the name of all that is Holy, I pray for an end to the*

Book VI Seasonal Inspiration

degradation and abuse of girls and women throughout our world. Amen

30 *Outreach through the written word and illumination* +
Who will you bless with your scribed heartfelt words and beauty today?

February
***
Hearth Moon

Refer to a liturgical calendar for the dates for Ash Wednesday, the Lenten season, and Easter.

1 *A day for prayer, reflection, and expression of the sacred life-arts*
Write your monthly personal, spiritual, and creative intentions. Create and express beauty.

Feast Day of St. Brigit of Kildare (451-525) +
A Celtic nun, abbess, and founder of many monasteries, St. Brigit is a companion saint for nuns, midwives, and others. Contemplate the many religious and lay sisters throughout time and their works of service. Go into the monastery of your heart to meditate and receive St. Brigit's inspiration and wisdom. Record your reflections in your journal.

Blessed St. Brigit, pray with me for all religious and lay sisters. May the Holy Spirit inspire their ministries of prayer and service and may those they serve appreciate their acts of charity and kindness. I pray for the doulas tending

The Way of Belle Cœur

mothers and their babies, may their hands be blessed to assure safe deliveries and to offer needed assurance and comfort. St. Brigit, you are a way-shower for feminine courage and commitment. Bless my spirit with your wisdom. Amen

2 *The Presentation of Jesus in the Temple*
Luke 2:22-40

Meditate upon the Beloved as a child and adolescent. How do you imagine him? How did others perceive and experience him as he grew? How do you imagine the workings of his interior world and spiritual in his early years? What were Mary's perceptions of him as the mother of young Jesus?

The Celebration of Candlemas +

This is day of celebration with reflection upon Jesus as the Light of the world. Gather the candles you will burn in the months ahead for a blessing: tea lights, tapers, pillars, etc. Place them on your altar. Choose one particular candle to mark this day of Candlemas. Offer the following prayer and light the candle at the appropriate moment within the prayer.

Jesus, our Beloved, You are the Light of the world. May the brilliance radiated by these candles serve as a blessed reminder of your illuminated presence and peace. Help me to shine brightly as a beacon of your love and hope, always in all ways. I light this candle today, in gratitude for the gift of life and light and all things that come through your extravagant Love. Amen

5 *Feast Day for St. Agatha* (231-251)

Book VI Seasonal Inspiration

St. Agatha is the companion saint of breast cancer patients and wet-nurses.

Today you're invited to pray for those who have died from breast cancer, those living with the disease, and breast cancer survivors and their families. Contemplate the blessings of mother's milk and Beatrice as "soothie." (*I&H:* 93, 399, 438)

11 *Our Lady of Lourdes*

Meditate upon the meaning of the words spoken by Mary, "*I am the Immaculate Conception,*" to the young peasant girl, Bernadette Soubirous in Lourdes, France, 1858.

If Mary appeared to you today how would she reveal herself? What would she say to you?

14 *Saint Valentine's Day*

A day dedicated to love. How will your love manifest today? How will you share God's Love? How will you receive love?

Craft a banner of love. Cut paper hearts of varying sizes from an assortment of papers.

Write the names or glue photos of your beloveds on the individual hearts. You may also write a word or a prayer for each person on the opposite side of the hearts. At the top of each heart punch two small holes ¾ inches apart. Thread a large darning needle with an appropriate length of kitchen twine or narrow ribbon. Weave the twine in and out of the holes of each heart. Space the hearts to create a banner effect. Hang the banner near your altar.

The Way of Belle Cœur

17 *Petronilla's Birthday +*
(*I&H:* 4-5)
Contemplate the concepts of spiritual awareness, the oratory within, and mystical understanding. What is your prophecy? How do express your mystical wisdom? Spend time designing a page for your codex that is dedicated to your prophetic and mystical understanding.
Study Petronilla's iconotypal portrait in Book IV.

27 *Outreach through written word and illumination*
Who will you bless with your scribed heartfelt words and beauty today?

March
***
Birthing Moon

1 *A day for prayer, reflection, and expression of the sacred life-arts*
Write your monthly personal, spiritual, and creative intentions. Create and express beauty.

10 *Ravenissa's Birthday +*
(*I&H:* 168-170)
Contemplate your relationship with God's creatures. Create a visual prayer to honor the animal kin-dom. Spend sacred time communing with your pet or animals in nature today.
Study Ravenissa's iconotypal portrait in Book IV.

Book VI Seasonal Inspiration

19 *The Feast Day of St. Joseph*
Today is dedicated to the contemplation of St. Joseph, carpenter, earthly father of Jesus, and companion saint of workers. Reflect upon the meaning of fatherhood for today's children.

20 *Vernal Equinox +*
You're invited today to renew and bless your altar as spring arrives. Clear your altar of winter's offerings. Gather your spring touchstones, sacred objects and treasures from nature. Dress and bless your altar to reflect spring's themes: resurrection, new life, the greening of the earth, the budding of possibility.

Wisdom Sophia, you infuse Creation through the birthing season of spring as the greening of the earth resumes. Help me to cultivate my creative and spiritual gifts while I embrace and appreciate the beauty of the earth at this fertile time. Mother of Nature's miracles, you bless my spirit with renewal! Amen

25 *The Celebration of the Annunciation of the Beloved*
This is the Feast Day to celebrate the angel Gabriel's announcement to Mary that God had chosen her to be the mother of Jesus. Reflect upon what it means to be called by God and to live life guided by prophetic obedience.

27 *Spring sharing*
What are you ready to release and share?

30 *Outreach through the written word and illumination*
Who will you bless with your scribed heartfelt words and beauty today?

April
***
River Moon

1 *A day for prayer, reflection, and expression of the sacred life-arts*
Write your monthly personal, spiritual, and creative intentions. Create and express beauty.

2 *Cibylle's Feast Day and Grace's Birthday* +
(*I&H*: 411-425)
Gather sticks, moss, leaves, tree bark, and other bits from nature to craft a small shrine for your altar as an homage to Cibylle. Offer a prayer for all the souls that will cross the thresholds into life and life everlasting today.

Study the iconotypal portraits for Cibylle and Grace in Book IV.

14 *Sabine's Birthday* +
(*I&H:* 112-133)
Sabine reminds you to pray for those who have lost their way. Contemplate a time when you have offered guidance or mentored someone. Remember a time when you felt lost. How did you find your way?

Study Sabine's iconotypal portrait in Book IV.

Book VI Seasonal Inspiration

27 *Brother Paul's Feast Day* +
(*I&H*: 30-37, 41-68)
Today marks a day of remembrance for your teachers and mentors.

Call to mind the mentors, teachers, and spiritual advisors who have made a difference for your life. Is there someone you desire to call or write to today to say thank you for his/her teaching, coaching, or guidance? Reflect upon the blessing of shared wisdom and mentorship with gratitude for life's teachers.

29 *Outreach through the written word and illumination*
Who will you bless with your scribed heartfelt words and beauty today?

May
***
Rose Moon

Traditionally, May is dedicated to devotions to the Blessed Mother. You may wish to add a statue of Mary to your altar this month, incorporate prayer beads or the Rosary weekly or daily as devotion, or create a visual prayer collage to represent the Mother. What additional ways are you inspired to celebrate Wisdom Sophia this month?

1 *A day for prayer, reflection, and expression of the sacred life-arts* Write your monthly personal, spiritual, and creative intentions. Create and express beauty.

4 *Belle Cœur Day of Prayer* +

The Way of Belle Cœur

Today is dedicated to prayer: for the needs of your beloveds, friends, the people of the earth, Creation, and your personal petitions. It is a day to also wear the color blue and to pray for the sisters, companions, and all who walk the Way of Belle Cœur. The invitation is to experience prayer, embody prayer, and share prayer. Pray aloud, pray within the silence of your heart, dance your prayer, sing your prayer, color your prayer, craft your prayer, cook a meal as a prayer, write a prayer and send it to someone, become a living, breathing prayer. You might also choose to offer prayer to Wisdom Sophia, to Mary in all her myriad forms as we celebrate May.

10 *The Blessing Celebration of the Bees, Beekeepers, and Hives* +

(*I&H:* 47)

Contemplate how you might plant flowers or scatter seeds to attract the bees.

Wisdom Sophia, your bees bless life with the miraculous creation of honey. They ensure the perpetuation of the crops and flowers. Their way of living within the hive teaches us about community. I pray today for the protection, health, and sacred work of the bees. Bless the beekeepers, the guardians of the hives who deliver the honey. May their service be honored as holy necessary and blessed. Amen

13 *Our Lady of the Rosary of Fatima*

The feast day celebrating the visions of Mary as experienced by three children in Fatima, Portugal

1917. Contemplate the mystery and miracle of the miraculous appearances of the Mother.

23 *Mabille's Birthday* +
(*I&H*: 237-238)

She held intentional, sacramental, presence and prayer with the dying. Today you are invited to pray for hospice workers and others that care for people through life's final days.

Study Mabille's iconotypal portrait in Book IV.

29 *Outreach through the written word and illumination*
Who will you bless with your scribed heartfelt words and beauty today?

30 *Feast Day for St. Joan of Arc* (1412-1431) +
St. Joan of Arc is the companion saint of soldiers and France. She is also a companion saint for those who follow the Way of Belle Cœur. She was martyred at the hands of the Inquisition and she fully lived her mystical truths. She is our spiritual inspiration as a model of courage, faith, and fidelity to God's guidance for her life through her mystical experiences in the midst of persecution.

St. Joan's Feast Day calls for the remembrance of those who lived faithfully unto death. Especially those who were deemed heretics and witches and killed during the medieval European Inquisition (12th-13th centuries) and Salem, Massachusetts trials (17th century). Meditate upon the words of the *Ink and Honey* Prologue. You're invited to pray for those who are unjustly incarcerated and held captive as a form of religious persecution.

Blessed Saint Joan, your faith and trust in God and the mystical guidance of your guides and angels changed the course of history and herstory. You call me to holy fearlessness in the face of injustice and discrimination against those without voices. You died for your witnessing, your beliefs, and your convictions. Your life was not in vain but rather your spirit lives on to inspire and illuminate the pathway of Service. I pray to be brave, to speak truth to power, and to follow God's prophetic call for my life. Amen

31 *The Visitation* +
Luke 1:39-45, Luke 1:46-55

Today you're invited to reflect upon the story of expectant Mary's visit with her pregnant cousin, Elizabeth. The child Elizabeth carried, John the Baptist, leapt in her womb with the recognition of Jesus within Mary.

Contemplate a time when someone recognized the gift you were carrying. How do you acknowledge the sacred gift within another?

June
***
Solo Moon

1 *A day for prayer, reflection, and expression of the sacred life-arts*

Write your monthly personal, spiritual, and creative intentions. Create and express beauty.

7 *Marie's Birthday* +
   (*I&H*: 267, 297)

Marie reminds you to practice unconditional love and to value the gift of time for play.

Is there someone in your life today you feel called to reach out to offer unconditional love and compassion? How will you play today?

Study Marie's iconotypal portrait in Book IV.

21 *Summer Solstice* + **Altar renewal/blessing**

The arrival of summer invites you to renew and bless your altar.

Clear your altar of spring's offerings. Gather your summer touchstones, sacred objects, and treasures from nature. Dress and bless your altar to reflect the season's themes: cultivation, growth, and fecundity.

Wisdom Sophia, you infuse Creation through the fertile season of summer in all her glory. I pray to nurture what was planted within me in spring to grow my wisdom in preparation for the autumn harvest. May I be reminded to revel and enjoy your magnificent sunny days, the ocean's splendor, and the sun's mysterious rising and setting. Mother of Eternal Beauty, you bless me with nature's extravagant wonders! Amen

25 *Summer Sharing*

What are you ready to release and share?

29 *Outreach through written word and illumination*

Who will you bless with your scribed heartfelt words and beauty today?

The Way of Belle Cœur

July
ᵅ ᵅ ᵅ

Child's Moon

1 *A day for prayer, reflection, and expression of the sacred life-arts*
Write your monthly personal, spiritual, and creative intentions. Create and express beauty.

11 *Feast of St. Benedict* (480-543)
This is a blessed and sacred day for reflection upon the monastic teachings of St. Benedict.

18 *Beatrice's Birthday* +
(*I&H:* 185, 264, 267)
Beatrice inspires the sacred life-art of hearth tending and nurturing. Bake little honey cakes today in honor of Beatrice. Contemplate the various ways you nurture others and the ways that would like to be nurtured at this time in your life. Read Beatrice's iconotypal portrait in Book IV.

22 *St. Mary Magdalene's Feast Day* +
John 20:1–2, 11–18
(*I&H:* 3, 123, 132, 141, 240)
St. Mary Magdalene is celebrated today as the first woman to see the risen Jesus. She is also a companion saint for Belle Cœur sisters and companions.
The suggested color for the day (often associated with Mary Magdalene) is red.

Blessed Mary Magdalene, you walked with the Beloved. You knew him, ate with him, and anointed him. You are a witness to the resurrection, beloved to the Beloved, and Apostle to the Apostles. As the embodiment of Sacred Feminine wisdom you are also a companion in prayer. Set my heart afire with your holy passion, purpose, and prophecies.

Inspire my dreams and visions. Bring me closer to the Mystery.

Amen

29 *St. Mary and St. Martha of Bethany Reflection* +

Luke 10: 38-42

Refer to Book IV and read the section: *Mary and Martha of Bethany*. Contemplate how you will balance your inner Mary, the contemplative, with your inner Martha, the doer. Mary and Martha's story is important as you seek to weave the sacred within everyday tasks and responsibilities.

30 *Outreach through the written word and illumination*

Who will you bless with your scribed heartfelt words and beauty today?

August
***
Chrism Moon

1 *A day for prayer, reflection, and expression of the sacred life-arts*

Write your monthly personal, spiritual, and creative intentions. Create and express beauty.

The Way of Belle Cœur

6 *Comtesse's Birthday* +
(*I&H:* 354-359)

Comtesse invites you to notice your shadow today. When do you feel defensive and speak inappropriately? Are there times when you feel compelled to act out to express hidden feelings of jealously, rage, insecurity, and shame?

The shadow is an aspect of human nature. Recognizing your shadow opens the space for spiritual and emotional growth and healing. Comtesse encourages the importance of *shadow work* and prayer for strength, courage, and stamina to address the darkest and most needful places within your heart and spirit.

Study Comtesse's iconotypal portrait in Book IV.

12 *Replenishment of anointing oil* +
John 12:1-3
(*I&H:* 144-147)

The ancient Sacrament of anointing is a valued facet of Belle Cœur spirituality. Today celebrates the annual replenishment of your anointing oil. Magdalene anointed Jesus. Their senses were filled with the scent of costly spikenard, a generous offering from beloved to Beloved. He was deeply moved by her generosity and honoring of him.

What selfless offering will you offer the Beloved today as a personal Sacrament?

You will find a recipe for anointing oil and prayers for anointing in Book IX.

30 *Outreach through written word and illumination*

Who will you bless with your scribed heartfelt words and beauty today?

Book VI Seasonal Inspiration

September
***
Forest Moon

1 *A day for prayer, reflection, and expression of the sacred life-arts*

Write your monthly personal, spiritual, and creative intentions. Create and express beauty.

4 *Goscelin's Birthday* +
(*I&H:* 271-272)

Ink and honey are important elements for Goscelin's spirit and creativity. Today you are invited to embrace the story that is currently prevalent in your life. Put pen (ink) to paper and scribe the essence of your current story. Afterwards make a cup of tea. Add a spoonful or two of honey while you contemplate the sweetness in the present moment.

What prayer arises within your heart? How do the substances of ink and honey hold meaning for you?

Study Goscelin's iconotypal portrait in Book IV.

15 *Our Lady of Sorrows*
Luke 2:35

Mary is honored today as the Mother that endured profound suffering. With her eternal compassion she prays with us in our lives during times of grief and challenge.

17 *St. Hildegard of Bingen's Feast Day* +
Read (*I&H:* 207-210)

Saint Hildegard is a Belle Cœur companion saint. Her spirit encourages curiosity, study, and the

The Way of Belle Cœur

cultivation of wisdom. Today, Saint Hildegard's deep mystical understanding of Creation and Wisdom Sophia invite you to engage your senses as conduits to the Divine Presence.

Take a walk in nature and breathe, touch, taste, listen, and see the miracles all around you. Burn incense upon your altar. Break bread with prayer and gratitude for your senses and God's miraculous and mysterious gifts.

23 *Autumnal Equinox* + Altar renewal/blessing

Today you're invited to renew and bless your altar as autumn arrives. Clear your altar of summer's offerings. Gather your autumn touchstones, sacred objects, and treasures from nature to represent summer. Dress and bless your altar to reflect the seasonal themes: harvest, bounty, and fruition.

Wisdom Sophia, you infuse Creation through the breathtaking, colorful, abundant season of autumn. I pray to harvest the gift I have been nurturing and growing within me.

May autumn bring forth the spiritual bounty within my heart and spirit as I prepare for winter's call to hibernation. I surrender to autumn's rapture and revel in her beauty.

Mother of Holy Generosity, you call me to the feast of Life! Amen

25 *Autumn Sharing*

What are you ready to release and share?

Book VI Seasonal Inspiration

29 *Feast of St. Michael, Gabriel, and Raphael* +
Matthew 24: 31
The angels are our guardians, advocates, and intercessors. Reflect upon the angelic realm and the gifts and mysteries of the angels. Write a prayer to honor your angel and place it on your altar with a white candle.

30 *Outreach through the written word and illumination*
Who will you bless with your scribed heartfelt words and beauty today?

October
***
Cornucopia Moon

This month is dedicated to praying the Rosary or another prayerful practice.

1 *A day for prayer, reflection, and expression of the sacred life-arts*
Write your monthly personal, spiritual, and creative intentions. Create and express beauty.

Feast Day for St. Thérèse of Lisieux (1873-1897) +
Saint Thérèse is a Belle Cœur companion saint. She modeled the grace of deep faith and determination in spite of pain, illness and other challenges. She is lovingly referred to as "The Little Flower." Roses are her symbol. We remember her courage and her belief that God never inspires one of us with an idea or vision that cannot be realized.

The Way of Belle Cœur

Contemplate whatever may be worthy of completion in your life and ask the spirit of St. Thérèse to pray with you for the perseverance and wherewithal to bring your project, task, or vision to completion.

14 *Blessing of the Harvest* +
Today you're invited to contemplate the blessings of life's bounty. Think of this as a time for thanksgiving, honoring, and celebration of all that has come to fruition in your life during the past year. Bless the harvest of wisdom, creativity, work, and fulfillment that you have experienced. Create a visual prayer collage of gratitude for the wisdom you have grown and the wisdom you have yet to discover.

18 *Imene's Birthday* +
(*I&H*: 156-158)

Imene's caregiving spirit blessed her sisters and those she nursed at the infirmary.

Her skills of midwifery helped to welcome many new lives into the world. Contemplate how you care for others. Where do you feel called to offer nurturing and support? Reflect upon Imene's invitation to serve the great planetary transformation as a *spiritual* midwife. How do you envision the metaphoric themes of the developmental stages of conception, gestation, and birth? What stage of spiritual/creative development are you currently experiencing?

Study Imene's iconotypal portrait in Book IV.

30 *Outreach through written word and illumination*
Who will you bless with your scribed heartfelt words and beauty today?

31 *Samhain* (Halloween, All Hallows' Eve)
A Gaelic feast day celebrating the harvest.

November
***
Ancestral Moon

1 *A day for prayer, reflection, and expression of the sacred life-arts*
Write your monthly personal, spiritual, and creative intentions. Create and express beauty.

All Saints' Day
Hebrews 12:1
This is a blessed day to remember, celebrate, and pray with the spirits of the Saints and angels. What are the qualities you consider *saintly?* Have you known someone in your life you consider to be a saint? Is there a saint that holds particular resonance for you? Dedicate the day to the study of the saints. Enter into prayer with your personal companion saint. Create a visual prayer to honor him/her.

2 *All Souls' Day*
Wisdom 3:1-9
According to ancient Christian tradition, today we remember the dearly departed. Add photos and cherished mementos to your altar in memory of friends and beloveds that now live in the world of Spirit.

The Way of Belle Cœur

27 *Helvide's Birthday* +
(*I&H:* 165-167)

Helvide's wisdom of the earth and all her properties blesses the season. Simmer spices such as clove, cinnamon, and nutmeg in apple juice or cider on your stove. Fill your home with scent of earth's bounty as you contemplate Helvide's knowledge and the pungent fragrances and medicines she brought to Belle Coeur. Bring an amaryllis or narcissus (paper whites) plant to your living space. Observe the blooming process as the leaves fall outside your window. Helvide's iconotypal portrait can be found in Book IV.

30 *Outreach through written word and illumination*

Who will you bless with your scribed heartfelt words and beauty today?

December
***
Pomegranate Moon

The Season of Advent is celebrated this month. + Advent begins on the Sunday closest to November 30th and spans four weeks prior to Christmas. It is a fertile and prayerful time of expectancy, preparation, and devotion as we await the Nativity of Jesus and the return of Light for our world.

1 *A day for prayer, reflection, and expression of the sacred life-arts*

Book VI Seasonal Inspiration

Write your monthly personal, spiritual, and creative intentions. Create and express beauty.

12 *Feast Day for Our Lady of Guadalupe*

The appearance of Mary to Mexican peasant, Juan Diego, in 1531, and the mysterious and beautiful image of her that was mystically imprinted on Diego's tilma (cloak) is celebrated today. The image of Our Lady (the Virgin) of Guadalupe is stunningly detailed with symbols, colors, and details that are meaningful to the culture of the area and also representative of Creation. Wisdom Sophia is celebrated in all her miraculous forms.

17 *Myrtle's Birthday* +
Read about Myrtle (*I&H:* 273-292)

Myrtle's wisdom is rooted within the earth. Her spirit draws near with each changing season. Stand on the ground in your bare feet and feel the heartbeat of the earth through your soles. Fill your bones with the blessings of this time of in between, twixt autumn and winter. Embody Myrtle's wisdom.

Read Myrtle's iconotypal portrait in Book IV.

22 *Winter Solstice* +

Today you're invited to renew and bless your altar as winter arrives. Clear your altar of autumn's offerings. Gather your winter touchstones, sacred objects, and nature's seasonal treasures. Dress your altar to reflect winter's themes: hibernation, rest, reflection.

The Way of Belle Cœur

Wisdom Sophia, you bless the earth with winter's slumber. I pray to enter the season of retreat and reflection to replenish my body and spirit for rebirth in the greening time. You call me to enter the darkness of hibernation with the promise of a new dream to awaken me in spring. Mother of Creation, you beckon me to sacred rest and I succumb to your invitation.
Amen

24 *Christmas Eve*
Beloved Infant, we give thanks tonight as you arrive to bless the world with your Light and Love. May there be peace, holy peace, upon the earth while our voices join the chorus of saints and angels and together we sing Alleluia, Alleluia.
Amen

25 *Christmas Day*
Ring bells, hug your beloveds, pray, feast, share, and celebrate! Merry Blessed Christmas! The Light of Christ is upon you and within you!

27 *Winter Sharing*
What are you ready to release and share?

30 *Outreach through written word and illumination*
Who will you bless with your scribed heartfelt words and beauty today?

31 *Open your blessing box and reflect upon the year's blessings.* +
You have been blessed throughout each season of the year. Tonight, as you prepare for the New Year's arrival, you may celebrate by revisiting your

Book VI Seasonal Inspiration

blessing notes contained in your blessing box. Light a candle and offer your prayer of gratitude (create your personal ritual) as you read each blessing you have experienced. You may wish to bundle and tie your blessings with ribbon. Empty the blessing box to receive the blessings that will arrive during the months ahead. Take time to contemplate your personal, spiritual, and creative intentions for the New Year.

The Qualities of Time

The earliest sisters of Belle Cœur
established their rituals
of prayer to take place
in the meadow
or near the hearth.
Evening prayer happened
when all were tucked
in before bed.
(I&H: 141)

Before we begin to circumnavigate the holy nature and properties of each season, it feels important to fully consider the concepts of linear and non-linear time. Clock time (*Kronos*) rules the day throughout the struggle to stay "on time and on task" in response to the demands of contemporary life. Belle Cœur spirituality, however, encourages living from a place of indwelling spaciousness assured with the knowledge that God's time, beyond human constructs and mathematics, is unending, eternal, open, and expansive (*Kairos*).

The earth's annual journey around the sun when viewed through the linear lens of clock or Kronos time can be summed up in the following way: *The calendar year is composed of twelve months, equaling fifty-two weeks, three hundred sixty-four days, eight thousand seven hundred thirty-six hours, and over one half million minutes.*

It can seem that time is actually moving more and more rapidly as the culture's dependence on technology adds an element of extreme immediacy to nearly all aspects of everyday existence. Life, lived in tempo with Kronos time fosters physical and mental exhaustion and excessive stress because the mind feeds the repetitive message, "*...there's not enough time!*" The Kronos worldview requires movement from one task or event to the next as quickly as possible with an ever-increasing and disoriented belief that time is slipping away.

However, from a spiritual perspective, we can never truly be short of time. Linear time, after all, is a human invention. The realm of Spirit is without time, there is only the present moment melting into the next present moment, and the next...eternally. We glimpse this *timeless* reality when we shift from the frantic state of doing (Kronos) to a contemplative place of being (Kairos). Kairos provides the opportunity to engage with feelings of spaciousness, calm, and direct relationship with the Divine Presence, within and without.

The *conscious* step from the intensity of Kronos time into the wide-open and expansive freedom of Kairos

Book VI Seasonal Inspiration

is a life-giving and generative practice. Engagement with the sacred dimension of Kairos is a prerequisite for spiritual awareness. In the midst of chaos there is a portal to access the center of the compass, True North, the Beloved, a Kairos state of being.

The entrance to the portal is the breath...breathing in and breathing out. The portal is opened through the full and conscious choice to move from *doing* to *being* as the shift from *action* to *contemplation.*

When the mind engages the rational world it works hard to stay on track and task oriented. A linear approach is necessary to accomplish the multitude of tasks required every day. However, there must also be time for the mind to turn away from clock-watching, endless details, and the frenetic rhythm required by the "to do" list. There is a very human need to slip across the borders of Kronos to enter the landscape of Kairos to rest and reset the mind through engagement with the creative heart and Spirit.

Imagine the way a traveler on foot navigates the Interstate with anxiety and trepidation. Suddenly, she can't take it anymore. She escapes the speeding reckless traffic to follow a path down an embankment that leads to a quiet sheltered place. The cacophony of traffic noise is now a faint hum. All that is heard is the gentle rhythm of her heartbeat and breathing. In the same way, the conscious move from Kronos to Kairos provides a palpable and visceral shift of energy, consciousness, and physical awareness.

The Way of Belle Cœur

Sacred practices to transition from Kronos to Kairos time

A Belle Cœur practice to signal the mind to shift from the dimension of Kronos to Kairos seems all too simple. Visual reminders and rituals initiate re-centering on all levels: physical, mental, and spiritual. The initial quest to stay within the center, to reside at True North on the compass in conscious co-creation with the Beloved, requires signposts to locate your inner sanctuary (oratory) in the midst of the whirlwind of everyday life.

Re-centering is a continual ongoing process and practice. Order and harmony in your surroundings illuminate the way. A sacred space, a special place in your home for journaling, meditation, reading sacred texts, or exploring your creativity is essential to living with Kairos awareness.

Naturally, you can't sit on a futon all day or never leave the confines of where you live. How is it possible to find peace within the endless distractions of work, errands, and the demands of our technological and frenzied paced world?

The simple practice of assigning specific responsibilities to your touchstones and everyday objects provides a network of prompts and cues to call you back to the center, to Kairos, as needed throughout the day. The assigned "helpers" assist you to maintain the calm interior you experience in your sanctuary at home.

For example…near my computer in my workspace I have created an altar of images and touchstones representing various saints who inspire my writing and

Book VI Seasonal Inspiration

other creative endeavors. Each time my eyes fall on these sacred icons, I am reminded to STOP and b r e a t h e. I'm invited to go within to draw replenishment for my center to renew my energy, creativity, and to receive guidance for my work.

Cherished photographs of family and friends are carefully arranged on my desk. As I shuffle papers or reach for the phone the faces of loved ones remind me to STOP and b r e a t h e. I place my hand to my heart to feel connected to Spirit and express gratitude for the precious people in my life. Peace washes over me. I have slipped the confining bounds from Kronos to the open potentiality of Kairos for an instant. Each time I experience a momentary interlude and feel the shift, I return to the task at hand renewed, energized, and centered.

When I'm caught in traffic by a red light, rather than responding with frustration and angst, the forced STOP gives me the opportunity to consciously b r e a t h e and move towards a Kairos moment...or not. It's a conscious choice. However, with practice there is the possibility for the shift to become an automatic response.

However, there are definitely instances when I am less than present and I stay locked in Kronos with angst and frustration as tenacious companions. To receive the full benefits a spiritual practice must be engaged regularly. Belle Cœur spirituality invites your creativity and inventiveness to discover, create, and foster practices that will best serve your needs.

Find your still point within. As you prepare to begin the next section of this book to contemplate how to inhabit the changing seasons with sacred awareness, you're invited to pause now in this present moment.

Place your hand over your heart and b r e a t h e. Inhale through your nose. Exhale through your mouth. Do this slowly five times. Close your eyes if you wish. With each breath, envision yourself syncopating your heartbeat with the heartbeat of the Beloved as you regulate your pulse with pace of Peace.

When you return to the present moment notice the overall effects of this common, simple, universal practice. Most importantly notice your bodily response to the distinct difference between your sense of Kronos and Kairos time.

This simple practice is only a starting place. The full invitation is to reach beyond self-imposed, habitual, and limited boundaries. Contemplate the countless and creative ways you can begin to embrace the spiritual peace within your own soul, as you navigate the changing seasons with Kairos awareness.

The Moon and Her Cycles

*Each month
when the moon was full
I let my long braid
fall loose and free.*

Book VI Seasonal Inspiration

*I suffered fits of crying
and my body swelled.
(I&H: 34)*

As the earth turns 'round and we move through the seasons we can't ignore the power and pull of the moon. It's scientific fact that the moon's cycles have a direct effect upon the changing oceanic tides. Interestingly, human bodies contain the same proportion of water as the seas covering the earth. These facts seem to explain why people, like the oceanic tides, also experience the physical and emotional effects of the moon according to her changing cycles.

The light of the moon and her gravitational pull, have the power to create myriad outcomes. Before electricity was invented it was common for women to experience their menstrual cycles according to the twenty-eight day cycle of the moon. Menstruation began in sync with the full moon. Women today that live together in community, or families where there two or more women under the same roof, often experience their periods at the same time in tandem with the full moon.

Women's bodies, psyches, and spirits are it seems, somehow inextricably connected to the moon and her rhythms. In ancient times women were the calendar keepers. They were healers and midwives, shamans, and priestesses. They understood that the power and pull of the moon's monthly cycle had a correlation with the planting of crops, times for hunting, and for celebrating ritual.

The Way of Belle Cœur

Fireman, paramedics, police and hospital workers understand how the full moon impacts sociological behavior in relationship to increased crimes and violence. The word, *lunacy*, speaks to the power of the moon and its impact on the shadow side of human nature. The new moon is another cycle where there are reports of a similar but lesser degree of instances of aberrant behavior. Curiously, the full and new moon cycles seem to also influence the occurrence of earthquakes.

Just as there is a shadow side to behavior patterns during the full and new moon, there is also documentation of many instances of blessing. Fishermen have expressed how their catches are most abundant during a full moon and for centuries astrologers have proposed that intentions made during a new moon can bring about fruition with the arrival of a full moon.

Belle Cœur spirituality incorporates the importance of the moon holistically. We stay consciously connected with the moon's cycles as we follow her ever-changing face and potency throughout each month. The practice of moon awareness is not rooted in magical thinking. Intentional awareness of the moon and her cycles provides a reconnection with ancient ancestral feminine wisdom that has been lost over the centuries.

The lunar month represents the triple goddess in this way: The crescent moon represents the Maiden. The full moon represents the Mother. The new moon correlates with the Crone. Each month the moon decreases (wanes) and also waxes (increases).

Book VI Seasonal Inspiration

Belle Cœur spirituality regards the moon as one of Creation's great mysteries. She is a conduit for poetic inspiration, a source of energy, mystical light, and meaning for our lives. She is a luminous spiritual and planetary tool.

The moon, with regard to Christian symbology and iconography, represents Mary (Wisdom Sophia). The Mother often appears in artworks and sculptures standing atop a waning crescent moon. The waning moon symbolically reflects the Old Testament. Mary is the "God bringer," the Mother of God. She ushers in the new. Her stance on the waning moon signifies her majesty and her transcendence of time and space.

In the Book of Revelation we are familiar with the passage: *"…a woman clothed with the sun, with the moon under her feet, and on her head a crown of twelve stars."* (Rev 12:1)

Theologians hold various beliefs with regard to the woman that is represented in this Scripture passage. Many believe the woman referred to is Mary. Others believe she represents Israel and Christ is birthed through her. The moon is thought to be the symbol for the seasons and ever changing time. The woman stands on top of the moon, as a sign of constancy and strength.

As you explore the seasons and refer to the Belle Coeur perpetual calendar please note the following:

- ❖ *The phases of the waxing crescent and new moon invite you to go inward. These two phases support the experiences of solitude, conscious intention, self-reflection, and discernment.*

The Way of Belle Cœur

❖ *The phase of the full moon and waning crescent are a period to be more extroverted. This cycle is the time for collaboration, to be task-oriented, to bring things to fruition, and experience community.*

As you begin to explore the following section please note that each month's moon has been given a name. The names refer to the energy of the moon according to the natural progression through the seasons. You're encouraged to integrate moon awareness into your spiritual practice.

Dominions and Graces Through the Seasons

Certain facets of the Way of Belle Cœur are inspired by wisdom contained within the ancient, sacred, mystery texts, *Dominions and Graces*, as described in *Ink and Honey*.

(*I&H*: 50, 52, 53, 54, 59, 81, 151, 188, 439, 482).

While we journey through the four seasons the various properties and elements of Winter, Spring, Summer, and Autumn as described in the various volumes of *Dominions and Graces*, are provided within this section for your reflection.

Book VI Seasonal Inspiration

Monthly Reflections

A Journey Through the Seasons of the Year

> *"You must use your senses*
> *to retrieve what God*
> *has coded in the sky,*
> *placed within the turn*
> *of the seasons, and hidden*
> *with the acorn*
> *and the bark of the tree."*
> (*I&H:* 76)

The following seasonal, month-by-month, calendar provides simple creative and spiritual practices. Sojourn through the year with Kairos time awareness, and notice how you experience the pull of the moon throughout her ever-changing phases. References for Scripture and *Ink and Honey* passages are provided each month for the spiritual practice of lectio divina. Engage your sacred imagination to create additional personal practices, prayers, and creative experiences to enrich your annual journey through the seasons.

Winter

***

...the seasons fell one

The Way of Belle Cœur

> *upon another.*
> *Scorching summer*
> *became radiant autumn*
> *that soon gave way*
> *to barren winter.*
> (*I&H:* p. 32)

Winter is the season that invites your Belle Cœur heart to rest within the stillness of the Divine Presence. The invitation for the winter months is to cocoon your creative heart and spirit. Create a space, within your soul and daily life, for new visions to gestate while you prayerfully prepare for the transformation of the earth that will arrive in spring. The spirit of Beatrice invites you to come closer to the hearth.

To nurture your body, mind, and soul with comfort this winter you may want to create a cocoon with soft blankets and pillows tucked within a special corner of your home. Imagine this as your gestation space where you'll receive spiritual and physical sustenance throughout the long nights and cold days of winter.

Additionally, prepare a basket or other container filled with things to inspire your creative heart and spirit and items that bless you with comfort. Suggestions include: a journal and your favorite writing tools, a book of prayers, your Bible and other sacred texts, or a book of cherished poems. You may wish to also include dark chocolate, your reading glasses, and a stack of seasonal postcards for writing little notes to friends, and anything else you feel called to add to your winter basket.

Book VI Seasonal Inspiration

Light a candle, put on your favorite music, wrap yourself in your shawl, and crawl into your cocoon near the hearth to contemplate the sacredness of the season. Fill your journal with your ideas and visions throughout the winter months while the snow falls and the wind blows outside your window.

The sacred Advent and Christmas seasons followed by the commencement of the New Year and Epiphany make winter especially meaningful as a time of promise, and prophecy. Essential to the Way of Belle Cœur's observance and celebration of the Advent and Christmas seasons is the spiritual presence of Mary (Wisdom Sophia), the mother of our Beloved. She offers the reminder of the importance of the awareness and intentional responsiveness to God's call and models how to live prayerfully in times of expectancy and waiting. She is the taproot of Holy Wisdom as Christ's mother and his first teacher.

Imagine the experience of reconnection with the miracle of your sacred imagination. Contemplate the sacred life-arts and creative projects you've been longing to explore and notice your dreams during winter's season of hibernation.

Winter invites pause, rest, and renewal. Embrace the opportunity to contemplate the true meaning of Advent and Christmas as you imagine the sacred mystery of *the Beloved being born within you.*

Prayer, reflection, ritual, and celebration are beacons of light during the darkest months of the year. Cocoon yourself to prayerfully witness the subtle and profound mysteries of winter's beauty.

The Way of Belle Cœur

*Dominions and Graces
Volume III: FIRE
Heart ~ **Winter** ~ Night
Gestation ~ Spider ~ Hawthorne ~
Transformation
Ashes ~ Burning Logs
~ Smoke ~ Gold.
(I&H: 63)*

You're invited to contemplate the meanings of winter and the properties of fire. Create a visual prayer collage to reflect your interpretation of winter and fire. Meditate upon your visual prayer and write a poem as another form of expression, while you grow your winter's wisdom.

December

***

*This season of Advent brings
a mood of sweet anticipation…
We have been helping the nuns
arrange boughs of pine,
bouquets of rosemary,
and red-berried holly branches
all about in preparation for Noël.
(I&H: 197)*

Pomegranate Moon

Advent is the spiritual season centered around preparation, hope, reflection and the anticipation of Christmas and the celebration of the birth of the Beloved. Advent is also defined as the liturgical period preceding Christmas, beginning in Western churches on the fourth Sunday before Christmas and in Eastern (Orthodox) churches in mid-November.

During the Advent season the hours of daylight grow exceedingly shorter. After the winter solstice the number of hours of light will slowly begin to increase day by day. The cycle of light and dark is eternal as the earth turns and the circumstances of our personal lives evolve and change.

Advent's darkness offers a womblike cocoon where you are invited to wait and to ponder what is gestating within your heart and spirit. For those with Christ-centered faith, it's a prayerful time to anticipate the return of Light to the world through the celebration of Jesus' birth.

December offers a gift of deep, dark, velvety interior spaciousness. This is the season when many of God's creatures hibernate. Meanwhile the current culture carries on in a way that is counter to our human, primal, animal nature for this time of year. Long dark nights stir our deepest longings for rest and renewal. All the while the media and advertisers encourage shopping and frenetic material consumption in preparation for the holidays.

Belle Cœur spirituality invites a more reflective and contemplative entry into the sacred season to explore the qualities and questions of inner holy longing and expectant waiting. Hope eternal is at the

The Way of Belle Cœur

heart of things as darkness moves toward the promise of the light's return with the birth of the Christ Child and the turning of the earth.

The Christ Child... I write this and with the ears of my heart I hear:

Awaken the sacred child that lives within your spirit. Invite your child-self to reveal your life through the lens of wonder, innocence, and awe. Embrace those who cross your path as though you are encountering them for the first time. Be Love in the world. Be the child who knows joy and imagines possibility without limitations through the impulse of every new idea and creative vision. While you await the birth of Jesus, become reacquainted with the sacred child that lives within you. Dream, explore, express, and re-imagine your life to be full with new potential. Be ready to step into innovative ways of living and being when the Light returns to the world. Celebrate this holy season as a sacred child of God.

The spiritual gifts of wonder and awe are part and parcel of every human's birthright. These qualities are meant to endure throughout life's journey, yet, somehow along the way it's easy to lose the connection, to embrace perceived constraints associated with adult responsibilities. Advent calls us to wakefulness and the remembrance of our Divine nature.

Reflect

John 1: 1-5

- ❖ Inspired by December's Scripture, reflect upon the contrast of Light and darkness and

the meaning these concepts hold for your life with regard to personal experience and understanding.
- When you contemplate the nature of "the Word" as expressed in John's Scripture, what images, feelings, and questions arise?
- In what creative way can you fully contemplate and experience Mary's role as Holy Wisdom and Christ's first teacher?
- How does it feel to imagine the coming of Christ as the embodiment of the indwelling Divine Presence within *your* heart and soul?
- Recall a Christmas memory from your earliest recollection that is charged with the feelings of wonder and awe. How might you re-engage this moment from your youth to serve you now?
- When you were a child did you create gifts, small offerings (les petits cadeaux de Noël) of love to give away to others at Christmas time? How would it feel to give something created by the work of your hands and heart? (*I&H:* p. 234)
- When you were a child did you have a dream or vision that felt very important? What small thing might you do this month to inspire a new dream or reactivate a long forgotten dream?
- Write a prayer through the voice of "wonder" that lives within your heart.

Express

As you cocoon to nourish the hopes, dreams and/or visions you're longing birth in your life, here is a simple winter ritual:

A Winter Prayer Jar Materials

- ❖ A small glass jar with lid
- ❖ An image to represent what you hope to bring forth in the spring (this can be a photograph or an image torn from a magazine).
- ❖ A sheet of paper
- ❖ Pen
- ❖ Glue stick
- ❖ Seeds (any kind of seed will work.... even something from your spice drawer)

Process

Glue the image representing your intention to the piece of paper. Take a deep breath. Breathe in peace and calm. Exhale whatever you need to release in the present moment; anxiety, doubt, fear, etc.

Spend some time meditating with the image. Notice the feelings that arise. Write your intention and prayer on the paper. Fold the paper and place it in the jar. Add the seeds to symbolically represent how your dream will grow to fruition in spring. Seal the jar with the lid.

Book VI Seasonal Inspiration

Find a meaningful place to bury your jar...in your yard, a nearby park, or a pot of earth. Feel the affirmation that you are incubating your winter's prayer during this season of cocooning and hibernation.

༺☙

Periodically, throughout the winter months, reflect upon your evolving process and thoughts regarding your visions and intentions. Make notations and a collage as a visual prayer to express what has been seeded within you. Trust that in the darkest time of the year there is transformation happening beneath the surface. Your vision, your winter's prayer will break forth with the return of the light in the spring. During the Advent and Christmas seasons, cocoon and give your Self the permission to withdraw from life's busyness to reflect upon the deepest Mysteries of this wondrous and holy time.

January

***

The New Year has begun.
January's cold wind blows
through the crevices
in the monastery walls without mercy,
and though we are grateful
for this shelter,
we miss Belle Cœur

our true home.
(*I&H:* p. 257)

Sentry Moon

You have crossed the threshold into a New Year. Doorways, portals, windows, and thresholds symbolize possibility and the potential for discovery. The invitation this month is to become attentive to the various openings that appear for your exploration within ordinary circumstances.

Notice the physical characteristics of the actual doorways and portals you encounter in daily life and contemplate the various metaphorical "inner" doorways that may be currently open, beginning to open, or closed within you.

- ❖ Are there new places you're longing to explore?
- ❖ Are there hidden forgotten passions locked away awaiting your re-visitation?
- ❖ What portals call forth your courage and commitment before your step into new terrain?
- ❖ How would it feel to fully enter the door of Mystery that leads to your deepest longing?

Imagine the opportunities that Goscelin might have missed had she not gathered her courage to enter the doorway to Brother Paul's hidden room for the first time. When she bravely stepped through that doorway she opened her heart to a world of possibility to become a scribe that would eventually "grow the wisdom." (*I&H*: 23, 46)

Reflect

Revelation 3:20

- ❖ What comes to mind and heart when you imagine hearing a knock at the front door of your home? You open it, and there you find Jesus awaiting you. How do you respond? How do you welcome him? What does He offer to you?
- ❖ When I reflect on the doorways and thresholds I have crossed during my life I recall and feel....
- ❖ A door that has been calling me to open it for some time could lead to...
- ❖ I have resisted opening this door because...
- ❖ The door I would like to close behind me is...
- ❖ When I imagine opening new doors I feel...
- ❖ My creativity and spirit are inspired when I open the door to...
- ❖ As the New Year begins I'm standing at a threshold leading me to...

Express

Take some quiet time for yourself. Gather together colored markers, pencils, or crayons, your pen, and journal. Collect a few magazines. Home décor magazines are especially good for this exercise. A glue stick and scissors will also be helpful to have nearby.

Rest in the stillness of the moment. Close your eyes, and contemplate three unique doorways you've encountered over time. These may be actual physical portals or metaphorical doors that have led you to an inner opening or transformational experience.

Your choice of doorways may include the following and feel free to choose other doors that have been especially important to you.

- ❖ The door of revelation that opens to reveal your creative heart and spirit.
- ❖ The door of mystery that opens to your biggest question at this moment in time.
- ❖ The door of potential that opens to your future.
- ❖ The door of closure that you have chosen to lock behind you.

Spend some time drawing your various doorways in your journal or you may wish to look through magazines to choose an image for representation. Paste these on individual pages in your journal. Use crayons or markers to embellish the pages or to record inspirations that may arise. Write a story about each door. Give each door a title. Record the wisdom you glean through this exercise in your codex.

Selected references pertaining to doorways (*I&H*: 12, 83, 126, 328, 344, 486)

Prayer

Beloved, it has been said, "When one door closes, another door opens." I pray for the courage to close doors that no longer lead to where I am called to go. Through grace, I pray to open new doors, to reveal your presence within my heart and spirit. Amen

Book VI Seasonal Inspiration

February

***

*I close my eyes to enter
the honey hive of my heart.*
(I&H: 1)

Hearth Moon

The human heart is one of the greatest mysteries we can ponder. The heart begins beating four weeks after conception and continues until death. The physical thumping of the heart keeps an ever-changing rhythm and tempo in syncopation with how we move, think and feel. Our innermost creative passions also influence the cadence of our heartbeat and pulse.

The heart and soul are connected. When you see the face of someone you love you feel affection as a palpable warmth within your chest, your pulse grows faster. When you grieve a loss you are aware of the suffering and pain at the very center of your being, at the heart of the matter. A broken heart is not only a descriptive phrase it's a visceral response in direct relationship with the experiences of grief, betrayal, loss, and abandonment.

Bliss, those moments when you meld into the flow of the Spirit, when you are creatively and soulfully engaged from the place of your deepest understanding and joy, in those instances your heart thrums praise for the Beloved. The ecstatic heart's rhythm is also unique in response to human recognition of the Divine Presence within.

The Way of Belle Cœur

This month's invitation is to enter into heart space with your creative spirit and passions. Spring appears to be closer on the horizon with the eternal promise of resurrection and new life. Your heart is a sacred vessel and wellspring for your creative dreams, visions, and inspirations. In preparation for the returning light and promise that accompanies the greening time reflect and reconnect to what makes your heart sing.

Selected references pertaining to the heart: (*I&H:* 10, 11, 12, 47, 86, 107, 113, 125, 152, 224. 267, 314, 355, 448)

Reflect

Ezekiel 11:19

- ❖ When you reflect upon this month's Scripture, how do you imagine your experience of a "*singleness of heart*" and "*new spirit*" as gifts from the Beloved?
- ❖ How would you describe your "*heart of stone*" and "*heart of flesh?*"
- ❖ When I contemplate the concept of "my beloveds" I think of…
- ❖ The last time I felt my heart meld with the flow of the Spirit was….
- ❖ My greatest source of creative inspiration comes from…
- ❖ I feel most connected to life's pulse when I…

- ❖ When I imagine the tune to my Divine Song is it an operatic aria, a ballad, a lament, a rap, a torch song or something else?
- ❖ The lyrics to my Divine Song go like this...

Express

Choose a favorite box, bowl, basket, or other container to represent your inner heart space. Place it where you will see it often throughout the day. Arrange your heart space reliquary on a scarf or cloth and add a candle nearby.

This month as a daily or weekly practice, light the candle and place your hands over your heart to feel its rhythmic pulse as it nourishes your body *and* soul. Offer a prayer of gratitude for the miracle of your heart while you contemplate your life as God's gift. Explore the questions and longings you carry within you. Meditate upon the persons, places, and work or activities that nourish and speak to your heart.

Periodically add a cherished photograph, an inspirational image from a magazine, a slip of paper with a quotation or poem, or other small object or something from nature to nurture your "heart-space." Throughout the month fill your sacred container with symbolic representations of the people, moments, creative inspiration, and worldly pastimes that inspire your heart's divine song. Add a symbol to represent God's love and presence within you as a blessing for all that your heart-space holds.

The invitation is to pause, reflect on the power of love and life within you, and to nurture your passions and longings with prayerful attention and intention to bring forth the full expression of your Divine Song.

Prayer

Place your hands over your heart as you pray the following prayer:

Beloved, you bless every moment of life with the ever-present reminder of your Love, my beating heart. You filled my heart and soul before my birth with a Divine Song that is uniquely my own. Help me to open my heart wide to share my song with confidence, passion, and delight. I pray for my voice to join with others to sing beauty, healing and love into the heart of our world. Amen

Spring

***

Spring winds blow the trees,
and the season of seeding
sets Creation in motion.
(*I&H*: 129)

Saints and poets have found inspiration in the garden. The word garden for some evokes a mental image of a peaceful place, a haven and sanctuary. It is a Belle Cœur tradition to keep a small dish garden as a sacred practice and a flourishing expression of Creation.

Weeds soon consume gardens that are left untended or forgotten. Weeds are an all too familiar sight and anyone who has ever cared for a garden knows how tenacious weeds can be.

As spring begins I invite you to consider the question: *How does your garden grow?* Not only the garden outside your window, but also the garden of your spirit.

Reflect

Isaiah 58:11

- If you were to place a statue or work of art upon the soil of your "interior" garden what would it represent?
- What do you long to seed, cultivate, and nurture to grow to fruition?
- How might you make a sanctuary of your interior world?
- Is there a neglected corner of your interior garden that is overgrown? What are the weeds in your garden made of.... too much busyness, boredom, doubt?
- Is there a missing ingredient from your life that you must add to nurture the soil of your spirit, to grow your longings and visions to fruition?

Express

Perhaps it's time to examine a long ignored corner of your heart and soul to determine what particular aspects of your life are no longer serving you. The removal of weeds from the garden creates space for the surrounding healthy and vibrant life to grow to full bloom.

Choose a large flowerpot or clay vessel and fill it with soil. Place it on your patio, balcony, or a sunlit patch on your lawn. Seed the earth with something you will cultivate, nurture and grow throughout the spring and summer... a plant, flower, fruit, or vegetable. As you tend this living example of God's creation, reflect on the possibilities for the growth of the interior garden of your soul. Invite the spirit of Helvide to assist you.

- ❖ What does your spirit require to grow and thrive?
- ❖ How might you make subtle and profound changes in your life to accommodate your hopes and dreams, to grow your wisdom?

Later in the year, with autumn's arrival, you may be surprised to discover a bountiful harvest of blessings, not only in your own backyard, but within your radiant spirit, as well.

Dominions and Graces
Volume II: AIR
*Breath ~ **Spring** ~ Dawn ~ Seeding ~*
Honeybee ~ Thistle ~The Mind ~ Feather

Book VI Seasonal Inspiration

~ Wind Moving Through the Trees ~ Roses ~ Silver
(I&H: 63)

March

***

*In spring we wove together:
clover, ivy, bright green grasses,
and strips of
colorful stained cloth
blessed with our prayers.*
(I&H: 283)

Birthing Moon

The nesting season has begun. The robins and sparrows are busy gathering twigs, dried grass, and the odd bit of string or fluff to weave together to create a home that will become the hatching and birthing chamber for their young. If you have the opportunity observe a bird as she selects her nesting materials. Notice how she appears to pick and choose carefully.

Her sense of design is acute. She knows what she's looking for. Her intention is clear and exploration and discernment for the most worthy materials are part of the process. Once her efforts have produced the comforting shelter and space she needs, she lays her eggs and then tends them with rapt attention until at last they open to reveal the new life within.

The Way of Belle Cœur

In winter you were cocooned to gestate your projects, dreams, and visions. The invitation for March is to refurbish your nest in preparation for new spiritual revelations and forms of creative expression. Contemplate what your uniquely personal nest for hatching and birthing will look like. What preparations for new life are calling to you as spring returns with her annual promise of increasing light and fecundity?

Reflect

Ezekiel 31:6

- When you contemplate the images within the Scripture above, how are you inspired?
- How does nature inform your spirituality?
- What does your nest for the incubation of your creative projects look like?
- March is typically a windy month. Are the winds of change blowing in your life this season? How will you respond?
- Is there a particular bird that inspires your spirit? Write a poem to express your inspiration.
- In this season of resurrection what facets of your life and spirit are in need of renewal and sacred attention?
- A project or dream I have carried for a long time that is ready to be hatched is…

Express

Walk through your living space to discern a place for you to nest this spring. You may want to settle near a window where you can observe Creation as she awakens from winter's sleep. Create a comfy resting place, not unlike the way you cocooned for winter. Again, call upon Helvide's spirit and passion for nature to inspire you.

Add a variety of things to your nesting place including: stones, representations of the elements (fire, water, air, and earth), and seasonal inspirational books to reflect how spring informs your spirit. Spring is a good season to begin a new journal. Gather simple art supplies; a glue stick, scissors, colored pens or pencils and put them in a basket to keep ready nearby.

When you're settled into your spring nest, make a sketch in your journal of your interior garden.

- ❖ What do you long to seed and grow within your creative heart and spirit?
- ❖ Where are there patches of weeds that need to be removed?
- ❖ How will you cultivate and nurture your seedlings of new ideas and inspirations?

Refer to your garden sketch frequently as spring unfolds to make any necessary adjustments to ensure a bountiful harvest.

Make a walking meditation in nature. Fill a bag with twigs, moss, vines and grasses. Look for things that catch your eye from a bird's eye view. Arrange your findings and begin to weave and shape them into a nest. Choose a personal symbol to place in your nest as a representation of what you are committed to birth this spring. Place your nest where you will often see it as a reminder that you are creative and your spirit is fertile with new life and possibility. Contemplate what the words *nest* and *birthing* mean for you.

Prayer

As you pray, place your hands in a cupped and open position, as if you are holding your nest containing your precious egg of promise.

Beloved Creator of the greening time, You bless me with inspiration for new life, creativity, possibility, and the fulfillment of my purpose. Help me to persevere and be attentive to the new life and creation I long to birth in the world. May this season of renewal yield the fulfillment of my hopes and dreams in service to Love. Amen

April

***

*The early morning was likened
to spring, a time of new beginnings,
the hours of resurrection*

Book VI Seasonal Inspiration

> *where gratitude for*
> *another day of living*
> *was at the center.*
> (*I&H*: 188)

River Moon

April showers often become a deluge. Spring storms blow across the landscape to shake loose all that is no longer serves natural growth, while dried creek beds and trickling streams fill to their banks. Everything becomes glistening, fresh, and renewed after the rain has ceased.

There is an errant quality within April's simple rhythm. It is a month that often still holds a remnant of winter's chill combined with the declaration of spring that grows stronger with each passing day. The senses long for the sight of the green shoots and first crocus and daffodil as they push through the earth after their long winter's sleep.

Wisdom Sophia's creative hand is everywhere. Animals birth their young. Luminous green leaves begin to unfurl from gnarly branches. The days grow brighter as the sunlight drenches the awakening earth with nourishment from the heavens.

There are blessings that await you on your morning walk. May your stride quicken as April spreads her promises at your feet with the invitation to awaken and revel in the splendor of resurrection and the gifts of Creation.

Reflect

Acts 14:17

- ❖ In what way(s) does your spirit thirst for a refreshing drink from the well of God's grace?
- ❖ What is beginning to flourish and with cultivation will thrive in summer?
- ❖ What aspect of your Self or your life is God inviting you to resurrect?
- ❖ Where in your life do you long for renewal?

Express

- ❖ Gather rainwater from the spring rains in a container. Before your morning shower, pour the water from the heavens over your head with a blessing for the new day. Contemplate God's gifts of Creation and the blessing of rain.
- ❖ Create a visual prayer collage to express your interpretation of the transition from winter to spring.

Prayer

Stand barefoot on the earth while you offer the following prayer:

Beloved, you bless us with Creation's splendor and renewal as spring arrives. We walk with you along the Via

Book VI Seasonal Inspiration

Dolorosa to Calvary as faithful witnesses of your selfless, lasting gift for humankind. We remember and reflect upon the cross, the tomb and ultimately your living promise of resurrection.

I pray to slow down this season, to open my eyes to behold the miracle of spring as she births abundant new life. Let me encounter your Love everywhere I turn. I will listen for your whisper within the gentle breeze and experience your touch when I bow my head to the oncoming rain.

My heart sings praises to you, for the miracle of Life and your assurance of Life Everlasting. Amen

May

***

*In spring Comtesse and I
went to the meadow
where we wove crowns
from daisies and clover.*
(*I&H*: 8)

Rose Moon

You enter into the heart of spring as May begins. The earth is once again frocked in her green dress. April's rains have awakened the colors of May's golden daffodils and purple iris. The garden flourishes and the light has fully returned.

The days grow longer while nights are starlit and blessed with the sounds of creatures singing their

The Way of Belle Cœur

praises to Creation herself. This is a holy, generative, life-giving season.

May is also traditionally known as Mary's month. The Ascension, the commemoration of the time when Mary and the women gathered with the apostles in the upper room for prayer, is a Marian celebration. It often falls in May, the Saturday after the celebration of the Ascension of Christ. The commemoration of the Visitation on May 31st is the acknowledgement of the important time when Mary pregnant with Jesus, visited her cousin, Elizabeth, while she was carrying John the Baptist.

This is a month to make crowns from flowers, and to revisit praying the Rosary as spiritual practice. May is bursting forth with Creation's brightest colors, the miracle of the rainbow, and the birth of new life in myriad forms. The Sacred Feminine is alive and visible for all to see!

Reflect

Luke 1:41

- ❖ How do you relate to Mary, the Mother of Jesus?
- ❖ How does her life's journey inform, inspire, or unsettle you?
- ❖ In this season when the Sacred Feminine is so readily visible within Creation, how do you draw upon her energy to feed your spirit?

- ❖ What invitation awaits you within the extended hours of daylight?

Express

- ❖ Use flowers from your garden or silk flowers to create a crown to honor Mary, Queen of the Angels. You may place the crown upon your altar or make a small crown to adorn a statue of the Blessed Mother.

Prayer

Hold a bouquet of flowers you will place upon your altar as you offer this prayer:

Sophia, Mother of Jesus, Holy Wisdom, Creatrix and Giver of Life, I offer these flowers as a living symbol of your blessing of Sacred Feminine presence throughout Creation. You inspire my heart to honor and cherish all you represent. I pray to grow my wisdom, enriched by your example of how to respond to God's call, to be strong in the face of adversity, and grow in grace through faith and devotion. As May reveals her particular splendor I celebrate you, Mother of us all, and give thanks for womanhood and your presence within all life. Amen

The Way of Belle Cœur

Summer

***

*For hours I walked
to the side of the narrow road
where the tall
summer grasses
and weeds hid me.
(I&H: 16)*

The bees are making honey in the hive and the garden is dressed in the colors of fruition. We celebrate the summer solstice as the daylight hours reach their pinnacle then begin to wane. Summer invites a paradox of movement and reverie. All of Creation is vibrantly alive with full bloom frequency. Messages of holy inspiration are everywhere. Be an active participant. Open your senses to fully experience the world around you.

Listen to the robin sing her love song to her mate from the treetop. Catch the sweet scent of jasmine on the warm breeze. Taste the juicy strawberries from the garden at the peak of ripeness. Take in the sight of the clouds when they darken on the horizon with the promise of rain. Put your hand to your chest and feel your heartbeat as you make your morning walk through the park. You are part of summer's phantasmagoria.

The intense sunlight, hot afternoons, and sultry evenings invite leisure and lingering. Summer invites you to ponder your heart's longings while you rest in the Divine Presence through nature's symphony of life.

Like Goscelin in the story of *Ink and Honey*, when she set out one summer's day from her home to find Belle

Book VI Seasonal Inspiration

Cœur, pilgrimage often calls the seeker to step on to the Holy Road as June arrives. Summer invites reconnection with places and also the people in our lives.

The long languid days of summer pass quickly and soon give way to the colors of autumn. Receive the blessings of the season of high noon and illuminate your life with renewal to last throughout the year.

Dominions and Graces
*Volume IV: WATER Blood ~ **Summer** ~ Day*
~ Tending ~ Fish ~ Clover
~The Emotions ~ Shell ~ Thunder ~ Rain ~ Green.
(I&H: 63)

You're invited to contemplate your personal understanding of summer's gifts. Engage your sacred imagination and create a visual prayer collage to express the complex layers of summer's gifts. Grow your wisdom while nature reveals her full bloom grandeur.

June

***

"Our book filled
with our stories,
will become a map
for the ones who

The Way of Belle Cœur

will come after us."
(I&H: 202)

Solo Moon

Before the invention of the GPS, a printed map was the primary tool for guidance from one place to another. There is a quality of mysterious beauty within the pages of a world atlas. Exotic names of faraway countries set atop the colorfully portrayed network of roads and highways assumes the appearance of a topographical crazy quilt, while an unfurled road map inspires the desire to set out for an adventure to explore new destinations and terrain.

Belle Cœur spirituality, as we have learned, incorporates a circular form of cartography, a template with four pathways, four chambers, and compass at the center. Your sacred practices, life experiences, and relationships create your personal cartography.

You are the cartographer of your life. Cartographers (map-makers) use their artistic skills to create accurate representations of the planet's geography. The vocabulary of map-making has a cadence and rhythm all its own. Latitude, longitude, and topography are words that evoke wanderlust and the desire for exploration.

The invitation for June is to travel *inward* to explore the map of your life. Become acquainted with your soul's image of the world as revealed to you through your sacred imagination.

Let June show you new terrain within your creative heart and spirit. What map will you create to chart your course for the months ahead?

Book VI Seasonal Inspiration

Reflect

Jeremiah 29: 11

- When you imagine yourself as the cartographer of your life, what images arise to inspire you?
- Can you recall a time when you were lost and you used a map to find your way?
- Write about the process you follow when you chart a new course for your work or personal life. Is your experience rooted within your intuitive understanding or is it more linear, step-by-step?
- List the particulars of your ideal place to live, be, or visit.

Express

Draw a map of your life's journey. Include your mountain peak experiences and the deserts where you wandered in search of something more. Where did you discover oceans where you dove deeply seeking previously undiscovered treasure? How will you depict life's valleys and meadows, those moments in time where you enjoyed peace and serenity?

Use an old road map as background for a visual prayer collage to express the map of your soul. Select images from magazines and combine these with copies of personal photos to depict your passions, longings, fulfillments, and desires. When the collage is complete write about why you chose particular images/photos. How does your soul map inform your life today?

The Way of Belle Cœur

Imagine you could choose a symbol for your soul. What image would you choose to describe the essence of who you are? Draw it.

- If you could chart a new course to discover a new pathway for your life, what would it look like? Give the path a name.
- How will you travel your new road?
- What will you take along?
- What will you choose to leave behind to lighten your load?

Prayer

Blessed Mapmaker of my life's journey, you reveal my choices to explore various highways and byways of discovery as I walk the Holy Road, inwardly and outwardly. I long to wisely choose the paths that will serve my highest good and lead me to the fulfillment of my life's purpose. Inspire my exploration so I may journey ever closer to you to live the life you have imprinted on my soul. Amen.

July

***

*Pictures thronged
my imagining.
They scurried forth
like playful children
rushing out of doors*

Book VI Seasonal Inspiration

on a warm summer's day.
(*I&H:* 25)

Child's Moon

This month's invitation is the spiritual practice of holy play. The Beloved invites us to *become like little children*, to reconnect with the experience of seeing the world through a lens of wide-eyed innocence, and to respond with unbridled creativity and joy.

Summer evokes memories of childhood when time passed slowly and sunny days were spent out of doors, playing with friends, enjoying nature, and imaginative games and adventures. Belle Cœur spirituality encourages moments of play to engage your creativity, encounter feelings of hope and delight, and to ultimately renew your spirit.

Play is all too often the forgotten ingredient in the prescription for how to live a balanced life. Sometimes play is the missing link to stay in touch with wonder and awe. Belle Cœur spirituality encourages abundant time for play.

The conscious intention to play might even be considered a spiritual rite, a Sacrament of Play. The sacred life-art of holy play is the expression of deliberate creative exploration, and imagination for pure enjoyment.

God has blessed you with the boundless and inexhaustible instrument of the sacred imagination. This month, engage, imagine, and experience pastimes and playful encounters to quicken your spirit and inspire your creativity. Become like a little a child and rediscover how the Sacrament of Play feeds your soul.

The Way of Belle Cœur

Reflect

Matthew 18:2-4

- ❖ List your most cherished books from childhood. Copy the passages that continue to inspire you within the pages of your journal or codex.
- ❖ Rent and watch a favorite film from childhood. Write about what you rediscovered about yourself, your interests, and creative spirit as you watched it.
- ❖ Name your favorite childhood games. Invent a new game and give it a name or make a deck of collaged playing cards.
- ❖ Write about the colors that inspire you. Paint your colors in your journal or codex.
- ❖ Write about your most memorable girlhood summer experience.
- ❖ Paste a photo of your eight-year-old self in your journal. What playful wisdom does the young girl have to share with you? Have a dialogue with her in your journal
- ❖ Write a poem about how it feels to be playful. Draw a picture with crayons to accompany it.

Express

Choose from the following list or explore the playful inspiration that arises in your mind and heart and then with engage one or more playful experiences.

Book VI Seasonal Inspiration

Notice what you feel and how your creative spirit is inspired through play.

- ❖ There are many adult coloring books available in bookstores. Choose one and purchase a big box of crayons with all the colors. Spread a blanket under your favorite tree and spend the afternoon coloring. Notice the feelings that arise within you.
- ❖ Blow bubbles into the summer breeze.
- ❖ Bake cupcakes and decorate them the way you would have done as a child.
- ❖ Invite a child to join you and play a favorite board or card game from your childhood.
- ❖ Fly a kite in the park or at the beach.
- ❖ Make adult size mud pies or cakes. Decorate your creations with offerings from nature. a Photograph your creations and add it to your codex. Write about your experience.
- ❖ Go to your closet and put your clothes and accessories together in a playful way. Play "Dress-up." Invent your alter ego.
- ❖ Catch fireflies and make s'mores.

Prayer

Creator of all that can be imagined, you, in your playfulness created the dragonfly and rainbow, the flying fish and the man in the moon. Help me to take time to play in your miraculous world. Let me recall what being young at heart truly means. *I open my heart to become more playful, to experience joy and wonder, and to celebrate joy.* Amen.

August

***

*The sun was about
to kiss the hills,
though the air
was still hot
and my cheeks burned.*
(*I&H:* 17)

Chrism Moon

August is the culmination and pinnacle of summer as we begin to prepare to make the turn towards autumn. God's hand is visible everywhere. Tree branches are heavy with young apples that will ripen for the autumn harvest during the weeks ahead. Fledgling birds have long since taken flight and vacant nests are shaken loose by the shifting wind.

We are in the season of in-between. August is the bridge that gently carries us from summer's fecundity to autumn's glory. In the northern places a fleeting chill rides the breeze, a portend to what is just around the corner.

August is the harbinger that announces the season's approaching change. Creation's invitation is to reflect and savor the last golden days of summer. This month of in between yields sun-kissed afternoons and night skies filled with shooting stars, while the earth turns round towards September and the waning time.

Reflect

Genesis 8:22

- If you were to give a title to this year's season of summer, what would you name it?
- As you anticipate the arrival of autumn what would you like to harvest?
- Contemplate your life's bountiful abundance. What would you like to share with others?
- In what areas of your life are you fully experiencing a season of in between?

Express

- Create a visual prayer collage in your journal or codex to express the concept of transition, as you experience the changing seasons.
- Contemplate if there are adjustments to be made within your environment such as: the rearrangement of furnishings, artwork, or the repurposing of various belongings during the season of in between.

Prayer

Beloved, I am grateful for the gifts that arrive with August's final exhale of summer, as the earth prepares for autumn's changes. Help me to remember to slow down to fully appreciate the subtle blessings that nature offers at this bittersweet moment of in between. While you turn Creation round to autumn, I take pause in wonder and awe and give thanks. Amen

Autumn

***

Autumn is a Sabbath season.
(I&H: 64)

Autumn is often accompanied by feelings of melancholy and nostalgia. Memories of years gone by seem to color the landscape of the heart, the way the russet and golden leaves color the earth.

It is also a fecund season with abundant gifts for the body and spirit. Autumn offers a harvest for aspects of life that are rich and plentiful with possibility, the result of creative and spiritual efforts extended throughout the previous seasons.

When the leaves begin to fall you are reminded to look at your life through autumn's lens. What is ripe for your inner harvest? How will you share your wisdom and creativity as offerings of blessing for others?

While the daylight hours wane and the evening hours grow longer, an invitation emerges. Imagine your journal as a logbook. Make notes in the margins (like a mariner's reference points) to document your swift passage through autumn to winter.

Late afternoon walks in nature feed your soul while you observe Creation's myriad changes that arrived while no one was watching. It's helpful for orientation to revisit the description of autumn in Dominions and Graces...

Autumn, the waning season of shedding corresponds to dusk. The purpose is the gathering and harvest of nature's bounty. All that has grown to fruition must now be collected and shared with the community. The earth gives of herself and in return she is tended by those she so generously serves.

Observe the creatures as they prepare for winter. Notice their frantic running about as they gather acorn and leaf. Dens and nests are warmed and fortified, and then all of nature grows still. God invites all of creation to rest and replenish what has been spent. Autumn is a Sabbath season. Gratitude is the prayer. Take stock of the blessings received, and succumb to tranquility. It is the dusk of the year, and the darkest months approach, heralded by the North Wind as she takes the remaining leaves from the trees. It is a time for sweet reverie, appreciation, and preparation as all the earth approaches the season of silence and gestation. (I&H: 64-65)

The red squirrels with their curled furry tails frantically scurry from branch to rooftop then race down the gutter spout. Their intuitive inner guidance nudges them on, "Prepare your house! Get ready!"

Geese fly overhead in their ancient V formation. They often soar above the house at night while they plaintively call to one another, lest one of their flock should be lost in the dark velvet sky. The same Guiding Voice that instructs the squirrels and geese to prepare for change is available for you.

There are signs of change everywhere. Meanwhile, the world continues to evolve day by day. Everything on the planet is moving through a portal of transformation and the experience sometimes feels unsettling, disorienting, chaotic, and challenging.

Autumn encourages a season of fervent prayer for courage to embrace change in all its complexity, and to seek the hidden beauty within the increasing darkness. In the depths of not knowing and at the threshold of change there lies the opportunity for both subtle and profound transformation. Let us seek the lesser-known shore as the destination for our autumn journey.

Autumn Embrace
Capture the beauty of the season

- ❖ Craft an autumn journal. Curate autumn's splendor within the pages.
- ❖ Take an afternoon walk with your camera and capture photos of fallen leaves, wet shiny stones, mossy pathways, piles of acorns, spider's webs,

Book VI Seasonal Inspiration

ripe orange pumpkins, busy squirrels, migrating birds. Paste these images in your journal.
- ❖ Paint your prayers in autumn colors.
- ❖ Choose a forgotten family favorite recipe and make it for supper. Invite someone you've lost touch with to join you.
- ❖ Dust off your birdfeeders and fill them with sustenance for God's winged ones as they follow their call to migration.
- ❖ Take a walk with a basket. Gather beauty from nature; acorns, leaves, stones, mossy twigs, etc. Create a little nature shrine in the spirit of Cibylle to honor God's season of autumn. Light a candle. Offer prayers of gratitude for autumn's splendor.

Dominions and Graces
Volume I: EARTH…***Autumn*** *is related to the following:*
bone, dusk, harvest, bear, acorn, the body,
stone, footfall upon fallen leaves, musk, vermillion.
(*I&H*: 63)

You're invited to contemplate the meanings of the properties of autumn. Create a visual prayer collage for your altar to reflect the particular character of the season.

The Way of Belle Cœur

September

***

*The land spread out
around us flat and
open like God's parchment,
ready for scribing
by autumn's hand.
(I&H: 314)*

Acorn Moon

September is the month when we turn our attention to hearth keeping and tending the home. September calls the children to the first day of school and marks the start of the New Year in Judaism. September also signals the return to *ordinary time* after the lazy vacation days of summer. It's the time to begin to prepare our homes for autumn and winter as the leaves begin to turn.

Home. Be it ever so humble or grand, shabby, chic, messy, tidy polished or neglected...home matters. Home is the place we long to be, whether a cottage, mansion, apartment, farmhouse, or a simple "room of one's own." Our homes are sacred spaces where we not only seek shelter at day's end and eat, sleep, and work...home is the place that nurtures our souls as a blessing place or sanctuary.

Home is where our routine and common daily rituals play out. While we experience daily life we sometimes forget to embrace the beauty of the familiar and common place. In our busyness we miss the sacred experience right before us.

Book VI Seasonal Inspiration

Contemplate how you begin each day with the ritual of awakening. Perhaps you open the blinds or curtains to welcome the morning light. You let the dog out for her run while you stretch and listen to the birds' sunrise song before you make the coffee. You open the kitchen cupboard and reach for your favorite bowl with the chipped rim before you fill it with hot oatmeal. You sit at the kitchen table to eat your breakfast and your daily rituals have only just begun.

This month the invitation is to bring your sacred awareness to the little daily rituals that enrich your life at home. Many animals are burrowing in and preparing for winter's arrival. They have much to teach us about the importance of ensuring our homes are nurturing places for comfort and sustenance. Allow September to offer you the blessing and joy of *being* home.

Reflect

Isaiah 32:18

- How will I express the shift from summer to autumn in my living space?
- What are my daily rituals at home from early morning until I climb into bed at the end of the day?
- How do I feel about my daily rituals? Are they fresh and enlivening or have they grown dull and rather life depleting?

The Way of Belle Cœur

- How might I renew my rituals with color, vibrancy, and sacred intention and meaning?
- Do I need a new ritual or two to bring sacredness and enrichment to the morning or evening hours?
- When I imagine nesting for the fall and winter months I feel…
- Some simple changes I can make in my living space to welcome fall are…

Express

- Write poems and/or prayers on velvety soft fallen leaves. Press them in your journal, leave them in random places for others to discover, or send your autumn offerings to your friends and beloveds.

Prayer

Sophia Wisdom, I celebrate the mystery and beauty of autumn. I pray to behold the ever-changing colors of the landscape and to stay open to the sweet surprises of the season. Bless my living space. May it be a haven for all who cross my threshold, Help me to be fully present to discover the sacred within the day's ordinary moments. In gratitude for the blessings of the season I say… Amen

Book VI Seasonal Inspiration

October

***

*It appeared at first glance
like a great sleeping beast,
nestled upon the
autumn landscape.
The enormity of the cathedral
caught my breath away.
(I&H: 317)*

Cornucopia Moon

We mark time through the change of seasons. Continuity and metamorphoses are inextricably woven together as one month flows into another. The shifting late afternoon sun scatters shadowy patterns on the kitchen floor. Days grow shorter. Dawn arrives more slowly with the invitation to slow down and enter the season of renewal while the blazing red sugar maple tree displays her radiant fall splendor.

Squirrel is busy running back and forth along the rail fence. Her cheeks full and round with bounty to be stored away. A murder of crows gathers each morning on the patio to wait for their breakfast of peanuts in the shell, a sure sign that its harvest time.

Ripe red pomegranates and black mission figs have replaced cherries and nectarines at the market. Bonfires fill the chilly evening air with an unmistakable smell that stirs long ago recollection held deep in the bones.

Enter into your Belle Cœur reverie while russet and golden leaves spiral to the earth outside the window.

What will arrive on the chill of the wind this year, as winter approaches? Is there something within your heart that is withering, changing color, in preparation to let go in tandem with the falling leaves?

October, you are God's harbinger of change. Autumn, you seduce and ravish the heart with your beauty. Please linger and stay, rather than depart to be replaced by winter's chill and pale, naked presence.

Your spirit is called to visit deeper inner terrain as fall covers the landscape. Feel the call to burrow in, make pots of hearty soup, and bring out your knitting.

This month's invitation is to contemplate whatever truly nourishes your heart and soul.

Journaling is a wonderful tool for excavating and exploring buried creative visions and dreams. This fall consider choosing a small blank book/journal that will serve as your autumn companion, a journal small enough to travel with you in your purse that is perhaps no bigger than your hand.

Think of your autumn journal as a sacred container for the inner harvest of what is most precious with personal meaning. You may want to keep your journal in a special cloth pouch to honor the sacredness of what it contains... your deepest truths, hopes, and heart's desires.

Reflect

Psalm 65:11

Take your journal and go to a place that nourishes your spirit...a favorite spot in your home, a place in nature, or another inspirational setting. Spend some time with each of the following questions.

- Right now in the present moment I would like to...
- My deepest longing at this time is...
- My song that is waiting to be sung is...
- The dream of my heart is...
- I feel a call to... I resist the call because...
- My sense of freedom is realized when I...
- My greatest joy is experienced when...
- My wisdom is...
- The two people who inspire me most at this time in my life are...
- I long to create...

Express

The landscape is alive with color this month. Be attentive to how colors affect your spirit. Create a mandala with the colors that inspire your creative passion.

Prayer

Wisdom Sophia, as October carries me inward, I pray for my heart to be opened to release my hidden secret longings and desires. Guide my pen to reveal wisdom for my life. I pray to reconnect to my sacred imagination to become a co-creator with you in this season of color, harvest, and reflection. I am grateful for the wonders of Creation and the inspiration that arrives within my dreams and is etched upon the falling leaves by you. Amen.

November

***

*Autumn was nearing
the turn to winter,
and we went about
our tasks as always,
with prayerful and
cheerful attitudes—
as best we could.
(I&H: 212)*

Ancestral Moon

At the beginning of November we celebrate All Soul's Day. This special ancient liturgical tradition is dedicated to remembering the souls of loved ones and friends. Many cultures believe that this is when the veil between the world of the living and the spirit world are thin. This month you're invited to contemplate the women of your *he*ritage, your feminine ancestors to reflect upon their legacy and wisdom and to reflect upon your mythology.

Book VI Seasonal Inspiration

Reflect

2 Corinthians 5:1

- List the names of the women in your lineage. Begin with your mother and move backwards in time; grandmother, great grandmother, great-great grandmother, etc. Write your list beginning: I am (your name), daughter of (mother's name), grand-daughter of (grandmother's name), etc.
- Make an autumn study of Fairy Tales and write about an episode in your life as though it were a myth. Who is the Queen? The dragon? Where is the forest? What is your quest?
- Create a time line in your journal to chart significant moments of transition in your life. Draw a horizontal line, above the line write the year. Below the line, name the event. Be aware of any patterns/repetitive themes. Is there a common thread?

Express

- Create a collage from copies of family photos of the women in your family. Add images from magazines to support the story within your photographs. Meditate with your collage to receive the story or poem hidden within it.
- Create a circle of stones in your yard or garden. Assign each stone a familial woman's name. You

The Way of Belle Cœur

may choose to paint the names on the stones. How will you incorporate the stones into your spiritual practice?
❖ Write a letter to a deceased female relative. Bury your letter and cover it with stones to honor her.

Prayer

Wisdom Sophia, I pray to embody the wisdom of my grandmothers' grandmothers. May their spirits bless my dreams with visions as I seek to discover the secrets scribed upon my bones by my ancestors. Amen

⁂

The year has circumnavigated its course and the holidays (Holy Days) have arrived once again. No matter where you might be on your life's journey this sacred season opens portals for a variety of experiences for your spirit, psyche, and heart. Contemplate how you will nurture your spirit in the midst of the frenetic busyness that accompanies this time of year.

Like so many aspects of life the holidays present the invitation to live in balance with the conscious awareness of personal needs and the needs of others...material, emotional and spiritual. Your senses provide conduits to engage fully with the people and experiences you encounter...to see, taste, smell, hear,

Book VI Seasonal Inspiration

touch, and intuit the deeper messages and meaning within this season of sacred celebration and Mystery.

When your senses are attuned and you're in touch with the present moment on multiple levels, the sacred meaning of the Holy Days delivers blessings in unexpected ways. In the midst of the busyness of your life give yourself time for a Holy Day, a Sabbath rest, or a day to simply explore your heart to reconnect to your creative spirit and sacred imagination.

During the holiday season practice reverent beholding of the people, sights, sounds, and experiences you encounter. Re-experience the feelings of child-like wonder, awe, and sacred awareness. Grow these simple practices of focus and intention during the Holy Days so they might continue throughout the New Year and beyond.

Embrace and embody the wisdom and sacred meaning within the seasons as God's presence is made visible through nature's ever changing face.

Book VII
Foundational Fundamentals

The Holy Mysteries and Twelve Elements of Wonder

*Our circle ended
with Helvide's recitation
of the Twelve Holy Mysteries.
These are the sacred
observations and practices
that are woven into
the day to day life
of the sisterhood.
(I&H: 139)*

Book VII Foundational Fundamentals

There are facets to Belle Cœur spirituality that require illumination and acknowledgement as twelve *holy mysteries*. Mystery is central to the spiritual experience because the realm of spirit is paradoxical. We encounter the sacred in moments that are miraculous and ecstatic, as well as, ordinary and commonplace. Our minds tell us that God is unfathomably great and beyond comprehension while our hearts often comprehend the peace of God's loving indwelling presence in a visceral way.

Each holy mystery is a portal to sacred understanding. You're invited to contemplate a particular mystery to discern the deeper personal meaning. Your understanding of a holy mystery may change form according to the particular season of life's journey you are navigating at a given time. Add your personal inspired exercises and reflections to deepen your experience.

Suggested related pages of *Ink and Honey* accompany the twelve holy mysteries. The reflections and practices/exercises for each mystery are offered for inspiration as a point of embarkation for your personal interpretation.

Scripture references are also provided. You're invited to explore the various Scriptures through the practice of lectio divina. Meditate upon the word or phrase within the Scripture that holds a particular resonance or captures your attention. Spend time in contemplation and discernment with your word or phrase and record your reflections in your journal.

You're invited to become familiar with the holy mysteries and to periodically revisit them as you encounter the Divine Presence in miraculous and ordinary ways.

It's suggested that you find your own rhythm as you slowly digest this material. You may discover additional holy mysteries to add to the list. There are no limitations to how the Beloved inspires and interacts to deliver sacred wisdom. Allow your creative spirit and sacred imagination to lead you.

The Holy Mysteries

I. ***The mystery of human love and the longing to know God***
Isaiah 26:9, Psalm 42:2, Revelation 22:17
(*I&H*: 4, 6-8, 12, 25, 53, 102, 125, 127, 162, 251, 339, 362, 396, 398)

Reflect

- ❖ How do you perceive the mystery that your human ability to love directly relates to and reflects God's love for you?
- ❖ How does your longing to know (experience) the Beloved's presence in your life manifest?
- ❖ In what ways do your body, mind and spirit express your longing?

Book VII Foundational Fundamentals

- ❖ When you imagine creatively expressing your love for God and others or creatively expressing your longing to know God more deeply, how are you inspired to respond?

II. *The mystery of holy silence and ecstatic praise*
Exodus 14:14, Psalm 62:5, James 1:19, Revelation 7:12
(*I&H*: 88, 97, 137, 139, 182, 230, 242, 287, 309, 324, 356, 393, 429, 486)

Reflect

- ❖ Describe your relationship with silence?
- ❖ Can you recall a time during your life's journey when silence delivered a spiritual awareness?
- ❖ Can you name the distractions that pull you away from the experience and blessing of holy silence?
- ❖ How do express ecstatic praise?
- ❖ Can you recall a time in your life when you were in ecstasy? Write about how this time impacted your body, mind, and spirit.

III. *The mystery of spiritual grace and anointing*
Exodus 29:7, John 5:14, Luke 7:46, Ephesians 2:8
(*I&H:* 6, 44, 77, 82, 88, 101, 120, 123, 128, 138, 141, 147, 180, 287-288, 424, 428)

Reflect

- ❖ Can you name a moment in your life when you recognized that you had received spiritual grace?
- ❖ How and in what circumstances have you extended grace for another?
- ❖ Have you ever been anointed (blessed by grace, forgiveness, healing) through an act of extreme kindness or the Sacrament of anointing?
- ❖ How do you imagine you might offer the Sacrament anointing?
- ❖ Is there a particular spiritual grace that you feel called to pray for yourself?
- ❖ What does it mean to be a grace-filled being?

IV. *The mystery of dreams and visions (Peramony)*
Acts 2:17, Luke 24:23, Matthew 27:19, Genesis 37:9
(*I&H:* 4, 12, 13, 16, 20, 32, 39, 53, 83, 84, 100, 139, 160, 240, 242, 254, 281, 284, 296, 362, 430)

Reflect

- ❖ If you imagine your dreams to be portals to understanding, prophecy, inspiration, healing or divine illumination…what past dream(s) hold wisdom and potency for you?
- ❖ How have you been changed, instructed, alerted, or creatively inspired by a dream?

Book VII Foundational Fundamentals

- How do you interpret the difference between a waking dream, a vision, and a lucid dream?
- When you contemplate the word *visionary* what emerges for you?
- In this present moment, what is the vision or dream that you are holding in your heart?
- Contemplate how you might cultivate your dreams and visions as inspiration for your life's journey.

V. *The mystery of the moon and stars (Shinorage)*
Genesis 1:16, Psalm 136:7-9, Job 9:7-9
(*I&H:* 33-35, 143, 165, 182, 184, 208, 255, 270-272, 280, 284, 287, 300-301, 373)

Reflect

- How do the changing phases of the moon affect your body, mind and spirit?
- It has been said that we are made from *star stuff*. What images arise for you as you reflect upon this concept?
- What symbol represents your astrological sign? Draw your symbol repetitively as a meditation to discover the personal meaning that it holds for you.
- Contemplate your relationship with the stars, planets, the changing face of the moon, the enormity of universe, space, time, and eternity. Write a poem to express whatever arises.

The Way of Belle Cœur

- ❖ Create a collage to illustrate your understanding of shinorage.
- ❖ How do you feel about other life forms beyond the earth? Is this concept unsettling or exciting for you?
- ❖ When you reflect upon the ideas of inner versus outer space what thoughts and images are evoked?

VI. *The mystery of signs and symbols*
2 Corinthians 12:12, Acts 14:3, Revelation 12:1
(*I&H:* 12, 50, 84-85, 88, 106-107, 141, 172, 183-185, 254, 301, 311, 473)

Reflect

- ❖ Write about a time in your life when you felt guided by a sign from God.
- ❖ How did this experience change you?
- ❖ How does your body validate or negate your intuitive understanding?
- ❖ If you were to choose one specific symbol as your cartouche or monogram what would it be?
- ❖ Draw or find an image to represent your symbol(s). Add these to your journal or codex.

VII. *The mystery of the changing seasons and Creation*
Genesis 1:14, Genesis 1:1, Ecclesiastes 3:1-22
(*I&H:* 7, 43, 47-51, 61-65, 76-83, 134-139, 143, 272, 275-278, 323-324, 333, 366, 448)

Book VII Foundational Fundamentals

Reflect

- ❖ Practice the observation of the rising and setting sun for a week while you meditate upon the wonders of Creation.
- ❖ Place a piece of fabric somewhere in your yard where it can remain for long period of time. Observe how the sun, rain, wind, heat, cold, etc. affect the fabric. Contemplate how the passage of time affects the physical world. Photograph the process.
- ❖ Contemplate what it means to live within the in between. As you've explored previously, in the weeks before autumn turns to winter, spring becomes summer, and summer changes to fall there is a season that is neither one nor the other. This is the season of in between. What does the seasonal time of liminal space hold for you?
- ❖ Choose the season that most resonates with your spirit. What colors, music, tastes, smells, textures, and images do you associate with your season? Create a visual prayer to pay homage to the season of your heart.

VIII. *The mystery of the angels and saints*
Revelation 8:3-4, Matthew 22:30, Psalm 78:25
(*I&H:* 24-25, 29-32, 41, 53-54, 84, 140, 147, 185, 208-210, 216, 241, 287, 311, 338, 354, 429)

The Way of Belle Cœur

Reflect

- ❖ Commit for one month to the practice of meditation with your guardian angel. Listen, with the ears of your heart, for your angel's wisdom.
- ❖ What is your angel's name? How have you been inspired or protected by your angel during your life's journey?
- ❖ Create an altar to honor the angelic spirits and saints that bless you each day.
- ❖ Choose a saint whose wisdom you value. Study your wisdom saint's teachings. Memorize one of his/her wisdom phrases as a meditation exercise.
- ❖ Write about a time when you became a human angel for someone and/or when you experienced an angelic presence, seen or unseen.

IX. *The mystery of the sacred imagination*
Ephesians 1:17-18
(*I&H:* 25, 40, 52-56, 59, 61-62, 146, 171, 189-190, 277, 297, 331, 365, 367, 472, 485, 487)

Reflect

- ❖ Take a blank piece of paper, 8 ½" x 11," and use your imagination to fold or tear it to make something new.
- ❖ Make a list of the ways God inspires your imagination.

Book VII Foundational Fundamentals

- ❖ Spend an hour in nature. How is your imagination inspired by the experience?
- ❖ Look around your environment. Engage your imagination to repurpose a room, an object or furnishings in a new way?
- ❖ Create a notebook full of words and images that inspire your imagination.

X. The mystery of holy ecstasy
Ezkiel 11:24-25, Acts 10:10-16, Acts 2:4
(*I&H:* 60-61, 142, 160, 175, 323, 332, 354, 361, 401, 408, 453)

Reflect

- ❖ Write about a time when you felt God's presence in a palpable way.
- ❖ Go out of doors and sing your morning prayer.
- ❖ When you imagine the experience of ecstasy what do you envision?
- ❖ How do you express yourself in an ecstatic moment?
- ❖ How do ecstatic feelings and your awareness of the Divine Presence inform and affect your body and spirit?
- ❖ Imagine how you might transform an ecstatic thought or feeling into your sacred artmaking?

The Way of Belle Cœur

XI. *The mystery of community and sisterhood*
Hebrews 10:24-25, Acts 2:42-47, Matthew 18-20
(*I&H:* 2, 3, 5, 64, 102, 107, 137, 153, 171, 185, 351, 355-356, 480, 483)

Reflect

- Write about a time when you were blessed by your participation of a community oriented experience.
- How has your community/sisterhood changed and informed your way of being in the world?
- If you were to call a community of kindred spirits together, what would you propose as your community's intention?
- When you imagine yourself as a sister within a sisterhood/community, what feelings arise?

XII. The mystery of fasting
Matthew 6:16-18, Daniel 10:3, Luke 4:2
(*I&H:* 30, 102, 157, 247, 258, 271, 306, 309)

Reflect

- How do you envision the concept of fasting as a personal spiritual practice?
- Do you feel called to fast from food, technology, alcohol, shopping, gossip…other?

Book VII Foundational Fundamentals

- ❖ If you make a conscious choice to fast, to what specific global cause or personal intentional prayer will you dedicate your fasting?
- ❖ How do you resonate with the idea of community fasting? How do you imagine a community fast might serve the greater good?

The Twelve Elements of Wonder

...I came to realize
the myriad ways
the sisterhood of Belle Cœur
was rooted in the elements,
in the body,
in the heart of God,
in Creation herself...
(I&H: 153)

The twelve elements of wonder are life enrichment principles and practices for the body, mind, and spirit. The elements of wonder offer the invitations to live, experience, and incorporate each element as a spiritual practice. In this way, the full embodiment and holistic benefit of the twelve elements is possible.

The Way of Belle Cœur

A suggested form for this inner work is to experience it as a yearlong process. Each month select one element as a spiritual/creative practice and focus. You may choose to work through the elements in sequence, as listed, or intuitively select the element that feels most appropriate for you at a given time.

When you have made your selection, contemplate how to weave the element (as a spiritual practice) into your life. Engage your creativity. Consider the following criteria:

- Does the element invite an active or passive form of practice?
- Is there an invitation to involve others or is this a solitary practice?
- Does the element call for a ritual or the incorporation of a sacred life-art?
- What is the ripple effect in other areas of my life as I incorporate the practice of this element?
- How does the element inspire additional personal revelatory response?
- How will I grow my wisdom as I embody this element?

Each element is accompanied by a Scripture reference and references to various *Ink and Honey* passages. These are provided as sources for the practice of lectio divina. You're encouraged to gather supplemental inspiration to fully support and express the elements through additional literary, poetic, or sacred sources.

Book VII Foundational Fundamentals

The Twelve Elements of Wonder

1. **Make your life a river of prayer.**
   Luke 18:1, 1 Thessalonians 5:17, Philippians 4:6
   (*I&H:* 2, 5, 12, 32, 100)
   Pray without ceasing. Bring your prayers to every gesture, action, activity, creation, interaction. With practice your life will become a river of prayer and there will be no separation between everyday life and your spiritual life. These two seeming separate portions of your existence will merge into one and you will be continually aware of the Divine Presence within you and surrounding you.

2. **Maintain a spirit of continuous gratitude.**
   Ephesians 1:16, James 1:17, 1Thessalonians 5:18
   (*I&H:* 42, 44, 65, 129, 403)

   Practice conscious gratitude for not only the obvious physical and material gifts but also for the spiritual and numinous blessings that you experience and receive each day. Prayerfully cultivate the intrinsic value for life's hardships and challenges as teaching moments and learning opportunities. When you experience feelings of ennui, despair, and sacrifice re-center your heart and spirit through the conscious awareness of your blessings. Begin with the thought…"God is within me. I'm alive. I can breathe. I feel my heart beating…"

3. **Seek joy in the small moments and celebrate often.**

The Way of Belle Cœur

Ecclesiastes 9:7, John 16:22, Psalm 30
(*I&H:* 18, 52, 87, 185, 233)
Momentous occasions of joy such as the birth of a child, the feeling of falling in love, or the return to health after illness are definitely cause for celebration. However, the discovery of joy in the simple everyday moments of life celebrated with gratitude and prayer create a harmonious flow within ordinary time. A cup of tea and conversation with a friend, the planting of bulbs in the fall, teaching a child to tie her shoes, or arising early to witness the sunrise these, too, are holy moments. Celebrate with gratitude the seemingly insignificant instances as the day-to-day threads that weave your life's tapestry with golden illumination.

4. **Practice self compassion and compassion for others.**
Matthew 6:14-15, Matthew 18:21-22, Colossians 3:12-13
(*I&H:* 124, 158, 183, 206, 372)

Compassion for others must also include the difficult and challenging persons that cross your path. Unlovable and disagreeable people are often the ones who have rarely been shown kindness or compassion. Pushing through judgment and negative feelings to begin to witness the vulnerable and tender places within another person, to genuinely touch compassion and empathy and be able to share it...this is true work of the soul. It can often be a very natural and free flowing process to be compassionate towards someone who is loving and giving and seen as deserving of compassion. The practice of compassion for your self is somehow much more onerous than the offering of compassion for another. Keep an open heart to allow kindness, compassion, and empathy to flow not only through you, but too you, as well.

5. **Practice self-forgiveness and forgive others.**
Psalm 51, 2 Corinthians 5:18-19, Matthew 6:14-15
(*I&H:* 120, 174, 315, 372, 474)

An open heart ensures the embodiment of a strong and healthy vessel. Forgiveness circulates through an open heart as one stream flowing in two directions. Forgiveness of self is poured inward in direct measure to the depth of forgiveness the heart extends to another. Forgiveness is compassion's sister. Practice compassion and forgiveness will follow.

6. **Engage through openhearted listening.**
Mark 4:24
(*I&H:* 123, 135, 194, 284, 355, 375, 474)
Openhearted listening is a body and soul experience. To listen attentively the body and senses must be fully engaged. Non-judgmental, active, compassionate listening is the highest

The Way of Belle Cœur

form of witness and presence for another's story or sharing. Eye contact is also important to ensure full engagement and connection to what is spoken. It is rare for our stories to be witnessed without interruption or comment by the listener. Practice openhearted listening to engage with others, soul to soul.

7. **Be consciously aware of others' needs and respond appropriately while offering hope,**
Romans 4:3-5
(*I&H:* 5, 30, 32, 108, 132, 137, 144-145, 183, 201, 219, 225, 237, 240, 243, 263, 278, 286, 359, 390, 418, 438).

The practice of conscious awareness for others' needs is the practice of compassionate response guided by the intuition. How to respond to another's needs directly or indirectly, calls for the discernment of the question: *Is it appropriate to respond to what I am currently witnessing? If so, how should I offer assistance?* Often the gesture of a simple touch, a word of acknowledgement, or affirmation of presence is all that is called for and can serve as an offering of hope. Most frequently the heartfelt offering of silent prayer for person's situation and circumstances is the highest choice of all.

8. **Practice self-nurturance.**
Ephesians 4:12-13
(*I&H:* 34, 158)

Book VII Foundational Fundamentals

Self-nurturance (the practice of extreme self-care) is perhaps one of the most important spiritual practices of all. Those who choose health, wellbeing, and spiritual centeredness as tenets for a balanced and radiant life offer an important example and model for others. Imagine a world where individuals assumed responsibility for caring for his/her spiritual, physical, and emotional health with conscious awareness and intention. Practice self-care and witness how your commitment blesses those around you.

9. **Speak your truth clearly with compassion.**
1Corinthians 1:1-13, 1 John 4:20, James 1:19
(*I&H:* Prologue, 136, 159, 180, 183, 277, 434)
Speak your truth with compassion as an ongoing, lifelong, sacred practice. The ninth element invites you to find your authentic voice. You are encouraged to practice discernment with regard to when to speak your truth and when to remain silent. Compassion for yourself, as well as, the listener is important. The qualities of courage, holy fierceness, and conviction are embedded within the practice of speaking the truth with clarity and compassion.

10. **Assume responsibility for the way you use, care, and revere your spiritual and creative gifts and the natural world.**
Genesis 2:15, Acts 14:17
(*I&H:* 41, 62, 64, 349, 484)

The Way of Belle Cœur

Our natural world and earthly resources deserve our full attention. The intention to discern right action, use, and reverence for nature's gifts and bounty is soul work and also an axiom of spiritual practice for this particular element of wonder. Where do you feel called to focus your attention with regard to nature's needs? You are part of the weave of Creation. Your distinct role and service to the web of life invites you to revere your creative and spiritual gifts (your charism). The practice of reverence is key for this element.

11. **Seek to connect soul to soul, beyond the obvious, with those who cross your path.**
Ephesians 4: 2-0, John 13:34, Luke 6:31,
(*I&H:* 95, 107, 188, 189, 240, 261, 448, 472)
Human connection is the full embodiment and expression of God's Love. Eye to eye, heart to heart, soul-to-soul. The spiritual conduit for this element is consciousness. The invitation is to become awake, aware, and present to everyday encounters with others. In the spirit of meaningful presence the soul is open to recognize human and spiritual connection with all. In this way the reality of being One with all manner of life is fully accessible, and the presence of God, within and without, is viably palpable.

12. **Carry your oratory (place of prayer) within you, even in the midst of chaos.**
Exodus 33:14, Joshua 1:9, Exodus 25:8

Book VII Foundational Fundamentals

(*I&H:* 5, 178, 189, 361, 352)

There are times in life when busyness, sudden change, challenge, illness, or uncertainty causes feelings of unsettledness, anxiety, and instability. The 12th and final element inspires the qualities of spiritual and sacred centeredness. The Beloved is at the center of Belle Cœur spirituality as the blessed assurance that God is always present within the heart and soul, no matter the circumstances of life. When your focus returns time and again to your oratory within you where there is peace, sanctuary and prayer the practice will become your reality. Walk in confidence with God's ever abiding and indwelling presence.

Book VIII
Illumination, Co-creation, and the Sacred Imagination

The Seven Facets of Illumination

*Behold what is all around you.
Illuminate your sacred faculty
of vision with prayer.
(I&H: 48)*

The Seven Facets of Illumination provide a way to envision your life from a spiritual and creative perspective. Become acquainted with the seven facets through the exploration of the sacred practices provided in this section.

Book VIII Illumination, Co-creation, and the Sacred Imagination

Contemplate your life as a sacred life-artisan. Imagine how your world would appear if seen through seven unique lenses of a kaleidoscope. When the creative and spiritual kaleidoscope of the heart is engaged everyday moments become illuminated with sacred and symbolic meaning.

Through your commitment to the practices for each of the seven facets you create the potential to experience balance, clarity, spaciousness, and serenity. New levels of untapped creativity arise when your visions, perceptions, and wisdom are illuminated through sacred practice and presence.

Be inspired by what you discover.

Live your life as a sacred artisan. In time, as you fully explore the sacred life-arts you will experience an ever deeper connection with the Beloved. Record your insights and observations in your journal as you embody the 7-facets of illumination. Add your wisdom to your codex while you engage your creative heart and spirit in new ways.

Facet I
Behold and cultivate beauty

"Our life at Belle Cœur cocooned us in beauty and our love for one another."
(*I&H*: 177)

Consider the way a wide-eyed child gazes with wonder and curiosity the first time she notices her shadow dancing on the wall. When you *behold* an object, a person, or a situation, you shift your consciousness from simply *looking* at the surface to *gaze* with reflection, fascination, and reverence to grasp the sacredness within. To gaze (in this context) means to regard or see with intention and full conscious awareness to fully contemplate and comprehend the deeper meaning of what is there before you. When you *behold* a person, place, a thing, or a set of circumstances you have the opportunity to connect with the Divine Presence within whatever is there before you.

Sacred Practice
Behold and cultivate

When you behold, you explore what you see with the eyes of your heart. Beholding requires you to drop judgment and to open your mind and spirit to experience awe. Embrace whatever you behold with the innocence and curiosity of a child. Allow questions to arise. Begin to reflect upon the following informative questions as you encounter various situations and circumstances throughout the day.

Reflect

- What sacred wisdom is being illuminated within this moment?
- How am I inspired by what I behold?
- What particular understanding am I being invited to cultivate from this encounter/experience?
- Is this encounter/experience a call to respond through specific action or loving and compassionate service?

These are helpful inquiries to return to time and again. Make notations in your journal regarding your awareness of subtle or profound interior shifts of consciousness as you engage with the first facet of illumination.

Belle Cœur spirituality encourages sacred life-artisans to recognize and understand the importance of personal resonance and engagement with beauty. The following practice offers a way to behold and cultivate beauty.

Sacred Practice
An ode to beauty: The tableau

Spread a cloth on a table in preparation for the creation of a tableau, a visual representation of objects, images, colors, and textures that are beautiful to your eye. Take time as you move about your home and in nature to carefully select those things that speak to you of beauty.

Think of your tableau as a continual work in progress. The objects you choose initially may be replaced or rearranged according to your needs and desires. On any given day you may want to embellish your tableau or simplify it. Allow the objects and images to tell you a story as though they are symbols within a waking dream. Resist the natural inclination to edit or make critical judgments with regard to your sense of aesthetic.

Cultivate the wisdom that beauty offers. Sketch your tableau in your journal. Photograph it at different times throughout the day as the light changes. Give a title to your particular understanding of beauty. Choose a descriptive name such as: natural, classical, eclectic, sacred, exotic, etc. to express your personal resonance.

Curate whatever catches the eyes of your heart to truly inspire your creativity, sacred imagination and spirit. Note your reflections about your creative process and add your photographs or sketches of your tableau to your codex with your commentary.

Facet II
Arrange your life as a sacred reflection of order, purpose, and simplicity

Belle Cœur's order and beauty brought to mind the memory of my home and the joy of my childhood days.
(I&H: 130)

The conditions that surround us, within our homes and workspaces provide a mirror of reflection for the climate of our interior lives and the acclimation of our spirits. The creation of an atmosphere of tranquility for daily life may be considered as spiritual practice. Order, purpose, and simplicity inspire serenity and foster feelings of equanimity.

Sorting and letting go of things (tangible and intangible) that no longer serve life's purpose, is a practice that promotes the healing and nurturance of the spirit. The reference to *Things,* in this context refers to material objects, possessions, places, circumstances, work, thoughts, activities, particular ways of living and being, and relationships.

When life is cleared of accumulated outworn or outgrown belongings, beliefs, and behaviors space opens for replenishment and renewal. Prayer and sacred intention are foundational to the creative and generative work of the establishment of order, purpose, and simplicity for your inner and outer worlds.

Sacred Practice
Discernment and letting go

Begin to arrange and claim order, purpose, and simplicity as a way of life. Assess the condition of the internal place where you store and hold onto things that no longer serve you. Create time for a journal experience. Draw a vertical line down the center of a blank page and label one column *Inner* and the second column *Outer*. Prayerfully contemplate and reflect on the following question:

> *What are the behaviors, addictions, relationships, and beliefs that no longer serve my life?*

Consciously acknowledge that you are making a committed intention, with God's Grace, to illumine your life with new awareness. Experience the following ritual to celebrate the process of letting go and to also acknowledge your openness to receive spiritual illumination.

Ritual
Release into new life

On slips of paper, write words that represent whatever you feel you are ready to release from your life or consciousness. Burn the papers in your fireplace or a safe place out of doors. Light a candle (a taper works well for this) from the fire of your letting go. Burn the candle in your sacred space to remind you of your commitment.

Add cooled ashes from your *fire of release* to pot filled with potting soil and add seeds or a plant. This is your symbolic welcome to the new life that has emerged from the ashes of your old ways of being. Tend the plant and your personal growth with reverence and attention as you nurture and grow your wisdom within your heart and spirit.

Reflect

Prayerfully contemplate and reflect upon the following question in your journal:

What are the material possessions in my life that no longer serve the woman I am becoming?

You may find it helpful to go from room to room in your living and work spaces and create a list on paper of what you are letting go. As you discern this process ask:

Whom do I know that will benefit from or appreciate this (material possession)?

Keep notes for how you will disperse the things you are clearing from your life.

Blessing and opening to the mystery

When everything you are choosing to release has been gathered, celebrate with a blessing ceremony. Give thanks for the service you've received from your possessions. Bless your belongings and release them to wherever they are meant to be. Open your arms wide in a gesture to acknowledge you are both releasing the old and creating space to welcome the new into your life.

Pass along your possessions

- ❖ Plan a garage or estate sale. Consider the donation of a portion of the sales to a personally meaningful cause.
- ❖ Donate useful possessions to a shelter or local organization or charity.
- ❖ Give things away to friends and family.
- ❖ Leave small objects or articles of clothing in public places where you know someone in need will find them.

If you find it difficult to let go of something but you truly want to let it go it might be helpful to dialogue with the object. Ask the image or the object the following question and imagine the object's response. Scribe your revelations in your journal. Ask the question:

What is your hold on me?

You may wish to photograph the things you are releasing. You might choose to print the images and create a collage as a visual prayer with the intention of blessing and release.

Keep an empty bowl or basket in a prominent place where you will see it often throughout the day. This empty vessel is a reminder that you have spaciousness within and around you. You are ready and open to receive new inspiration, experiences, abundance, joy, and health for your renewed life.

Facet III
Tend your heart and hearth to nurture your relationships and surroundings

We gathered in our circle near the hearth. Mabille lit the candle at the center.
(I&H: 453)

When you discern the beneficial vitamins or supplements that are necessary to ensure your physical health, you practice self-care for your body. The third facet of illumination offers the invitation to discern necessary spiritual vitamins to ensure the emotional and spiritual health of your heart and your hearth, your relationships, and your environment. Contemplate the following questions:

- ❖ *What soothes your soul?*
- ❖ *What nurtures your body and mind?*
- ❖ *What are the colors, textures, sights, and smells that deliver comfort for your tired or wounded spirit?*
- ❖ *How do you celebrate joy?*
- ❖ *How do you serve others?*
- ❖ *How do your gifts and talents uplift the spirits of your friends and beloveds with hope, and inspiration?*

Sacred Practice
Discern your needs

The practice to discern what the heart and soul truly need often takes coaxing and patience. It is ongoing soul work to discern reasons for self-denial of experiences that hold potential for personal fulfillment. Quiet reflective time out of doors allows the workings and wonders of nature to shift the mind from rational thought to more primal forms of understanding that extend beyond language. In nature, you are free to connect with Creation and your innate (and perhaps forgotten and ignored) animal instincts. Information awaits us within the stillness of nature.

Reflect

In your journal, work with the following questions and honor any additional inquiries that arise:

- ❖ When my heart and spirit are feeling low I know I need to...
- ❖ When I think of practicing extreme self-care I feel...
- ❖ I foster and tend my precious relationships with friends and beloveds when I...
- ❖ There is a relationship I long to reconcile. When I think of... I feel...
- ❖ When I tend my home as a sanctuary I...

- The concept that my home is an outward representation for the internal world of my heart inspires me to…

Return to these questions periodically. Tend your heart and hearth as an ongoing process. Create time and space often for reflection and discernment regarding how to nourish and enrich your ever-evolving spiritual and creative longings.

Contemplate and create

Consider the following questions and select one or more as a creative and spiritual focus to actualize:

- Where do you find spiritual medicine and tonic for your heart and soul?
- Will you write your prayers on stones or gather poetry and words of inspiration, images and symbols as a collection of kindling for your creative fire?
- Will you collect roots, tree bark, shells, and seeds and wrap them in cotton soaked in lavender oil, frankincense, or spikenard?
- Will you send postcards to your beloveds from sacred sites or catalogue old photographs of your kindred spirits?
- Will you create a welcoming space in your home in preparation for an unexpected visitor/pilgrim?

- Will you prepare a festive meal on a random day and invite your neighbors to join you for a celebration of LIFE?
- Today will you phone the person you've been thinking about for months?
- Today will you forgive yourself for whatever troubles your heart?

Create your Cozy Basket

Gather things to nurture your body and spirit such as; your favorite teas, hand cream, a favorite DVD or music, prayer beads, devotional and spiritual books, aromatic oils such as lavender or spikenard, chocolate, photos of your beloveds, a special journal to hold your deepest thoughts, colored pens or pencils, postcards to send to friends or relatives, a stuffed animal or doll, knitting or needlework, tissues, a soft comfortable wrap or shawl, a candle, etc.

When you have made your selections arrange them in a basket or tote bag so your comfort collection will be portable. This is your personal pharmacy for your soul. When you're feeling depleted, tired, depressed, or out of balance go to your comfort basket and select something that feels right. Choose the prescription that will best serve your current need.

Physical activity is also very comforting. Take your dog for a walk or go for a swim. Ask your heart to reveal what will best serve your present need. The answer may surprise you.

Correspond

E-mail is a wonderful tool but it has become an ever-ready substitute for many for the blessing of a hand-written card or letter. As you contemplate ways to tend your hearth and the relationships of your life, here's a suggestion:

Keep a bundle of post cards readily available. Make a list of names and addresses (the friends and beloveds you want to keep in touch with) on slips of paper and put them in a little box or bowl. Each morning or once a week as a meditation, draw a name at random from the bowl and write a one or two-sentence message, create a little sketch, share a quote, or offer a prayer on a post card.

This practice is simple, fast, meaningful, and satisfying for you and for the one who will receive your heartfelt blessing. Hand-stamp the postcard with an image of your personal symbol. This sacred practice is a simple way to cultivate beauty and offer your loving presence. Additionally, this practice compliments the Belle Cœur perpetual calendar monthly practice of outreach through the written word and illumination.

Facet IV
Pray, listen, and dedicate your spirit to co-creation with God

I observe my sisters and listen to them carefully. I pray to capture their stories the way Ravenissa gently scoops the fat speckled caterpillar from the garden path.
(*I&H*: 375)

St. Paul reminds us to... *"Pray without ceasing."* The fourth facet of illumination centers upon prayerful devotion and the contemplative practice of listening with the ears of the heart for God's guidance.

The senses, as we've explored previously, inspire and activate your sacred imagination and create sensory pathways to connect you with the heart of God. The practices of prayer, deep inner listening, and sensual awareness enrich your internal environment for co-creation with the Divine Presence.

Sacred Practice
Mark Life's Rhythm

As a co-creator with the Divine, it's important to understand the various ways you experience resonance and dissonance. Your intellectual and spiritual responses to daily life and the world around you invite your engagement through an open and receptive heart.

Be conscious of the tempo of life throughout each day. There are eight cycles of measurement to consider: dawn, morning, noon, afternoon, dusk, evening, night, pre-dawn. Begin to notice and pay attention to the following:

- ❖ Where do you resonate and where do you experience discord with regard to the various cycles of the hours throughout the day?

- ❖ *Which* particular hours offer your *still-point*, the time when the veil between the worlds is thin and you are most aware of the Divine Presence?
- ❖ Are you a *morning or night person?*
- ❖ Contemplate the ebb and flow of your energy, your life force. When is your physical and mental energy the most effective?
- ❖ As the day progresses from dawn to dark, do you require periods of absolute silence to periodically renew your spirit?
- ❖ How do your physical, mental, and emotional capacities change during a twenty-four hour period?

Be attentive to your particular affinity or deference to the various hours of the day, the seasons of the year, the changing climate, and phases of the moon. Self-comprehension creates an atmosphere for your spirit's syncopation with the heartbeat of God.

Sacred Practice
Energetic and sensual awareness

Create a chart on a blank page in your journal. Draw eight, equally spaced, horizontal lines to create eight horizontal rows. The eight rows designate the eight cycles of time throughout the day. Label the eight rows from top to bottom on the left side of the page: pre-dawn, dawn, morning, noon, afternoon, dusk, evening, and night.

Next, on the same page draw seven, equally spaced, vertical lines to form seven vertical columns. Label the seven columns across the top of the page, from left to right with the days of the week, Monday through Sunday.

Dedicate one week to the practice of energy awareness. Use your chart to indicate the various cycles of time throughout each day when you are aware that your energy has peaked or waned.

Draw a plus sign (+) in the columns to indicate the hours when you feel at your maximum energy level, when your senses are attuned, and you experience your optimal connectedness with life. Draw a minus sign (-) for those hours when your energy is diminished, your senses are dulled, and you notice feelings of depletion. Be sure to add additional helpful notations to your chart to support your findings.

At the end of the week refer to the chart to discern particular patterns or themes. Use this information to make correlations and discoveries with regard to how diet, exercise, sleep, stress, and other factors affect your energy levels and sensual awareness.

The following additional criteria will deepen the practice of energetic and sensual acclimation:

- Are you warm natured or cold natured?
- Do you enjoy the bright sunny warm golden palette of the tropics or the gentle foggy gray coolness of the forest?
- What sounds soothe your mind or irritate it?
- Do you prefer the taste of sweet or savory?

Book VIII Illumination, Co-creation, and the...

- What textures attract your sense of touch?
- Do you refresh and recharge your energy when you interact with others or when you retreat to silence and solitude?
- Does exercise energize you or make you feel tired?
- How does your energy respond to caffeine, sugar, veggies, etc?

Practice sensual awareness as a sacred practice. When you're cold, notice how your body and emotions respond. Become consciously aware of how cold affects you and bring your awareness to a global perspective. Shift your discomfort to become a prayer for all those in the world who have no way to find warmth and comfort.

Likewise, when you're uncomfortable due to the hot summer sun and temperature, be fully present to how heat affects you and pray for your brothers and sisters who are parched and thirsty.

If you are suffering from physical pain, be present to the pain. Dedicate your suffering to the suffering of the world. Stretch the bounds of your physical body to feel connected to others who are suffering through your suffering. In this way your pain becomes a prayer through your conscious awareness.

If you are hungry, before you eat, offer the following prayer: *Merciful Beloved, I pray that someone with an empty belly through your grace, will be nourished and filled through the partaking of this meal.* Amen

There are myriad ways each day to connect with our brothers and sisters on this earth. Let us pray for one another without ceasing.

The Way of Belle Cœur

Blessing prayer

Prayer is your form of intimate language between you and the Holy One. Choose a favorite line of Scripture or sacred poetry or select a sacred word or name of your choosing such as:

Beloved	Jesus	Holy One
Wisdom Sophia	Yahweh	Creator
Mother of Mercy		Keeper of my Soul

Repeat your phrase or name throughout the day and night in silence. Silently pray your blessing word or phrase as you go about your work, drive carpool, cook a meal, fold laundry, and as you fall asleep at night.

When intrusive, anxious, or distracting thoughts pull you from your center refocus your mind and heart, in silence, as you return your attention to your word or phrase. Embody your sacred word as a blessing for your body, mind, and soul. Become a living, breathing prayer.

Facet V
Craft your creative tools and sacred practices for your authentic life

I believe God has placed me in this monastery's scriptorium so I might be privy to the needed tools to complete my scribing of our sisterhood's stories.
(*I&H*: 174)

Creative tools and sacred practices for your authentic life are important. Throughout time there have been archetypal symbols, patterns, and experiences left behind by our ancestors to inform our lives as sacred life-artisans. Creative tools and spiritual practices are limited only by our imaginations. It is suggested that you spend time with your journal to explore a variety of sacred tools and practices.

Sacred tools do not necessarily refer to expensive creative accouterments such as: pens, scissors, paints, etc. purchased at the art supply store. A stick or twig dipped in ink is a tool. A favorite symbol carved into a raw potato or rubber eraser becomes a stamp when pressed onto a colorful stamp pad or dipped in beet juice. Brown paper lunch bags when cut and sewn together with kitchen twine can be fashioned to become a journal. Begin to keep a list of forms of creative expression that connect you with your earliest recall of inventiveness and inspired response.

Sacred Practice
Your pilgrim symbols

This section provides journal steppingstones to get you started. Please have colored pens and markers nearby. Think of this creative time as a blessing. You are invited to visit the well of your sacred imagination to drink deeply to quench your creative thirst.

The Way of Belle Cœur

Light a candle. Take a deep breath and as you exhale, let go of your anxieties, preconceived notions, resistance, and anything that hinders your full engagement with this process. Inhale what you need in this moment: an open mind and heart, spontaneity, trust, or fearlessness. Offer a prayer to honor your intention to bring forth whatever will best serve your creative heart and spirit.

Spread your colored markers, crayons, and pens on the table. Turn to a fresh page of your journal and date the page.

Select a variety of colors to reflect the concepts of *serenity* and *peace*. Without editing or judgment engage your sacred imagination to find an image to represent serenity and peace. Draw what you see with your inner eyes. Take as much time as you need for each drawing. These sketches may be as literal or abstract as you choose. You can't make a mistake.

When your first drawing feels complete choose colors that you feel reflect *courage* and *safety*. Again, without self-criticism, draw a personal symbol to reflect the elements of courage and safety.

Lastly, choose colors to radiate *love* and *trust*. Once more, give yourself permission for total freedom of expression and draw your intuitive and imaginative image to exemplify love and trust.

When your three drawings are completed, reflect upon your symbols for serenity and peace, courage and protection, and love and trust. Have a written conversation with each symbol in your journal. Refer to the following example to understand the dialogue process:

Book VIII Illumination, Co-creation, and the...

YOU : Courage and protection, why did I choose red and purple to represent you?

Next, respond as the voice of your symbol. Your higher self will guide the process. Don't think about your response. Simply record whatever flows into your heart and mind.

SYMBOL: Red and purple speak to royalty. I am the eternal protector and guardian your strength and virtue. I offer you the imprint of courage.

The journal dialogue is a powerful process. You may choose to write both voices using your dominant hand. You may also pose the question with your dominant hand and respond to your question with your non-dominant hand.

The next practice will help you to synthesize your symbols in a three dimensional way.

Pilgrim tools and ritual objects

Keep your images of your three symbols nearby for this practice. Contemplate your life's journey as a pilgrimage of discovery while you walk with the Beloved into the Mystery of the truth of who you are meant to be…a co-creator with God and the sacred artist of your life.

In medieval times when pilgrims made their pilgrimage they carried their spiritual tools and ritual objects with them. These included but were not limited to the following:

The Way of Belle Cœur

- ❖ *A coquille shell.* This is a symbol for pilgrimage carried by pilgrims and used as a marker on the road for other pilgrims to help them find their way. The shell was also used as a scoop for one portion of food or drink. The grooves upon the surface of the shell converge into one point. Symbolically the grooves represent the various routes of pilgrimage that lead to a singular destination. The coquille shell is also a liturgical symbol for Baptism. (*I&H:* 122, 311, 433)
- ❖ *Pilgrim badge.* These shell shaped symbols were made of fabric or lead and collected at various sacred sites and worn by pilgrims. (*I&H:* 325)
- ❖ *Pilgrim staff.* A walking stick made from a tree branch. It may be carved, plain, or painted and embellished. (*I&H:* 256)
- ❖ *Vade Mecum.* As we know, pilgrims carried a special guidebook containing maps, prayers, and guidance for the pilgrimage. It was also a place to store souvenirs gathered along the journey. (*I&H:* 208, 325)
- ❖ *Pilgrim Satchel* A small cloth or leather tote bag to hold the *Vade Mecum,* a coquille shell, and things found along the Holy Road. (*I&H:* 20, 69, 75)

Tools for your life's pilgrimage

The following suggested crafts are offered to inspire the creation of your personal pilgrimage tools. Allow your sacred imagination to guide you in whatever way feels right for you.

- ❖ Draw from the inspiration of your three symbols as a starting point to imagine the creation of your personal pilgrim badge. You may choose to sew your badge from a patchwork of scrap fabrics. Add charms, embroidery or buttons or whatever else your imagination offers. Another choice might be to make your badge from a flat wooden disc from the craft store. Paint and embellish it. Glue or sew a brooch pin to the reverse side so the disc or fabric badge can be worn.
- ❖ Notice the predominant symbol that informs the creation of your walking stick. You may choose a tall branch (5') from nature that you use in its natural state, or paint a wooden pole. Embellish your walking stick with your symbol or symbols, add ribbons, yarn, or colorful strips of fabric to make it beautiful.
- ❖ Glue the front of an envelope (flap side facing you) to the inside back cover of your journal or codex. Think of this as a sacred container for life's souvenirs, your prayers, and "found" tokens of inspiration.

- ❖ For your version of the pilgrim's coquille shell, use an actual coquille shell from the beach or craft store. Keep this sacred symbol on your altar as a reminder to keep an open heart as you journey life's Holy Road.
- ❖ Craft your pilgrim's satchel from a readymade canvas tote that you paint with acrylic paints or handcraft your bag from fabric or leather. Add your symbols and other touches of beauty. Use it to carry this book, your journal, and codex when you journey.

Facet VI
Archive inspiration to quicken your sacred imagination

Divine inspiration lives and breathes within our imaginations. (I&H: 52)

The sacred life-artisan is dedicated to the process of gathering and archiving inspiration. Become a curator of the images, experiences, ephemera, symbols, and other tangibles that inform your heart and spirit.

Why is inspiration critically important? Inspiration is the kindling for your creative fire. Inspiration is also the key that unlocks the door to your sacred imagination.

How do you archive inspiration? It's a simple gathering process. If you have begun to craft your sacred codex, it's likely that you are archiving fuel for your spirit. For review (with regard to what to include) refer to the list below and add or delete to fit your needs and desires. Gather and collect images, samples, articles, and all forms of papery items that pertain to the following:

- *People* Those you know and don't know, living and deceased, historical, fictional, or familial
- *Nature* Weather, animals, plants, trees, flowers, seasons
- *Pets* Past, present, and imagined
- *Fabrics* Patterns, textures, colors
- *Colors* Found within nature, your favorite clothing, or environment
- *Textures* Fabrics, furnishings, food, nature
- *Sounds* Music, nature
- *Tastes* Salty, savory, sweet, bitter
- *Smells* Pungent, perfumed, peppery
- *Images* Magazines, photos, books, Internet
- *Artwork* Personal or favorite artists'

Be attentive where you experience resonance or dissonance within the context of the various categories listed above. Feel free to expand the list of possibilities as you grow your wisdom and gather and curate inspiration to become your creative kindling.

A cabinet of curiosities

Several years ago I was inspired by an artist friend to begin to collect bits and pieces of creative stimuli including: various kinds of string, yarn, inks, imagery, rubber art stamps, seed pods, snail shells, bones, twigs, stones, and other found objects. I contained my discoveries in glass jars of every size and variety. My oddities, curiosities, and inspirations are visibly displayed in a hall cupboard with glass doors. Over time this cupboard has become my Cabinet of Curiosities.

The curation of my collection throughout the years has become a personally beloved sacred practice. Only the most treasured inspirations are selected and added to the cabinet. My grandmother's pearl earrings, black and white photos of beloved family members now gone from this world, a bundle of greeting cards received on my 60th birthday tied with ribbon, my bridal veil and gloves, a note written to me by a friend the week before she died. All of these precious items are lovingly housed in my cabinet of curiosities, a reliquary dedicated to the treasured tangible objects and symbols of my life.

Contemplate how you will the curate your cabinet or cupboard of inspiration and personal treasure. You may also choose to create a shadow box filled with your curiosities to illuminate your story and legacy. Engage your sacred imagination and become a curator and archivist of inspiration.

Facet VII
Share your creative/spiritual gifts with others

As each woman, one by one, became a sister, she brought her inspired gifts to share with the whole of the community.

(*I&H:* 136)

You carry a particular and unique brand of wisdom and creativity. Your gifts and talents are purposefully cultivated and nourished through your prayers, intentions, and sacred practices. Over time these gifts come to fulfillment like fruit of the Spirit. The gifts God has graced in you are of you... but they do not belong to you. They are given to you to share with others.

Contemplate how you will share your gifts, as your illumination for the benefit of our world.

The gifts within us

The "Visitation" story (Luke 1:39-45) is especially inspirational. The Scripture tells how Mary, while pregnant with Jesus, travels to Judea to visit her cousin, Elizabeth. She is also pregnant. When the women greet one another, Elizabeth, feels the child within her womb leap with his recognition of the blessed infant in Mary's womb. Elizabeth's child will later be known as John the Baptist. Mary and Elizabeth *behold* the gift within one another.

This story reflects how women are called to support one another. We are also called to recognize each other's inner blessings and spiritual/creative gifts. The invitation arises through our mutual recognition to become spiritual midwives, in service to the rebirth of the Sacred Feminine through the work of our hearts and hands.

The Way of Belle Cœur

Intuition and the Sacred Imagination

*Comtesse illumined linen
the way I illumined parchment,
from the inspiration
that was born
in our sacred imaginations.
(I&H: 140)*

"*You say God speaks to you, but it's only your imagination.*" These are the words spoken by the inquisitor to Joan of Arc during her trial for heresy. "*How would God speak to me, if not through my imagination?*" Joan replied with confidence.

The story of Saint Joan and her visions and voices that led her to victory for France several centuries ago is familiar to most women. Her sacred imagination was the fertile field where her human talents and creativity merged with the inspiration of the Holy Spirit. Her clever ingenuity combined with her intuition, devotion, and profound readiness to serve God in ways that changed the course of history and *her*story.

It is every person's birthright to be blessed with the potential to engage the sacred imagination in co-creation with God. When intuitive urges are fully engaged there is the possibility for inspired (*inspirited*) forms of creative expression. In this state of conscious awareness it's possible to birth new visions, problem solve, and reimagine renewed ways of living and being. In short, when there is the commitment to become a co-creator with the Beloved, the potential for transformation, innovation, and discovery await.

If intuition is the voice of the soul, the sacred imagination and creativity are the heart and hands of the soul. Intuition delivers guidance from Spirit. Creativity transforms the guidance from within into a tangible form.

Intuition is born within a place of mystery within an effable space between the heart and soul, beyond the psyche's ruminations and calculated left-brain thinking. Often intuition speaks in a whisper and occasionally it shouts to the senses as a mystical invitation to enter new terrain beyond the boundary of the familiar.

When intuition calls, active participation is necessary to fully engage the sacred imagination with the process of creative expression. Initially, the message from the intuition may seem unclear. Sacred artmaking offers a way to crack the code imbedded within the message. The intention to dialogue with intuition through creative exploration most often leads to opportunities for original and innovative discovery. This process may be thought of as the dance of co-creation.

The Way of Belle Cœur

The abilities of conscious listening and focused awareness are conduits for connection with your inner broadcast system. When an intuitive message is received your sacred imagination offers a myriad of possibilities to express the information you have been given. The choice to accept the invitation to begin the co-creative dance or to refuse it rests with you.

Consider how different the story might have ended if Saint Joan had denied her intuitive guidance and hadn't called forth her courage and creativity to express what she knew as her absolute truth. Her intuition (the wisdom of her highest Self in relationship with guidance from the Spirit) spoke to her and she responded through creative action and fierce prayerful commitment. Her clear statement to her inquisitors *How would God speak to me, if not through my imagination?* This echo from centuries past holds spiritual wisdom for our lives today.

My definition of the sacred imagination is that place within each of us where there is a field of pure creative potential. It is the place where the Divine Presence inspires and ignites the full potential of our humanness to fully co-create with Spirit to birth something new.

Each of us carries unique gifts and talents and a particular way of seeing and experiencing the world. Given a ball of clay no two of us would create the same work of art.

Inspiration sparks the heart in countless ways through a myriad of circumstances. As mortals we are free to decide whether or not to respond to and act on the inspiration we receive.

This time on earth calls for active participation with the Creative Wisdom that birthed the world into being. If the sacred imagination is fully engaged, consciously and reverently, it's possible to bring forth the visions, beauty, healing, and sacred awareness necessary for personal and global restoration, blessing, and renewal.

Reflect

- How do you experience the call to serve the Beloved during this time in human history/herstory?
- What vision, dream, creative expression, or yearning within your soul awaits your exploration?
- How will you create an environment to nurture your sacred imagination?
- How will you engage your senses to enlarge your inner landscape?
- What are the necessary tools to alchemically transform your ideas and dreams into full and vibrant fruition?

A Belle Cœur Sister shares her wisdom

"My Sacred Imagination began in a different and new way on the first day of our formation retreat together as sisters of Belle Coeur. It was there, when I began to create my Belle Coeur Codex of Sacred Wisdom. I saw the community art table filled with a sampling of assorted creations. So, along with my personal art supplies and other art forms, I worked at my personal art space in silence and listened to beautiful, creative, and meditative music for four days while my Codex took shape and became very special to me. What is so inspiring is that it is still ongoing. It is a sacred piece still being created as I collect pictures, prayers, quotes, and add my own calligraphy and flourishes."

Margaret McNealy,
Sister of Belle Cœur

Six Steps to Fulfillment

God's Call to Co-creation

Is this how it is with mortals
who are struck deeply
by God's arrow?
By God's flaming arrow
of holy passion
and calling
for the human soul?

Book VIII Illumination, Co-creation, and the...

> *...How many times in a lifetime*
> *are we hunted, dropped to our knees,*
> *and changed by God's grace*
> *to find the strength to begin again?*
> *(I&H: 395-396)*

Co-creation with God is an embedded and recurring theme within Belle Cœur spirituality. When the Beloved calls the human spirit to wakefulness and intentional action, the opportunity is set in motion to fully embody a sacred and co-creative relationship with the Divine Presence.

What does it mean to say, "Yes!" to God's call? The following six-step outline offers illumination for the process of mystical co-creation of the human imagination (matter) with the indwelling Presence of God.

I) **Divine Inspiration: The numinous call to become a co-creator with God**

The call begins when the Divine spark (the Spirit's arrow of intuitive awakening) is delivered to the seeker's heart and mind. The thrust of the arrow may be experienced as an initiatory dream, a fleeting thought, the inkling of an idea, or the sudden realization of intellectual or spiritual understanding. The initial engagement may be subtle or profound as the Holy One inspires human intuition to engage as a co-creator for good. Free will ensures the choice to accept or deny the call.

II) Sacred Fusion: The agreement to answer the call

The seeker's call to fully realize and engage with inner spiritual and creative gifts may initially induce a paradoxical experience. Feelings of elation and excitement combined with fear and confusion confound the ego. Indecision is encouraged by the egoic mind's need to control the soul's natural response to gravitate towards the Divine. Eventually, either the mind or the soul will decide the draw.

If, "YES!" is the response to the call, previously unexplored facets of the Self will soon become illuminated. The inclination to engage with familiar aspects of the psyche and soul in new and surprising ways is strong during sacred fusion, when Divine inspiration (the Spirit) merges with human creative gifts and talents (matter).

The sacred imagination is now inspired to reach new levels of creative potential. There is a period of transition when the heart and psyche yearn for the appropriate response to the Beloved's call. The human desire may arise to research and study subjects that previously held little or no interest. There may also be the sudden desire to make a pilgrimage to a sacred site in search of the ineffable mystery. It's important to note that the initial quest that begins during the fusion of matter with the Spirit through the intuition and sacred imagination is unique for each individual.

III) Wholly (Holy) Embodiment: The indwelling physical experience of yearning and desire through the senses

When co-creation commences it's possible to experience a sharpened focus through the senses. There is a sudden quickening of the faculties of taste, touch, smell, hearing, seeing, and intuitive understanding. The heightened awareness through the senses indicates that the body and the Spirit have signaled agreement to the commission. The awareness of sensory response dispenses a blessed, mystical, interior anointing perceived as the embodiment of serenity and peace.

This numinous experience initiates the healing of the sacred wound received from the arrow of Divine inspiration. Conscious connection with the natural world provides grounding for the body while the Spirit and human imagination and intuition continue to coalesce.

Embodiment of the call takes places when the yearning for God's presence is combined with the ardent desire to fulfill what has been set in motion. When the merging of Spirit and matter and the activation of the senses is complete, the interior rhythm settles into a stable cadence and the next phase of co-creation commences.

IV) **Alchemical Connections: Sacred implements and pathways to uncover the Holy Mystery**

The alchemical process continues as synchronicities occur to provide necessary guidance and additional inspiration for the fulfillment of the call, while the spiritual realm provides ready assistance. Angels from the invisible realms and those in human form, show up to provide guidance to lead the seeker to the fulfillment of the call's highest possible outcome.

The journal, pen, paintbrush, clay, altar, mixing bowl, camera, and the needle and thread are potential alchemical implements. Full expression of the creative heart through sacred artmaking, ecstatic prayer, and additional inspired actions opens the door to the deepest resources within the soul. There is affirmation that the embarkation point of transformation has been reached when the physical body and daily life return to a steady gentle rhythm and tempo.

V) **The Sacred Work: The commitment to prayerful dedication and co-creation with God**

Arrival at the fifth stage ensures that inspiration has been received and there has been movement through dedicated and focused study or a pilgrimage, the result of yearning. Also, the benefits of immersion within nature, has grounded the body within a new reality. The discovery of the necessary alchemical tools to support the specific call creates an open portal to the next phase of co-creation, the sanctification of a personal and prayerful space for the Sacred Work.

The commitment of the body, mind, and spirit to the co-creative work is made in tandem with dedicated prayer for a global or personal cause. Intentional devotion enlarges the purpose of the Work from the focus upon *Self* to the greater *Oneness* of humanity.

Daily sacred practice and extreme self-care during this period require a measure of grace to engage the specific call through active or contemplative service for the greater good. The alchemical tools and senses act as the rudder and compass while the soul's sturdy vessel sets sail into the sea of co-creation.

VI) **Gratitude and Perseverance: The evolution of the call and continual commission**

When the manifestation of the co-creative Sacred Work is complete it is time to begin a season of contemplative or active service. With a thankful heart for the sacred experience of awakening and for the opportunity to serve as Christ's heart and hands in the world, the resulting contemplative or active service begins.

Lastly, the soul offers itself anew for God's next commission and prepares once again to receive the flaming arrow of Divine Love. With each holy bidden and unbidden wounding may the spirit enters ever more deeply into the burning Sacred Heart of the Beloved. This is the nature of God's call to co-creation. This is how sacred wisdom is grown.

Book IX
The Oratory

*"Be still and go within
the oratory of your souls, Sisters.
God is there.
We don't have far
to travel to find our Beloved
patiently waiting.
Make your art and craft a prayer.
Fashion each moment
of your life
into a sacred gesture
of affection to the One
who dwells within you."*
(I&H: 361)

Book IX The Oratory

The Oratory is a place of prayer, sanctuary, and peace. Here you will find seeds of inspiration to deepen your devotional and spiritual practices. It is suggested that you initially explore this section in its entirety to become familiar with the various prayers and practices. Scripture references are provided for the practice of lectio divina.

When you enter sacred space for prayer, meditation, or ritual or to share Communion or the Sacrament of Anointing, you step out of ordinary time and space and enter a numinous reality. To add another element of beauty to the experience, wrap yourself in a shawl. The Belle Cœur color is pale bluish green or you may choose another color for your shawl that holds personal spiritual resonance. Donning a shawl as a spiritual practice signals the heart and spirit that you desire to bring your full awareness to the Divine Presence, within and without.

Additionally, during a time of ready making and preparation for a ritual, a sacred celebration, or Communion you might choose to wear an apron as a symbolic garment for hospitality and hearth keeping. An apron with a pocket can be very beneficial. The pocket may be used as a reliquary, a sacred place to hold a meaningful touchstone or carefully folded written prayer. As you enter your oratory or go about your sacred work, contemplate how you might incorporate a shawl, apron, and other garments and objects as *gestures of reverence and sacred presence. (I&H: 7, 13, 32, 83, 87, 89, 109)*

The Daily Hours

> *Praying the hours marked*
> *the portions of the day,*
> *night, dawn, morning, noon,*
> *afternoon, dusk, evening*
> *and the return of night.*
> *I pondered how the hours*
> *were like seasons,*
> *folding one into the next.*
> *(I&H: 187)*

Belle Cœur spirituality incorporates the ancient, monastic, spiritual practice of praying the Divine Office (Daily Hours). This meaningful and rich process for reflection acknowledges eight specific times for devotion and prayer throughout the day. (*I&H:* 186)

Our busy contemporary lives for most of us, don't allow the spaciousness to stop for sacred reading and prayer throughout the day. However, if we believe we carry our oratory (place of prayer) within us at all times, we can hold the awareness of the sacred passage of the hours from pre-dawn and throughout the night.

An outline of the daily hours is provided here. Scripture notations for lectio divina, and a suggested prayer accompany each designated time.

A suggested simple practice

Choose two or three of the specific hours and commit for one day, week, or month to make pause at the appointed times for a brief period of prayer and reflection. Find your particular rhythm and experience the spiritual gifts of sacred presence and prayer throughout the day.

Matins or Vigils
Luke: 6-12
The hour prior to daybreak or in the middle of the night (3 a.m.)
Many women of a certain age experience a sudden onset of repetitive awakening throughout the night. Matins or Vigils may be regarded as a time of prayer known as the night watch. If you happen to awaken in the deep velvet of night at three or four a.m. take comfort. Others across the world in monasteries and cloisters are also praying.

In silence, breathe deeply, and rest your body within the heart of the Beloved. Feel God's love and peace and open yourself to serve as a conduit of grace through prayer. Pray for those who have no one to pray for them, for the suffering world and her people, for the children, the homeless, the broken, for those who are taking their last breath and for those who are taking their first breath, for your personal needs and the needs of your family and friends.

During the night watch you may wish to pray and meditate upon a simple phrase such as:

Beloved, have mercy. Be near. Hear my prayer or repeat the name of the Beloved, *Jesus, Jesus, Jesus* in cadence with the rise and fall of your heart's rhythm. Select a word or phrase that holds sacred meaning for you. Repeat this (within the silence of your heart or aloud) while you envision those you are praying for, held safe, within the heart of God.

If you choose to pray in silence with the voice of your heart be assured God will hear you. Feel your connection with countless others praying throughout the world in bedrooms, monasteries, on park benches, in hospitals, and at kitchen tables.

Lauds
Isaiah 33:2
A prayer before rising (5 a.m.)
It is a holy moment when the eyes first open to welcome the new day. If you awaken at this hour take time to rest in the stillness of the Divine Presence.

Beloved, I return from my nightly journeying to wakefulness. I give thanks for blessed rest and your purpose and promise for my life today. Amen

Prime
Titus 3:5
A prayer as the day begins (6 a.m.)
Wisdom Sophia, the sunlight streams through my window, while Creation awakens. I may feel weary but I welcome this day and the mystery of how it will unfold. I pray to take time to touch the earth, to feel the wind on my face, and listen for the robin's call. Help me to move slowly to savor the delights of nature's gifts and the sacred gift of my own heartbeat as I breathe in the miracle of life. Amen

Bathing as a morning ritual and prayer
While you're in the shower contemplate the ruminating anxious thoughts that you long to release

before the day begins. Pray to be baptized anew as the water flows over you. Envision your anxieties and concerns being washed away. While the water pours over you imagine God's love and protection fortifying and sealing your body, mind, and spirit for whatever the day may bring. You may wish to anoint your body with oil and prayer before you dress to complete this ritual.

A prayer while dressing for the day (Proverbs 31:25)

While you select your clothing and accessories for the day contemplate the colors and textures that will best convey the uplifting spiritual and creative inspiration you hope to radiate. Be aware of your physical body as you dress. Give thanks for God's miraculous creation. Step into your clothes with intentional awareness as you "*Put on the full armor of God so that you can stand firm against the tactics of the Devil.*" (Ephesians 6:11-18)

Beloved, I give thanks for the blessing of my physical body, my soul's vessel made to your perfection. My bones, blood, and flesh are your creation and encoded with ancestral wisdom. I choose my garments and adornment today as a reflection of my love for you. Bless my earthly costume with purpose and meaning as I step into the day as your co-creator of beauty, hope, healing, and inspiration. Amen

The Morning Prayer of Belle Cœur
(*I&H*: 142)

Beloved, please guide me in my desire to live as your faithful servant. May my eyes be your eyes, to recognize the depths of human suffering and the ecstasies of divine beauty. May my

ears be your ears, to hear the hidden truths within the hearts of those who bring their stories to my door. May my hands be your hands, so your healing love may gently fall on each fevered brow I touch and each task that I perform. May my words be your words. Inspire my tongue to utter your guidance and encourage me to rest in silence, when silence is needed. O Blessed One, keep my heart, forever open to fully feel life's pain and delight. Help me to not turn away from those things that are difficult to witness, or those that cause me to be fearful. Still my trembling, and strengthen me through your presence within me. Make me brave and guide my every action. Bless my work to your glory. Amen

Terce
Psalm 91:11
Mid-morning devotion (9 a.m.)
  Blessed angel, holy messenger, come near with your sweet breath and ethers of inspiration. Stay near with your protection and whisper into my heart how I may best serve God's Creation today. Amen

Sext or the Sixth Hour
Ephesians 5:8
Noon devotion (12 p.m.)
  Beloved, I pause from my daily tasks to praise you for the illumination of the daylight, as I grow my wisdom and faith through you. You radiate my path with symbols and guideposts. Help me to stay awake to recognize the gifts you lay before me, as I continue my journey through this day. Amen

Early afternoon devotion
  Choose one of the following Psalms, or a reading of your choosing to be read and savored, twice. Notice

Book IX The Oratory

the phrase or word within the Psalm that holds special resonance for you. Carry the word or phrase within your heart for the remainder of the day as a blessing and meditation.
Psalm 26, 84, 104, 108, 126

None or the Ninth Hour
Acts 3:1
Mid-afternoon devotion (3 p.m.)
Blessed Mother, I pause to contemplate you, the Beloved's first teacher, his guardian, and way-bearer. O, Holy Wisdom, teach me to carry your virtues of strength and compassion. You are the Mother of life's greatest Mystery. You are the womb of the world. Birth me ever anew, ever closer to Christ. As the day continues I dedicate the prayer of my heart to you. Amen

Vespers or Evensong
Luke 24:29
Prayer at dusk (6 p.m.)
Beloved, the daylight wanes and soon night will spread her starlit canopy across the sky. Be near me at this holy hour of in between. I pray to release all concerns and distractions and enter my oratory within where you patiently await my prayers. I go there now to share sweet reverie with you. Amen

Compline or Night Prayer
Genesis 28:11-12
Prayers at day's end before sleep (9 p.m.)
Loving God, the dark has settled around me, and I feel held within the comfort and shelter of your Presence. I enter my dreams with the assurance that morning will awaken me

when your sunlight blesses the world with the illuminated promise of the new day. Amen

Myrtle's bedtime prayer
(*I&H:* 276)
Job 12: 7-10

> *For the four-legged ones in forest and meadow, bless them.*
> *For the creeping ones on the ground, bless them.*
> *For the flying ones of the air, bless them.*
> *For the swimming ones in the river and Blind Spring, bless them.*
> *For the honeybee, the butterfly, the spider and all the ones that crawl or fly, bless them.*
> *For fire, we give thanks.*
> *For air, we give thanks.*
> *For water, we give thanks.*
> *For sky, we give thanks.*
> *For plants, stones, metals, we give thanks.*
> *For Grandmother Tree and her brothers and sisters, we give thanks.*
> *Mother Goddess, we give up this day to you. We see you in all of creation and we give thanks. Turah. Turah.*

Marking Time

A Sacred Practice

Let each day unfold
hour by hour

Book IX The Oratory

*as God reveals your markings
and fills you with grace.
(I&H:* **139**)

Portions of the day
A spiritual practice

The four distinct quadrants or portions of time within each twenty-four hour period: dawn, day, dusk, and dark present distinct vantage points for sacred awareness throughout the year. Consider the potential spiritual benefit that exists within a momentary pause to pray as the earth turns round and moves from dawn to day, dusk to dark. Keep your journal nearby for your reflections as you explore your relationship with time.

☙

Each portion of time is accompanied by questions that may be used as journal prompts. Add your additional questions as they surface with the rising and falling of the hours. Work with the questions daily or weekly and notice how your responses change in tempo with what is happening during the present moment. Scripture and *Ink and Honey* references may be used for lectio divina.

The incorporation of assorted colorful pens or markers will add to the experience and help to delineate the identity of each particular portion of time. Bring sacred awareness and your creative spirit to the process.

Dawn

Isaiah 58:8
(*I&H:* 76, 141, 187, 188)

As you awaken, reflect upon the blessing of morning, Creation, and the wisdom of the remnants of dream images that linger beyond sleep. Respond to the following questions using a marker in a color to reflect the dawn.

- ❖ Today, what loving act of kindness will express my gratitude to God for my life and the gifts of the Spirit?
- ❖ What creative expression might I offer as a gesture of beauty and hope in my workplace?
- ❖ How might I create an opportunity to spend time in the natural world today?
- ❖ What symbols and images did I receive from my dreams last night that I might embody and learn from?

Day

Genesis 1:1-31
(*I&H:* 2, 3, 66, 177)

The light of day provides myriad opportunities to serve as Christ's heart and hands here on earth. Choose

Book IX The Oratory

a colored marker to reflect the golden radiant light of day as you work with the prompts.

- ❖ How might I best serve friends, family, my ministry, and co-workers today?
- ❖ What negative thought am I holding onto that blocks my full presence to recognize and embrace the Divine Presence within others? How will I release it?
- ❖ What area of my life calls for fasting? To what cause or person will I dedicate my fast?
- ❖ Do I feel called to fast from spending, eating, gossiping, e-mail, complaining...?
- ❖ How will I express my ministry of presence today?

Dusk

Psalm 113: 3-9
(*I&H:* 20, 28, 64, 65, 186)

Sunset begins the new day as you move towards the dark. This is the signal to shift from *doing* to *being* in preparation for night. Take a reflective pause for prayer to witness the fading light and become mindful of the day's departure. Select a colored marker with a smoky, dusky hue for your responses to the following questions.

- ❖ What do I need to release through prayer as I prepare for night?
- ❖ Who do I need to forgive?
- ❖ What past issue is calling for self-forgiveness?

The Way of Belle Cœur

- What is keeping me from physical, spiritual, or emotional rest?

Dark
Luke 6:12
(*I&H:* 21, 153, 188, 276)

Blessed rest. Before sleep and dreams, time for reflection, prayer, contemplation. Contemplate these questions and use a black or dark blue marker to write your responses.

- How did I help make the world a better place today?
- When was I hurtful or unkind to another…to myself?
- What correction for my life's course could I make tomorrow?
- How do I experience gratitude as I settle into night's darkness?

Prayers for Particular Needs and Occasions

Nearby my sisters take their rest
between the hours
of communal prayer.
(I&H: 4)

Book IX The Oratory

Beatrice's table blessing
Acts 2:42

Beloved, we gather at our bountiful table with gratitude. May this food bless and sustain us. We pray for a hungry stranger, somewhere in the world, to be mystically nourished and filled through your grace, in the breaking of the bread.
Amen

Prayer from the Heart of Community
For clarity and guidance
Matthew 18:20

Beloved, each of us holds a challenge and a question within the heart that disturbs her sleep and rattles her spirit. The path is strewn with obstacles and distractions that pull us away from your Presence. We pray you will shelter us and bless us with your eternal creative wisdom. Give us the inner strength to remember you are with us even when we feel bruised and weary from life's complexities.

We ask for angels to guide and guard us as we find our way home again to the Peace that passes human understanding. Help us to surrender ever more deeply into the Mystery. Ignite our sacred imaginations so we may co-create with you. Fill our dreams and waking visions with your signs and symbols to help us understand the nature of your call. Oh, God, our longings are deep and dear. Bless us with patience. Hold us within your Sacred Heart as we hold fast to the rim of this circle in anticipation of your guidance for our community.
Amen

Prayer when there is challenge within the community
1 Corinthians 1:10

Jesus, our Consoler, there is a tear in the fabric of our beloved community.

We pray to you to mercifully mend what has been torn while we trust the highest outcome for all concerned will be revealed through your grace. Amen   (*I&H:* 359)

A Journal-Keeper's Prayer
Job 19:23

Beloved, please inspire my heart and mind to record my story truthfully and to create beauty upon and within these pages. Open me to your Mystery, and teach my pen to dance my prayers. Set me free into the wonder of self-expression through my sacred imagination and creative spirit. Amen

A Pilgrim's Prayer to Our Lady of Chartres
Luke 1:28

Blessed Mary, the Beloved's mother, confidante and friend, you are seated upon the throne of Holy Wisdom. Open the door within my soul! Let loose the birthing waters! Bring forth new life in me! Make me your handmaiden!

I am ready and eager to serve you. I feel you reaching out to me, as I reach out to you in loving service. Hone your humble instrument. Reshape me through the molding of my understanding. I offer my body and soul to your service. Amen

A Blessing for Spousal Love

Come, beloveds!
Come to the celebration.
Come to the place where the wind whispers the lover's song.
Come feast upon the foods of remembrance.
Oysters from the salty sea and pomegranate seeds red as your passion.

Book IX The Oratory

Come now, beloveds!
Come to the sacred sands, to build a fire, to bless your union.
In sweet warmth kneel down together.
There within the flames is the map you have searched for.
Created from your love for one another.
A map sanctified by Spirit.
Delivered by the angels.
Come now beloveds!
For the blessing time is here.
Lie down together to dream a common dream.
In sleep you'll dance the lover's dance.
Earth's heartbeat marks the rhythm.
The changing moon marks time.
Come now beloveds!
Your ancestors' prayers encircle you.
On this sacred night,
Come now beloveds!
To the feast.
To the dance.
To the dream.
Spin, beloveds!
Spin a cocoon of your love.
Spin strength.
Spin wisdom.
Spin passion.
Spin Light.
Spin love, spin hope, spin Life. Amen

The Way of Belle Cœur

Sacred Rituals

*Prayer, ritual, healing and grace
colored each facet of daily life.*
(*I&H:* 153)

The Sacrament of Naming
A ceremony to be shared within community
2 Peter 1:10
(*I&H:* 72, 172, 176)

The Sacrament of Naming is celebrated when a sister or sisters within a community are designated and named as a *guardian* or *keeper* of a specific responsibility for the community. Examples include but are not limited to the following: Keeper of the Prayers, Guardian of the Portundae, Hearth-Keepers, Bread Bakers, Scribe or Keeper of the Stories (Community Codex), etc.

Each community creates a naming ceremony that is appropriate for their circumstances. The following is a suggested form that may be developed to meet particular needs. Be creative and incorporate your community's traditions and prayers to enrich the celebration.

Preparation

The Sacrament of Naming is a ceremony of celebration. The altar is set with flowers, a candle and other essentials for the ceremony such as: anointing oil and a gift such as a shawl or symbolic necklace, ring, or bracelet to represent the specific call of the sister that will be named (see below).

Chairs are arranged in a circle around the altar at the center. One sister serves as the leader of the ceremony and the entire community participates.

The sister being named will be presented during the ceremony with shawl or stole, or other symbol to mark the significance of her calling and charism. One or two of the sisters (the Vesters) volunteer to take care of all details pertaining to vesting the named sister with the shawl or symbol at the appropriate time.

If it is decided that the named will receive the Sacrament of anointing during the ceremony, a designated sister will come forward to anoint her at the appropriate time.

The Ceremony

The community gathers and is seated in the circle. The leader approaches the one to be named and they stand together facing those around them.

Leader: *Creator of all life, you inspire our hearts and minds and bless us with spiritual and creative gifts to share as a special charism. You have inspired Sister* (name) *with the call to serve our community through her charism of* (Example: recording our community's stories). *We gather together to bless her calling through the Sacrament of Naming. We pray for your blessing for Sister* (name) *and her service. Inspire our community to support her in her responsibilities, as she grows her wisdom and lives her charism.* Amen

The Way of Belle Cœur

Community: *Sister* (name), *we are grateful for your response to your call and we honor you today.*

Leader: *Sister* (name), *do you commit to the fulfillment of your responsibilities including:* (list various responsibilities as you record our stories)?

Sister being named: *I commit to my calling and the fulfillment of my responsibilities in service to our community supported by God's guidance and my sisters' prayers.*

The vester takes the shawl/symbol from the altar and presents it to the named.

Vester: *We vest you with this* (shawl, necklace, symbol, etc.) *as an outward sign of your inner spiritual and creative gifts and your calling as* (The Keeper of the Stories).

Anointer: *May Wisdom Sophia bless you as your charism grows and flourishes through your shared wisdom and service. Amen*

The anointer dips her index and middle fingers in the sacred oil and draws a cross enclosed within a circle on each hand of the named while saying, "In the name of the Creator, Jesus, the Beloved, and Wisdom Sophia. Amen

Leader: *You have responded with your "Yes!" to the inspiration of the Spirit and to your calling. Sister* (name) *we name you* (Keeper of the Stories).

Book IX The Oratory

Community: *Keeper of Our Stories, we put our trust and faith in you to carry out your calling.* (The community extends hands in blessing) *We pray for your loving service for our community to be blessed by the Spirit and to be fulfilled through your wisdom. May God's blessings flow to you and through you, Sister* (name) *as the Keeper of Our Stories. Amen*

The Sacrament of Anointing

*I offered the old gentleman a blessing
and anointed his heart
with Imene's golden serum.
(I&H: 147)*

Mark 6:13

Anointing is a Sacrament of Belle Cœur that may be offered with prayer for a variety of needs as outlined in the *Path of Sacrament* section of Book I. You may wish to carry a small container of anointing oil with you to have ready for needs as they arise, such as: an offering of blessing and healing, a final blessing for a friend or beloved during a vigil at the time of death, for the blessing of a pet or the blessing of hands before beginning new work, etc.

A blessing sign for anointing

When I was heavy with oncoming dreams, I was startled to my senses by the scent of rose oil. I opened my eyes to feel Myrtle finger a cross and circle on my forehead with her sweet anointing. (I&H: 287)

When anointing, dip the thumb or index and middle fingers into the oil. On the forehead of the person receiving the blessing, draw a cross with your fingers and continue as you draw a circle to enclose the cross. As you draw the vertical branch of the cross, say the words: *In the name of our Creator.* Draw the horizontal branch of the cross with the words: *Jesus, the Beloved.* Draw the circle to enclose the cross while you complete the blessing with: *and Wisdom Sophia.* Amen

You may choose to bless an alternative appropriate place on the body such as: the hands of the sacred life-artisan, the feet of the pilgrim, the soft space of the neck of the brokenhearted, the forehead of the student beginning her studies, etc.

Prayers appropriate for the circumstances may be added to the above blessing. The following are suggested prayers for various needs. You are encouraged to write additional prayers, as inspired.

Myrtle's Recipe for anointing oil

Mix 2 parts olive oil with 1 part petroleum jelly. Use a wire whisk to mix until smooth and thickened. Add several drops of rose or spikenard oil. Mix well and pour into a small glass jar or other appropriate container.

A prayer for anointing and healing
(*I&H*: p. 147)
Lay down your miseries, beloved of God, and rest in the peace of Christ. Lay down your miseries, weary traveler of life and be healed. Amen

A prayer for a sacred life-artisan when starting a new creation/project/body of work
Exodus 35:35
(*I&H:* 349)
Anoint the hands, forehead, and the artists' tools with the sign of Belle Cœur and these words…
May the work that (name) *begins today be inspired by her wisdom as a co-creation with you. May her hands forge beauty with the tools of her craft to inspire others to know the creative power of the sacred imagination.* Amen.

A prayer of blessing for the Sacred Wisdom Codex
Anoint the front and back covers of the codex with oil, making the sign of Belle Cœur, while offering the following blessing.
In the spirit of my ancestors and the Beguines I dedicate my Sacred Wisdom Codex as my reliquary of truth and presence and the heart of my legacy. May the ancient tradition of women's recorded stories continue to reveal the illuminated knowledge yet to be lived and grown. In the name of our Creator, Jesus, the Beloved, and Wisdom Sophia. Amen

The Way of Belle Cœur

Table Community

The Feast of Life

*I took the cup of wine after
the bread had been passed
and offered it to Helvide...
"The cup of compassion."
My sister took the cup
and sipped from it
then passed it on.
(I&H: 251)*

The Bread of Life and the Cup of Compassion
A shared sacred meal for communities, friends, and families

Acts 2: 44-47, Matthew 26:26-29, 1 Corinthians 11: 23-26
(*I&H*: 193, 250-251, 474)

To fully express the blessing and meaning of Communion it's important to return to the taproot of the early followers of Jesus. After the resurrection, there were table communities of men, women, and children that sought the sacred through the sharing of the stories of Jesus. These were people who came together to break bread and share a cup of wine while

Book IX The Oratory

they remembered and reflected upon the Beloved's teachings.

In the beginning they gathered two by two on rocky hillsides, or in small groups hidden away in caves, or in secret at one another's homes. Over time the growing community of believers began to build sizable structures for worship to house the increasing crowds of followers. Women were active leaders and participants of the earliest house churches that began spread throughout the countryside and beyond.

The physical centerpiece to their shared experience was a table, the place where they broke bread and shared the cup of the New Covenant. The table's physicality differed from place to place and was dependent upon the location where the people met. It may in one instance have been a flax-cloth spread on a dirt floor, or in another place it was a small low table made of cedar, or in a more permanent setting a large flat stone set on stone pillars. Perhaps the women of the earliest Christ-centered communities took turns to bake the bread and the men shared the weekly offering of a goatskin filled with wine that was carefully poured into a common cup.

The stories about Jesus were told and questions that arose from the stories were discussed, while prayers for the community's myriad needs were also shared. The people (men, women, and children) gathered about the table, broke the bread, and passed the cup as they remembered their Teacher, his parables, his miracles, and his Way. They were fed and nourished by the bread, the wine, the prayers and their common experience.

The Way of Belle Cœur

Contemporary life is vastly different from the world of the first century followers of Christ. Many today are spiritually hungry.

- ❖ What is today's pilgrim truly seeking?
- ❖ What is the invitation within the current common longing for community and spiritual sustenance?
- ❖ How might the inclusivity of the table communities of our long ago brothers and sisters in Christ serve our culture today?

The Feast of Life
Communion supper

The following story offers an illustrative guidance for the celebration of Communion within the context of a contemporary table community. Read slowly and imagine yourself at the table. Notice any additional ideas or visions that arise. Names are inserted as placeholders for the persons you would add to the scene. Build and elaborate upon the foundational concepts offered here, as you are inspired. The cornerstone principle for this experience is openhearted hospitality. All are welcome to the table!

⁂

Imagine you have invited several kindred spirits to your home for a Feast of Life Communion Supper. Everyone is encouraged to invite and welcome additional others not previously known to the group

Book IX The Oratory

to come to the table. You made a personal call earlier in the week to Sam, Carol, Mary, and Paul to ask them to serve as the celebrants of tonight's gathering at the table. They will each play a part during Communion. The guests arrive with their carefully chosen and prepared prayers, Scripture, and inspirational readings.

Sam will read from the Book of John and he has prepared a question that relates to the Scripture for shared reflection around the table before the bread is broken and the cup of wine is passed. Carol will contribute a spiritual poem by the poet, Hafiz, and she will also lead the opening prayer. She volunteered to print a one-page outline of tonight's Communion and she has copies for everyone so the others can follow along and join in the prayers. Mary will lead the prayers for the breaking of the bread and passing of the cup, as well as, offer the closing prayer. The elder of the group, Paul, brings his guitar. He will play a musical interlude to weave the Communion with the Feast of Life that will follow. His sister, Maggie, has joined him tonight.

Earlier today you prepared the table and baked a round loaf of bread with prayer and intention.

"May this bread be enriched with Christ's Peace and Promise to bless and nourish those who will feed one another."

Jack arrives with the wine and he carefully pours it into a wine glass. You place the bread in a basket and cover it with a linen napkin. These gifts of the Spirit are placed at the center of the table flanked by an unlit candle on either side.

The Way of Belle Cœur

Your remaining guests arrive with a variety of delicious contributions for the Feast of Life celebration that will follow Communion. There is an array of dishes from savory to sweet. These are brought to the kitchen to be kept warm or chilled until later.

༺࿇༻

When everyone is present they are invited to take their seats at the table. Susan lights the candles.

Envision the sacred unfolding that begins with a prayer of gratitude for the opportunity to come together to share in the Divine Presence within the bread and wine. Carol shares the poem and Sam reads from the Scriptures. He poses his question for discussion and after a moment of silence, for the next twenty minutes, people have the opportunity to share his/her reflection of what the reading meant to them.

Mary asks if anyone has a prayer request. Several guests request prayer support for themselves and their friends and beloveds. There are also prayers for the needs of the world and Creation.

Next, the story of the Beloved's teaching of the meaning of the bread and wine is offered as a shared story. Paul begins, "The men and women gathered with Jesus around the table…" Mary adds, "It was evening and they were enjoying one another's company." Susan says, "Their Teacher took the bread and said…." and so the story continues to unfold through the spontaneous telling around the table.

Book IX The Oratory

Afterwards, Carol leads the Jesus Prayer. After the prayer you open your arms wide and say, "*Christ's Peace be with you,*" and each one turns to the one on his/her right or left and shares The Peace.

Next there is a brief pause for silence and then everyone around the table extends their hands towards the basket of bread and cup of wine to offer a simple blessing prayer led by Mary. The basket of bread is passed. Each person receives the basket, breaks a piece of bread from the loaf, and offers the piece of bread to the person on the left with the blessing, "*The Bread of Life.*" The glass of wine is passed in the same way with the blessing, "*The Cup of Compassion.*" A napkin accompanies the wine to wipe the rim after each sip.

When all have received if bread and wine remain, the basket and glass are passed again, in silence, until all is consumed. After Communion, you remove the basket and glass from the table and there is a moment or two of silence. Mary leads the closing prayer while Paul plays a peaceful melody on his guitar.

Dinner follows with personal sharing around the table. Tonight's feasting is in celebration of God's extravagant love, present within each person gathered here as a table community. Stories, laughter and tears, and spiritual and global questions are shared. There is music and feasting.

The evening winds to a close it's agreed you'll meet at Carol and Mary's home next month and details will be worked out in the interim. There are hugs all around and everyone goes into the night full to the brim with spiritual sustenance.

⁂

In this dark season on our planet when so many are struggling from religious confusion and spiritual starvation perhaps it's time, once again, to look to the past to inform the present. Perhaps it's time to return to the taproot…to the gift and spiritual sustenance that lives within a table community. Let us gather round the table and be fed by God's loving Presence alive in the bread and wine and within each of us.

⁂

You're invited to take the story you have just read and make it your own. Imagine celebrating Communion with your kindred spirits followed by feasting and heartfelt conversation. Allow the Spirit to move among you as you plan your Communion and sacred feasting. Incorporate Scripture, various forms of prayer, music, poetry, and readings from a variety of sacred texts and add touches of beauty including: color, flowers, candles, and song.

Co-create and plan your sacred gathering with reverence and abundant joy. Celebrate often and always have an empty seat at your table for the unexpected guest.

Book IX The Oratory

Don't neglect to show hospitality to strangers, for by doing so some people have entertained angels without knowing it.
Hebrews 10:12

The co-creation of intentional meals to serve the various ever-changing needs of a family or community might include:

- ❖ A Feast of Ideas, when collaboration is called for
- ❖ A Feast of New Life, when a baby is born
- ❖ A Feast for Healing, when someone becomes ill
- ❖ A Feast of Remembrance, when there is a death
- ❖ A Feast of Beginning, when someone moves to a new home or begins a new job

There are many possibilities and themes for the creation of a feast. Most importantly, may Communion be at the heart of the experience as a blessing for those gathered to worship, celebrate life, share stories, and bear witness to God's extravagant and radical love.

Recipe
Le Pain de Dieu
Communion Bread

2 C. whole-wheat flour
1 C. regular bread flour

The Way of Belle Cœur

2 T. oil
2 t. salt
1 t. baking powder
3 T. honey
1½ C. water

Mix the flours together and stir in thoroughly the salt and baking powder. Sift this mixture 3 times. Mix the honey and water completely. To this mixture add the oil and stir well. Add this syrup to the flour and knead until a dough effect is attained. Be careful not to over knead. Allow the dough to be sticky. Knead about 2 minutes.

Cut into 6 portions. Roll each portion into a ball then pat each ball directly onto a lightly greased cookie sheet. Each patted circle of dough should be approximately 5 inches in diameter, 1/4 inch thick. Using a table knife dipped in water, carefully score (do not cut all the way through the dough) into bite-size squares or score into larger pieces if desired.

Yield: approximately 25 pieces per 5" loaf. After patting and scoring, even the circular edge using a spatula dipped in water to make the loaves uniform in height and thickness.

Bake at 325-350F for about 10-13 minutes. Watch your oven's baking carefully. The bread will not brown, but the bottom must be checked for browning. Do not let them become more than a golden color. After removing from the oven, lightly brush each with a pastry brush dipped in oil.

An additional recipe that can be served for celebrations is included here.

Les Petits Gâeaux au Miel
Little Honey Cakes

Combine all ingredients in a large bowl…
2 C. ground oatmeal (process oatmeal in a food processor or blender)
1 C. oat flour
¼ C. sugar
¼ C. light brown sugar loosely packed
½ C. melted unsalted butter
¼ C. amber honey
1 t. almond extract
½ t. orange zest
¼ t. cinnamon
½ C. chopped toasted almonds
1 T. crushed edible lavender, optional (available at fine grocers)
Heat oven to 375 F.
Grease two sheet pans.

Stir ingredients with spoon then knead with hands or use food processor on pulse mode.
　Batter should form a firm dough.
　Make a ball. Flatten it.
　On a floured counter or pastry board, use floured rolling pin to roll dough to ¼ inch thickness.

Use a biscuit cutter or rim of a small glass to cut dough into circles.

Rework, roll out, and cut remaining scrap dough.

Lift circles of dough onto the cookie sheets with spatula. Allow 2-3 inches between each circle.

Bake at 375 for 10-12 minutes. (Inspired by Christina Baldwin's oatcake recipe)

The Fast

A Sacred Practice

Prepare your spirits with fasting
to make a welcoming place
within you so you
may be filled with Jesus.
(I&H: 157)

Fasting is an intentional and prayerful sacred practice. During the Lenten season we remember how Jesus fasted for forty days and forty nights. His fasting was a conscious choice and the result of his spiritual need and desire, rather than a practice of austere self-denial. With the Beloved as our teacher, the practice of fasting becomes a way to deepen spiritual understanding and connection with the Divine Presence and a pathway to prayer for the greater good.

The following list provides suggestions for a variety of intentional and prayerful fasts. A fast is a particularly meaningful practice when there is a discerned call to contemplate a specific personal or global issue for conscious awareness. Add additional intentions for fasting as they arise. (*I&H*: 30, 102, 140, 157, 228, 247, 271, 306, 320)

The technology fast

Genesis 11:6, Daniel 12:4, 1 Corinthians 6:12

In spite of the many advantages of instant communication, global networking, and immediate access to every imaginable form of information, technology consumes precious time, affects various health issues, and opens gateways to addiction. The technology fast involves turning off the computer, putting away the cell phone, and unplugging from any other form of connection that involves technological gadgetry including television.

Many of us have succumbed to the rush of online, instant gratification, notoriety, and interaction. A technology fast invites the rediscovery of lost time and forgotten pastimes. Unplugging from all manner of devices frees the body, mind, and spirit to explore forgotten interests beyond the latest app or social media video post.

If you feel called to make a technology fast, notice if there is resistance or relief when you unplug, shut down, and power off. Journal your responses and become aware of how technology plays a part in your life. Notice where you rediscover pockets of time and spaciousness for prayer, sacred study, reading, writing, creating, or extra hours with family and friends.

The Sabbath is traditionally a day of rest. If you choose to fast from technology, the Sabbath may be an appropriate day for this practice.

Reflect

- ❖ When I unplugged all my electronics I became instantly aware that I…
- ❖ I spent my technology free time in the following way(s)…
- ❖ When I imagine the life before computers, cell phones, etc., I….
- ❖ The fast from technology has changed the way I…

The fast from material consumption

Luke 12:15, Matthew 6:19-21, 1 John 3:17

A fast from material consumption raises consciousness and awareness regarding the difference between something that is desired versus something that is necessary to sustain a healthy, functional, and vital life. The invitation to make a fast from consumption is to spend a designated period of time (one week, one month, or longer) without purchasing personal material goods, other than the essential for your existence such as food, medication, and shelter.

Notice what arises when you begin to ask the question, "Do I desire this (pair of shoes, book, lipstick, etc.) or is this item essential for my existence?" This fast offers the opportunity to experience solidarity with those who never have the opportunity or luxury of buying something simply because it's desired. Consciousness regarding material consumption holds important spiritual truths. Practice lectio with the Scripture references and journal your reflections as feelings arise during your fast.

Reflect

- I define my *desires* as…
- My *needs* can be expressed as…
- When I practice discernment with regard to what I want versus what I truly need to survive I experience feelings of…
- My greatest learning and conscious understanding from this fast are…

Fast from food

Matthew 4:1-11, Luke 4:2, Acts 13:3

Fasting is most commonly associated with the non-partaking of solid food especially animal flesh. Fasting from food means the diet is limited to liquids and/or one very small meal a day with abstinence from animal flesh.

The call to make a fast from food is to enter into the experience of prayerful solidarity with the people of the world that live in a state of perpetual hunger. When fasting from food, there is awareness for those that awaken every morning and go to bed every night with an empty belly. A fast from food raises consciousness and awareness with regard to world hunger.

If you are called to prayerfully explore your conscious awareness of global hunger, be sure to respond responsibly with regard to your health and physical needs. A limited fast one or two days a week might consist of one small meal without animal flesh and ample liquids (to prevent dehydration). Wednesday and Friday are traditionally days of fasting in some Christian communities. It's important to use discernment and be health conscious when fasting from food and if you have health issues be sure to check with your physician before fasting.

After your fast when you go to a restaurant or grocery shopping, maintain awareness of the issue of world hunger. Observe the extreme abundance of food, water, and nourishment that's readily available. Contemplate how you are called to respond to your experience of fasting and your inner and outer observations.

Reflect

- During my fast from food I realized…
- The most challenging aspect of my nutritional fast was…
- When I see the abundant array of food, water, and all forms of sustenance available at the market I feel…and I'm aware that I…
- My fast from food has changed me in the following way(s)…

Additional suggestions for a fast include fasting from:

judgment
gossip
self criticism
procrastination
energy consumption

Book X
The Belle Cœur Lexicon

*Brother Paul patiently taught me
the sound of each letter,
how they all connected
together to form words,
and then how the words
fell into order
to create language.
(I&H: 31)*

Belle Cœur symbology

The following definitions are reflective of Belle Cœur spirituality with regard to each specific, meaningful, and pertinent symbol. Symbolic

Book X The Belle Cœur Lexicon

understanding and appreciation enriches the sacred imagination and inspires the spirit. Contemplation of the various symbols listed here may reveal additional personal associations and meanings.

You are encouraged to imagine additional symbols that hold personal relevance. Dedicate pages of your codex for your symbolic reflections. Incorporate symbols within your creations and add them to your altar. Grow your wisdom through your symbolic exploration and understanding.

Belle Cœur Symbology

*...flying two-headed beasts,
twisted vines and countless flowers,
a fiery sun, milky moon,
and all manner of symbols
covered the walls
of our one room home.
(I&H: 278)*

❖ *Acorn*
(*I&H:* 63, 112, 285)
The acorn symbolizes pure potentiality as the seeding of wisdom. It is the Belle Cœur symbol for autumn.

The Way of Belle Cœur

- *Angel*
  (*I&H*: 24, 41, 54, 164)
  The angels are our messengers, guardians, and intercessors. When we prayerfully intend to co-create with the Divine the angels serve as our spiritual companions and guides. The Way of Belle Cœur also honors and celebrates the Archangels: Gabriel (the herald), Michael (the protector), and Raphael (healer).

- *Birds*
  (*I&H*: 23, 41, 55, 316)
  Birds have been said to be God's messengers between heaven and earth. Bird feathers, nests, and eggs, hold resonance as metaphors for birth, self-care, gestation, and messages from the Divine. These are also symbols for spring. The crow is especially significant as a daimon. The stork is also important to Belle Cœur as the harbinger of birth and change.

- *Coquille Shell*
  (*I&H*: 122, 311, 325)
  An identifying symbol for pilgrims and for marking the pilgrim road to sacred sites. The coquille (scallop) shell is also a symbol for baptism and new life.

- *Doll*
  (*I&H*: 1, 13, 44, 205)
  In the story of *Ink and Honey*, Goscelin's tiny doll, Henriette, lives in Goscelin's apron pocket. Henriette is her comforter and treasured companion. She represents Goscelin's intuition and wisdom. A doll is a very potent symbolic presence when created with sacred

and prayerful intention. Spirit doll-making is a beloved sacred craft for Belle Cœur sisters.

❖ *Fleur de Lis*
From the French, meaning *Flower of the lily*. The lily is symbolic for the resurrection, and is also a symbol for Mary, the Mother of Jesus.

❖ *Grandmother Tree*
(*I&H:* 276, 284, 352)
The Grandmother Tree is a particularly grand and ancient tree and not unlike the Tree of Life. It provides a home and shelter for many creatures. She is a tree with deep roots and a broad canopy. Grandmother Tree is symbolic of the life giving and birthing qualities of the Sacred Feminine and Creation, and the merging of heaven and earth.

❖ *Honeybee and Queen Bee*
(*I&H:* 47, 49, 163, 323)
The Queen bee symbolizes Mary, the Mother of God. Honey is symbolic for Christ. The honeycomb and the hive are also indicative of sacred community and service. The honeybee is a very cherished and meaningful symbol for Belle Cœur spirituality.

A Belle Cœur Sister shares her wisdom.

"If ever you have a chance, to visit a bee yard, do so. Stand very still, close your eyes and simply listen. Allow the strength and steadiness of the sacred hum to mesmerize you and draw you ever closer to the world as God created it. Within the

hive lie the answers to perfect community. The hymn of the hive beckons me near to hear all that deep meditation and contemplation call me to learn."

Katherine Hempel
Sister of Belle Cœur

- *Labyrinth*
  (*I&H*: 333-335)
  The Chartres Cathedral labyrinth is meaningful for Belle Cœur spirituality as a symbol for life's journey and spiritual continuity throughout the ages. We journey from the rim to the center and return to the rim as a cyclical experience, time and again. The labyrinth is a revered spiritual tool for those who follow the Way of Belle Cœur.

- *Lavender, Rosemary, and the Sunflower*
  (*I&H*: 165, 386, 79, 197)
  Lavender and the sunflower are important symbols for French culture. Belle Cœur's relationship with the French sisters of *Ink and Honey* inspires these symbols. Lavender and the sunflower are also symbolic for summer. Rosemary is often associated with the Blessed Mother as an herb that is symbolic for "remembrance."

- *Moon*
  (*I&H*: 34, 35, 41, 139, 184, 236, 271, 284, 300, 301, 373)
  The moon symbolizes the cyclical nature of the feminine journey. She represents the stages of a woman's life: Maiden, Mother, and Crone.

Book X The Belle Cœur Lexicon

- *Pomegranate*
 (*I&H:* 61)
 The multi-seeded, crimson, succulent pomegranate is another symbol for the Sacred Feminine. With reference to Belle Cœur, the pomegranate engages and activates the senses as conduits for sacred awareness.

- *Portal*
 (*I&H:* 241-244, 329, 339)
 A portal leads from one space to another. A portal is symbolic of entry points to other realms and mystical understanding.

- *The Sign of Belle Cœur: The Equidistant Cross within a Circle*
 (*I&H:* 85, 141, 183, 473)
 These symbolic forms create the template for the Way of Belle Cœur. There are four pathways: Spirit, Sacrament, Sisterhood, and Service and four alchemical chambers: Craft, Devotion, Story, and Study. The Beloved (Jesus, the Cosmic Christ) is within the center of the cross as our compass and true north. The circle represents Sophia Wisdom, as the all-encompassing circle of life, nature, and the cosmos.

- *Stone*
 (*I&H:* 8, 13, 20, 63, 65, 241, 248, 275, 280, 297)
 Stones represent strength, resilience, and they hold the energy of the earth.

Belle Cœur Vocabulary

"I wish I understood her.
She's a mystery to me.
Perhaps she'll teach me her language."
(*I&H*: 266)

Belle Cœur spirituality incorporates monastic terms, special, and coined words specifically meaningful for the Way of Belle Cœur. The following is an overview of the most frequently used Belle Cœur terms.

Belle Cœur Vocabulary

- *Anchoress*
  (*I&H:* 304-308, 460-461, 468, 480)
  With regard to Belle Cœur spirituality, an anchoress is a sister or companion that is called to solitude, prayer, and reflection without connection to a community.

- *The Beloved*
  (*I&H:* 53, 76, 88, 125, 141, 240, 331, 361, 368, 375, 437, 467, 480)
  Jesus, the Cosmic Christ at the center and heart of the Way of Belle Cœur.

- *Belle Cœur Journal*
  A journal dedicated as a workbook for personal response to the reflection questions and material provided in *The Way of Belle Cœur*.

- *Cescies*
  (*I&H:* 403-404)
  A Belle Cœur term for tiny, unexpected gifts from nature given from one sister to another.

- *Circle*
  (*I&H:* 102, 107, 137, 182, 190, 252, 373).
  The group process form used for all Belle Cœur gatherings based on the teachings of *The Circle Way: A Leader in Every Chair* by Christina Baldwin and Ann Linnea. The circle is also the sacred symbol for community and the presence of Wisdom Sophia within Creation.

- *Cloister*
  (*I&H:* 10, 99, 217, 347, 355)
  With reference to Belle Cœur life, the cloister is a woman's interior world and/or physical

The Way of Belle Cœur

environment and workspace for her craft. It is also her sacred place for spiritual sustenance and retreat.

❖ *Companion*
A reflective, reclusive, hermitic friend of Belle Cœur.

❖ *Community*
An intentional circle of women seekers or reference to a Belle Cœur sisterhood circle.

❖ *Cosmic Christ*
Jesus the Christ, the Anointed One, the Alpha and Omega, and Logos.

❖ *Divine Office (Daily Hours)*
(*I&H*: 186, 486)
A cycle of daily prayers of the canonical hours performed by members of religious orders and the clergy throughout the centuries. The cycle of eight canonical hours for the performance of the Divine Office: Matins (three a.m.), Lauds (five a.m.), Prime (six a.m.), Terce (nine a.m.), Sext (twelve noon), Nones (three p.m.), Vespers (six p.m.), and Compline (nine p.m.).

❖ *Grow your wisdom*
(*I&H*: 46, 47, 63, 66, 134)
A Belle Cœur phrase to reflect the ongoing intellectual, spiritual, and creative process of life-enrichment, and the pursuit of sacred knowledge and understanding.

❖ *Hanswere*
(*I&H*: 244, 264, 373, 403, 438, 454)
A Belle Cœur method for democratic voting (coined word). Voters pat their hearts for

agreement or cover the eyes with the hands in disagreement.

- *Hope and wisdom*
  (*I&H:* 252, 254, 432, 446, 475)
  A Belle Cœur phrase of upliftment that is shared as a blessing.

- *La Ruche*
  From the French meaning, *The Hive.* La Ruche refers to the meeting place (Chapter House) for a Belle Cœur community.

- *Les Petits Cadeaux*
  (*I&H:* 234, 270)
  Small, handcrafted, gifts and offerings that are exchanged, sister-to-sister.

- *Oratory*
  (*I&H:* 5, 361)
  A sacred space or place for prayer. Belle Cœur spirituality encourages the concept of carrying a personal vision of an oratory (a sanctuary) within the heart and spirit.

- *Peramony*
  (*I&H:* 139, 240, 242, 246, 455)
  A Belle Cœur ritual for dreaming and visioning. (coined word)

- *Portundae*
  (*I&H:* 456, 458, 460, 464-468, 472)
  A sacred bundle of personal relics and sacred objects. (coined word)

- *Reliquary*
  (*I&H:* 235, 322, 323, 459, 484)
  A sacred vessel or container to hold portundae or other sacred relics, objects, and touchstones.

The Way of Belle Cœur

- *Sacred Life-Arts*
  (*I&H:* 178, 199, 349, 350, 365, 485)
  All forms of creative expression, as well as, the awareness of a conscious creation of beauty and sacred/prayerful purpose in all areas of daily life.
- *Sacred Life-Artisan*
  A practitioner of the sacred life-arts.
- *Sacred Wisdom Codex*
  A book of personal wisdom, inspiration, and beauty created by a Belle Cœur sister or companion as her legacy manuscript.
- *Shawl*
  A pale blue wrap worn about the shoulders by Sisters of Belle Cœur during circle gatherings, for rituals and celebrations, or while going about their work.
- *Sister*
  A woman becomes a Sister of Belle Cœur when she has completed a prayerful discernment process and preparation to affirm her call to sisterhood.
- *Sisterhood and Sisterhood Circle*
  (*I&H:*1, 102, 106-107, 111, 137, 142, 153, 224, 355, 480)
  Belle Cœur Sisterhood encompasses the entirety of individual Belle Cœur circles of sisters. A sisterhood circle is formed during a Way of Belle Cœur retreat between those participants that feel called to become sisters. Not all women that attend a Way of Belle Cœur retreat are called to become sisters.

Belle Cœur Vocabulary

The choice to become a sister is personal and requires discernment. Each sisterhood circle is autonomous, though all sisters of Belle Cœur share particular devotions, rituals, prayers, and sacred practices.

❖ *The Way of Belle Cœur Template*
(*I&H:* 84-85, 88, 107, 141, 183, 184, 245, 254, 346, 373, 470, 475, 480)
The sign of Belle Cœur, as depicted in the story of *Ink and Honey* is an equidistant cross, enclosed within a circle. This sign is also the spiritual and creative template for the Way of Belle Cœur, represented as four pathways (Spirit, Sacrament, Sisterhood, and Service), four chambers (Devotion, Craft, Study, and Story), the Compass at the center (The Beloved), enclosed by the circle (Wisdom Sophia).

❖ *Wisdom Sophia*
The Sacred Feminine including: Mary (the mother of Jesus) in her myriad forms, Mary Magdalene, and the generative Spirit of Creation/Nature. Wisdom Sophia is represented as the all-encompassing circle that surrounds the Belle Cœur cross and sacred template.

Bibliography

Michelle P. Brown, *Understanding Illuminated Manuscripts: A Guide to Technical Terms*, (The J. Paul Getty Museum and The British Library Board, Malibu, California, 1994) Robert M. Place, *A Gnostic Book of Saints*, (Llewellyn Publications, St. Paul, Minnesota, 2001)

D.J. Conway, *Moon Magick: Myth and Magic, Crafts and Recipes, Rituals and Spells*, (Llewellyn Publications, 1995)

Laurel Glen, *The Art of the Medieval Manuscripts*, (Laurel Glen Publishing, San Diego, CA.,1997). *The Inclusive Hebrew Scriptures, Volume i: The Torah* (AltaMira Press, a division of Rowman & Littlefield Publishers, Inc. Lanham, Maryland, 2000).

The Inclusive Hebrew Scriptures, Volume ii: The Prophets, (Alta Mira Press, A Division of Rowman & Littlefield Publishers, Walnut Creek, California, 2004).
The Inclusive Hebrew Scriptures, Volume iii: The Writings (Priests for Equality, Brentwood, Maryland, 1999).
The Inclusive New Testament, (AltaMira Press, a division of Rowman & Littlefield Publishers, Inc. Lanham, Maryland, 2006).
The Inclusive Psalms, (Priests for Equality, W. Hyattsville, Maryland, 1999).
Saskia Murk-Jansen, *Brides in the Desert: The Spirituality of the Beguines,* (Wipf & Stock Publishers, Eugene, Oregon) Introduction.
Glenn E. Myers, *Seeking Spiritual Intimacy,* (InterVarsity Press, Madison, Wisconsin, 2011).
Laura Swan, *The Wisdom of the Beguines,* (Bluebridge, Katonah, N.Y., 2014).
M.E. Warlick, *The Philosopher's Stones: Let the magic of Alchemy transform your life,* (Eddison Sadd Editions Limited, London, 1997).
Macrina Wiederkehr, *Seven Sacred Pauses,* (Sorin Books, Notre Dame, Indiana, 2008).

Online Reference
The Last Beguine (article, *The Economist*) April 27, 2013 www.economist.com/news/obituary/21576632-marcella-pattyn-worlds-last-beguine-died-april-14th-aged-92-marcella-pattyn
The Mystica, www.themystica.com/mystica/articles/~alchemy/moon.html St. Teresa of Avila Quote: http://www.internetmonk.com/archive/11749 hccfl.edu/media/724354/

Bibliography

archetypesforliterary analysis.pdf campus.udayton.edu/mary/meditations/crownmed.htm en.wikipedia.org/wiki/General_Roman_Calendar#January_.28General_Calendar.29 The University of Dayton Campus, campus.udayton.edu/mary/questions/yq/yq244.htm Bible Hub, http://biblehub.com/revelation/12-1.htm

Acknowledgements

My writing process for *The Way of Belle Cœur: A Woman's Vade Mecum* has been blessed and enriched through the support, encouragement, and wisdom of many creative and spirited women. Deep appreciation to Belle Cœur sister, beloved friend, and teaching partner, Pamela Jean Sampel, for her Christ-centered companionship on the writing journey.

My profound gratitude goes to our contemporary Sisterhood of Belle Cœur for the blessings of your enthusiasm and support. You are the life, breath, and inspiration of Belle Cœur. Thank you to all who shared your stories and wisdom within these pages. Your prayerful presence, enthusiasm, and illuminated spirits continue to bless the journey.

The Way of Belle Cœur

Thank you, Gina Bogle, Mary Anne Dorner, Nancy Dunckerly, Anne Ellen Fuquay, Deborah Hansen, Katherine Hempel, Carolyn Hewlitt, Terri Hubbard, Carol Luster, Margaret MacNealy, Mary Ann Matthys, Millie Mellgren, Mary Montayne, Trish Morris, Evelyn Pope, Edelle Rose, Pamela Jean Sampel, Ruth Turner, Sharyn Turner, Sheryll Shepherd, Jill Westbrook, and Stacy Wills. Onward we go...

For your creative enthusiasm and beautiful Belle Cœur template illustrations, Judy Alkema, heart pats and gratitude. Thank you, Katherine Hempel, for your generous contributions of time, creative energy, honey and beeswax. Christina Baldwin and Ann Linnea, bless you for your transformative circle work and support. Thank you, Lacy Clark Ellman for your creative guidance and website design

Thank you, beloved creative and wise women, sister bishops, and women priests:, Kathryn Poethig, Victoria Rue, Suzanne Thiel, Olivia Doko and Roman Catholic Womenpriests. Bridget Mary Meehan, Mary Teresa Streck, the Association of Roman Catholic Womenpriests, Nausicaa Giulia Bianchi, thank you for your support.

Laurie Sandblom, thank you, dear faith-filled partner in prayer for your ministry of Presence. Tricia Kibbe, continued gratitude and awe for you and our shared adventures. Elizabeth Murray you are a shining star and inspiration.

I'm grateful for the love, support, and wisdom within my beloved APC circle: Christina Baldwin, Kimberly Gilbreath, Ann Linnea, Sarah MacDougall, Pamela Jean Sampel, Linda Secord, Clare Taylor, Kit

Acknowledgements

Wilson, and dear Harriet of Ost who now resides with the angels and saints, within the eternal circle of the ancestors.

Always and forever gratitude for my precious family: Jason, Amy, Brad, and Haley, you bless each day with meaning and inspiration. To my beloved, Don, my eternal gratitude for your unending support, your wise and generous spirit, and caring heart. You are my anchor, and editor in chief par excellence.

Thank you to my elegant mother, for sharing your passion for beauty and hearth tending and for teaching me to embrace my elder years with joy and grace. Stacey, Chris, and Alex you inspire me and bless life's journey.

To my muses from the story of *Ink and Honey*, the 13th Century Sisters of Belle Cœur and to the spirits of the Beguines...*Merci beaucoup!*

For the call, the work, and the journey that continue to carry me ever deeper into the Mystery and the heart of Belle Cœur, I give thanks to the Beloved, Jesus the Christ, and Wisdom Sophia. Amen

Belle Cœur Resources

Please visit the author's website,
SibylDanaReynolds.com.

The *Belle Cœur FAQ Page* at the website provides answers to frequently asked questions pertaining to all things Belle Cœur. You will also find links for details about Belle Cœur Retreats, Belle Cœur Sisterhood, and upcoming online courses and workshops.

Additionally, the Belle Cœur page offers a suggested reading list for topics including Spirituality, Hildegard of Bingen, the Beguines, the Mystics, and Creativity, as well as links to resources for art supplies and journals.

Visit often as new information and materials for your exploration are continually added.

Printed in Great Britain
by Amazon.co.uk, Ltd.,
Marston Gate.